CULTURAL HERITAGE, ETHICS AND CONTEMPORARY MIGRATIONS

Cultural Heritage, Ethics and Contemporary Migrations breaks new ground in our understanding of the challenges faced by heritage practitioners and researchers in the contemporary world of mass migration, where people encounter new cultural heritage and relocate their own. It focuses particularly on issues affecting archaeological heritage sites and artefacts, which help determine and maintain social identity, a role problematised when populations are in flux. This diverse and authoritative collection brings together international specialists to discuss socio-political and ethical implications for the management of archaeological heritage in global society.

With contributions by authors from a range of disciplinary backgrounds, including archaeologists, philosophers, cultural historians and custodians of cultural heritage, the volume explores a rich mix of contrasting, yet complementary, viewpoints and approaches. Among the topics discussed are the relations between culture and identity; the potentialities of museums and monuments to support or subvert a people's sense of who they are; and how cultural heritage has been used to bring together communities containing people of different origins and traditions, yet without erasing or blurring their distinctive cultural features.

Cultural Heritage, Ethics and Contemporary Migrations is a crucial text for archaeologists, curators, policymakers and others working in the heritage field, as well as for philosophers, political scientists and other readers interested in the links between immigration and cultural heritage.

Cornelius Holtorf is Professor of Archaeology and holds a UNESCO Chair on Heritage Futures at Linnaeus University in Kalmar, Sweden. He also directs the Graduate School in Contract Archaeology (GRASCA). In his research he is particularly interested in the significance of archaeology and heritage in present and future societies.

Andreas Pantazatos is Assistant Professor in the Philosophy Department, Parliamentary Academic Fellow, University College Fellow and Co-Director of the Centre for the Ethics of Cultural Heritage at Durham University, UK. He is also Research Associate at the Collaborative for Cultural Heritage Management and Policy at the Department of Anthropology of the University of Illinois, USA. His interests are philosophy of cultural heritage and archaeology, ethics of stewardship and trusteeship, epistemic injustice and museums, ethics of identity and politics of the past (including post-war heritage reconstruction) and ethics of heritage and immigration.

Geoffrey Scarre is a Professor in the Philosophy Department at Durham University, UK. In recent years he has taught and published mainly in moral theory and applied ethics. His books include *Utilitarianism* (1996), *After Evil* (2004), *Death* (2007) and *On Courage* (2010), and he has co-edited two previous collections of papers on ethics in archaeology. In 2009 he was a co-founder of the Durham University Centre for the Ethics of Cultural Heritage.

CULTURAL HERITAGE, ETHICS AND CONTEMPORARY MIGRATIONS

Edited by Cornelius Holtorf, Andreas Pantazatos and Geoffrey Scarre

Routledge
Taylor & Francis Group

LONDON AND NEW YORK

First published 2019
by Routledge
2 Park Square, Milton Park, Abingdon, Oxon OX14 4RN

and by Routledge
52 Vanderbilt Avenue, New York, NY 10017

Routledge is an imprint of the Taylor & Francis Group, an informa business

British Library Cataloguing-in-Publication Data
A catalogue record for this book is available from the British Library

Library of Congress Cataloging-in-Publication Data
Names: Holtorf, Cornelius, 1968- editor. | Pantazatos, Andreas, editor. | Scarre, Geoffrey, editor.
Title: Cultural heritage, ethics and contemporary migrations / edited by Cornelius Holtorf, Andreas Pantazatos and Geoffrey Scarre.
Description: Abingdon, Oxon ; New York, NY : Routledge, 2018. | Includes bibliographical references and index.
Identifiers: LCCN 2018025087 | ISBN 9781138788213 (hardback : alk. paper) | ISBN 9781138788220 (paperback: alk. paper) | ISBN 9780429464300 (ebook) | ISBN 9780429875229 (ePub) | ISBN 9780429875236 (web pdf) | ISBN 9780429875212 (mobi kindle)
Subjects: LCSH: Cultural property. | Cultural pluralism. | Emigration and immigration—Social aspects.
Classification: LCC CC135 .C834 2018 | DDC 363.6/9—dc23
LC record available at https://lccn.loc.gov/2018025087

ISBN: 978-1-138-78821-3 (hbk)
ISBN: 978-1-138-78822-0 (pbk)
ISBN: 978-0-429-46430-0 (ebk)

Typeset in Bembo
by Swales & Willis Ltd, Exeter, Devon, UK

Printed and bound in Great Britain by
TJ International Ltd, Padstow, Cornwall

CONTENTS

FIGURES

CONTRIBUTORS

Michael Blake is Professor of Philosophy, Public Policy and Governance at the University of Washington, where he is appointed in the Department of Philosophy and in the Daniel J. Evans School of Public Policy and Governance. He writes on global justice and migration. His most recent book, written with Gillian Brock, is entitled *Debating Brain Drain: May Governments Restrict Emigration?* (Oxford University Press, 2013). He is currently writing a book on the relationship between justice, migration and the virtue of mercy.

Denis Byrne is a research fellow at the Institute of Culture and Society, Western Sydney University, Australia. He is an archaeologist who has worked both in the government and academic spheres of heritage conservation and has been a time contributor to critical debates on the practices of archaeology and heritage conservation in Southeast Asia and Australia. He is author of *Surface Collection: Archaeological Travels in Southeast Asia* (2007), and *Counter Heritage: Critical Perspectives on Heritage Conservation in Asia* (2014). His current research interests include a study of the China–Australia migration heritage corridor.

Laia Colomer is an archaeologist with extensive professional and academic experience in archaeological heritage management and public archaeology. The question currently driving her research focuses on how particular heritage communities use and develop cultural heritage to reinforce or redefine their identity in an increasingly globalised world. She was educated in Barcelona (PhD in Prehistory Archaeology, Autonomous University of Barcelona) and in London (MA in Public Archaeology, University College London). She has combined an academic career in the Netherlands, the UK, Spain and Sweden, with a professional career in cultural heritage management in Spain and Italy, including in both paths several European Commission projects. Currently Colomer is a researcher in the Archaeology Department, Linnaeus University, Sweden.

Jason De León is Professor of Anthropology and Chicana/o Studies at the University of California Los Angeles. He is also Director of the Undocumented Migration Project. His 2015 book *The Land of Open Graves: Living and Dying on the Migrant Trail* was awarded the 2016 Margaret Mead Award by the American Anthropological Association and the Society for Applied Anthropology. De León's work has been featured in numerous popular media outlets including The New York Times, National Public Radio, and Al Jazeera. He is co-curator of the award-winning exhibition State of Exception and a National Geographic Emerging Explorer.

Margarita Díaz-Andreu is an ICREA Research Professor based at the University of Barcelona. She is the Principal Investigator (PI) of the Public Archaeology and Heritage Group (www.gapp.cat) and was the PI of the Spanish team for the 'Heritage Values Network' European JPI project. Her areas of research are the history of archaeological heritage, archaeological tourism, migration and the politics of heritage. She has published widely in international journals on these matters.

Cynthia Dunning Thierstein studied archaeology at the University of Geneva, Switzerland, where she presented a PhD thesis on the Early Iron Age. She also obtained a Master's in Advanced Studies in Cultural Management at the University of Basel, Switzerland. From the beginning of her career she was always very interested in the theory of archaeology and its management, which she applied to the institutions she led (the Schwab Museum in Biel and the Archaeological Service of the Canton of Berne, Switzerland). In 2011, she founded a company specialising in the development and management of archaeology, conservation and museology projects. The use of archaeological heritage in the domains of sociology is a theme she developed while working with multicultural school classes in her hometown of Biel. On an international level, she participated in the development of principles of good practice in archaeological archives and started an archaeology and tourism network which will help to raise standards in archaeological tourism.

Ivan Gaskell is Professor of Cultural History and Museum Studies at Bard Graduate Center, New York City. Using non-written traces of the past, he addresses intersections among history, art history, anthropology and philosophy. As well as writing case studies ranging from seventeenth-century Dutch and Flemish paintings, Native American baskets and Congo textiles, he works on underlying philosophical questions. He is the author or editor of twelve books, most recently *Tangible Things: Making History through Objects* (2015). He organised numerous exhibitions at Harvard University, where he taught and curated between 1991 and 2011. At Bard Graduate Center, as well as teaching in the Masters and PhD programmes, Gaskell heads the Focus Project, an ongoing series of experimental exhibitions and publications. He is a Permanent Senior Fellow of the Advanced Study Institute of the Georg-August University, Göttingen, Germany.

Paul Gilbert is Emeritus Professor of Philosophy at the University of Hull, where he taught from 1967 to 2007. He was Head of Philosophy from 1985 to 1994 and of Humanities from 1999 to 2007. His publications include *Human Relationships* (1991), *Terrorism, Security and Nationality* (1994), *The Philosophy of Nationalism*

(1998), *Philosophy of Mind* (with K. Lennon and S. Burwood, 1998), *Peoples, Cultures and Nations in Political Philosophy* (2000), *New Terror, New Wars* (2003), *The World, The Flesh and The Subject* (with K. Lennon, 2005), *Cultural Identity and Political Ethics* (2013) and *An Introduction to Metaphilosophy* (with S. Overgaard and S. Burwood, 2013).

Cameron Gokee is an Assistant Professor of Anthropology at Appalachian State University, USA. He collaborates with the Undocumented Migration Project to study and call attention to the ways in which undocumented migrants experience the dangerous physical and political landscape of the US–Mexico borderlands. His fieldwork in the upper Senegal–Niger region of West Africa takes a multi-scalar approach to the history of village communities over the past thousand years – a period that witnessed long-term climate change, the rise and fall of medieval empires, the violence of the Atlantic slave trade, the spread of Islam, and ulti-mately, the imposition of colonialism.

Johan Hegardt is Associate Professor in Archaeology (Uppsala University). His research focus is within critical heritage and museum studies and he is active in a vast amount of projects, among others the project Art, Culture, Conflict: Transformations of Museums and Memory Culture in the Baltic Sea Region after 1989. Hegardt has been a member of the research programme Time, Memory and Representations: A Multidisciplinary Program on Transformations in Historical Consciousness. In his contribution to this collection of essays Hegardt takes his point of departure from an ongoing project in the city of Örebro, Sweden.

Christopher Prescott is currently Director at the Norwegian Institute in Rome, Italy, Archaeology Professor at the University of Oslo, Norway and Docent at the University of Gothenburg, Sweden. He has served on numerous departmen-tal, faculty, museum and university boards, as well as been head of departments and teaching programmes – leading to an interest in the social aspects of recruit-ment and training in the humanities. He has been involved in several national and international archaeological projects as well as the Nordic graduate school in archaeology Dialogues with the Past and served as editor-in-chief of the *Norwegian Archaeological Review* from 1997 to 2001. His primary research interests have been Nordic Prehistory from the Late Neolithic to the end of the Bronze Age, the Northern European Bell Beaker Culture, the Archaic Period in southern Italy, migration and knowledge transmission, environmental archaeology and the rela-tionship between humanities and science, the illicit trade in antiquities, and the social and political implications of globalisation for heritage and archaeological knowledge production.

Robert Seddon conducted his doctoral research into the ethics of cultural herit-age at Durham University, where he retains an Honorary Fellowship with the Department of Philosophy and membership of the Centre for the Ethics of Cultural Heritage. His research interests within applied ethics have also extended into aspects of the philosophy of technology, from 'virtual' realities, through bioenhancement, back to the cultural heritage of the heavens as encountered in space exploration.

Jonathan Seglow is Reader (Associate Professor) in Political Theory at Royal Holloway, University of London. He is the author of *Defending Associative Duties* (Routledge, 2013) and of recent articles on hate speech, self-respect, religious accommodation and establishment in journals including *Ethical Theory and Moral Practice, Ethnicities* and *Critical Review of International Social and Political Philosophy*.

Helaine Silverman is Professor in the Department of Anthropology at the University of Illinois and Director of the Collaborative for Cultural Heritage Management and Policy (CHAMP). She is an Expert Member of ICOMOS' International Scientific Committees on Archaeological Heritage Management (ICAHM) and Cultural Tourism (ICTC). Her research focuses on cultural politics in the production and consumption of archaeological monuments and living historic centres. In addition to her own authored works she is the editor/co-editor of: *Archaeological Site Museums in Latin America* (2006), *Cultural Heritage and Human Rights* (2007), *Intangible Heritage Embodied* (2009), *Contested Cultural Heritage* (2011), *Cultural Heritage Politics in China* (2013), *Encounters with Popular Pasts* (2015), *Heritage in Action* (2017) and *Heritage of Death* (2018). She currently serves on the editorial boards of *International Journal of Heritage Studies, Heritage & Society, World Art* and *Thema*. She is the editor of two book series: Heritage, Tourism, and Community (Routledge) and Multidisciplinary Perspectives in Archaeological Heritage Management (Springer).

1

INTRODUCTION

*Geoffrey Scarre, Cornelius Holtorf and
Andreas Pantazatos*

The story of humanity is a tale of migration and we are all of us migrants or the
descendants of migrants. Truly aboriginal inhabitants are to be found nowhere on
earth. As Sir Thomas Browne put it in the seventeenth century, 'There was therefore never any Autochthon but . . . Adam' (1658: 334). Whether we conceive our
origins to have been in the Garden of Eden or the Olduvai Gorge, we should recognise that human beings have always been wanderers over the face of the globe,
moved to travel by a myriad of factors including increase of population, pressure
on resources, exhaustion of habitat, climate change, war, political strife, famine and
disease – to which should be added our natural acquisitiveness, ambition and curiosity. Current techniques of analysis, including genetic mapping, reveal just how
extensive the movement and intermingling of people over time has been and make
it clear that many of the more habitable parts of the earth have been contested
sites since high antiquity. Mass movements of people by land and sea have been a
constant feature throughout thousands of years of prehistory and history, a pattern
of things that continues to the present day.

This human heritage of migration poses problems and affords opportunities.
The problems arise in part because human beings are territorial animals accustomed
to stake exclusionary claims to land and resources. Hence the arrival of outsiders
who demand or request to have a share in the same goods is often resented and
resisted even where the newcomers are able in some way to 'pay' for the privilege,
for example by contributing their own goods and labour or providing new and
useful skills. Where the new arrivals are considered as 'strangers in our midst' (to
quote from the title of a recent book by David Miller (2016)), a conceptual obstacle impedes the formation of smooth social relationships. As Matthew Lindauer
remarks, 'Discussions of strangers walking among us forseeably evoke fear and distrust of these people (Lindauer 2017: 273). The advent of people who do things
differently can be a source of social and cultural enrichment for the host society but

it can also generate fear, suspicion, puzzlement and a sense of threatened identity, especially if migrants arrive in large numbers or speak unfamiliar languages. (Popular worries about the large scale of immigration into Britain in recent decades were a major factor influencing many UK citizens to vote for so-called 'Brexit' from the European Union in the referendum of June 2016.) The thought that we are all migrants or descended from such cuts little ice when it comes to welcoming newcomers, for even quite shallow ancestral roots in a particular location are commonly sufficient to make its people regard it as 'theirs' and act as jealous guardians of its boundaries. And once we are firmly entrenched behind our own borders (a situation which can develop in very few generations), those who are outside, as Edward Said has noted, are represented as the Other: alien, strange and potentially threatening (Said 1978).

No social phenomenon is more familiar to those of us who live in the developed world than the mass movement of peoples since the Second World War, with many countries receiving very large numbers of migrants; so by now we should be very well used to seeing new faces. Yet familiarity does not always bring with it acceptance. At the time of writing, US President Donald Trump would like to build a border wall to prevent immigrants entering the USA illegally from Mexico. Europe is experiencing an unprecedented wave of migration from the strife-torn countries of the Near- and Middle-East, especially Syria, Iraq and Afghanistan. Germany's decision, prompted by its Chancellor, Angela Merkel, to grant entry to close on one million immigrants from Syrian and neighbouring lands has been welcomed by many but not all Germans (reaction by the dissentients has resulted in the dramatic rise of the far-right party, the 'Alternative for Germany' (AfD), in elections in Summer 2017). Meanwhile a savage process of ethnic cleansing is underway in predominantly Buddhist Myanmar, where half a million Muslims from the province of Rohingya have been forced by the army to flee across the border to Bangladesh. All these large migrations of peoples, however, may yet be dwarfed in scale in the future if rising sea-levels and wide-scale desertification produced by climate change cause large areas of currently populated land to become uninhabitable.

While most of these migrants are asylum-seekers desiring to be accepted as refugees in 'safe' countries, recent years have also seen an increase worldwide in the phenomenon of economic migration and this affects all continents. Thousands of people from several African countries each year attempt the perilous sea crossing from Libya to Europe, and hundreds lose their lives as their overcrowded, ill-equipped boats founder in the Mediterranean. Although some of the African migrants are escaping war or persecution in their home countries, others are fleeing poverty and looking for a better life in Europe. There are many different categories of migrants and generalisations about them can be misleading. Some migrants are willing emigrants from their original countries, others are victims of forced removal or 'ethnic cleansing'; some are looking for permanent homes elsewhere, others for only a temporary place of refuge or employment. Attitudes to mass migration in the receiving countries have likewise varied, as much in the academic community as in the wider population. Writers on the liberal wing, while lamenting the bad conditions that have driven many people to seek a new life in a new land, have tended to see mass migration more in terms of opportunity than of threat from the point of view of the receiving countries. At one extreme, Ash Amin represents the Europe of the future as ideally the space of no fixed cultures but as an eternal melting-pot or marketplace of disparate cultural traditions, essentially a migrant space rather than a place of settled ideas and modes of life (Amin 2004). This radical vision contrasts markedly with that of more conservative thinkers who fear that, under the pressure of the new, the best of the old will be lost and European national identities and the well-being of the original population be diminished in consequence.

Cultural *heritage* is essentially an *inheritance* that reinforces ties among the generations, a mechanism by which we receive goods from our forebears and hand them down to our descendants. It is not a simple legacy to be used (or used up) in whatever way we like. Through the device of cultural inheritance a society preserves not simply its art and archaeology, literature, scholarship, monuments and other historical reference points, but its identity over time, linking its past, present and future members by a connecting chain of traditions, customs, values and beliefs. While, in David Lowenthal's words, 'most heritage comes already packaged by precursors' (Lowenthal 1998: 23), later generations generally make their own mark on it as well. Of course, not all cultural traditions deserve to be preserved and handed on: slavery and human sacrifice obviously do not, however central they may have been to a particular society's sense of identity. (On the other hand, the *memory* that these things were once practised should be retained, as a salutary warning to the future and an antidote to self-complacency.) One advantage of cultural mixing is that it can help a community, whether established or migrant, to achieve a better critical perspective on its own traditions, by revealing the existence of alternatives.

The cultural heritage of refugees and immigrants makes contributions to their lives in multiple ways. It sustains memory links between their homeland and those who are displaced from it, whether voluntarily or not. It retains connections with past forms of life that were a source of self-respect and happiness. Heritage can help displaced communities to construct meaningful futures for themselves, building on their past traditions and achievements. Cultural heritage enables displaced communities to maintain their relations with present and future generations of their homeland, even though they do not live there anymore. At the same time, they must forge viable relationships with the culture (or cultures) of their new country, otherwise they will never be able to feel at home there. It would be naïve to suppose that such personal cultural integration is always easy of attainment. Yet it is something worth striving for, as immigrants who are receptive to the cultural heritage of their old home and their new can enjoy what both have to offer.

It might be suggested that those who speak of 'native' or traditional culture as having to be defended against the influx of new customs and ideas demonstrate a wrong mindset from the start. For why should the imported cultural heritage of immigrants be seen as endangering long-standing traditions? Can there not be co-existence without rivalry or competition? Such co-existence is certainly possible where a spirit of 'live and let live' prevails and members of older and newer communities are prepared to extend the hand of friendship to each other. The trouble is that mutual goodwill between established and immigrant communities has too often been conspicuous by its absence. The advent of white European immigrants in the Americas, Australia and elsewhere had a calamitous impact on existing indigenous populations and their cultures (see, e.g., Lear 2006). Where native people have been murdered or marginalised, their land taken and their traditions disparaged, the damage to a culture may be permanent and irremediable. It is natural for members of both established and migrant communities to be anxious when they find themselves among new neighbours whose ways seem strange to them. As Miller writes: 'People feel at home in a place in part because they can see that their surroundings bear the imprint of past generations whose values were recognizably their own' (Miller 2005: 201). When those familiar surroundings become significantly marked by foreign imprints, the sense of being at home in them can become harder to sustain. And for recent arrivals who find themselves in culturally unfamiliar surroundings, the absence of the imprint of their own forebears can be even more disorientating, fostering a sense of loss and diaspora.

Seyla Benhabib notes that the boundaries separating cultures are typically 'contested, fragile as well as delicate', while 'the interpretation of cultures as hermetic, sealed and internally self-consistent wholes is untenable' (Benhabib 2002: 7, 25). When people from diverse cultural backgrounds live close together, as they have come to do in much of Europe in the last half century, a degree of cultural mixing is inevitable as people wax curious about the habits of their neighbours. One way in which this happens is by a blending of traditions, in which formerly disparate past patterns of action merge to form new wholes, or the broader social acceptance of practices that were formerly special to particular communities. This mixing and mingling of cultural traditions can be highly rewarding for all concerned. Take, as a homely example, the evolution of the British diet over the last half century. Where once the standard British dinner consisted of meat and two vegetables (varied by fish and chips on Fridays), followed by rice pudding and a cup of tea, nowadays Britons enjoy a vast range of cuisines from across the world. While the old menus remain available for those of more conservative tastes, no one could sensibly wish to return to the limited diet of earlier years. Here, as in many other cases that could be cited, the new supplements and enriches the old without supplanting it.

Admittedly, food (if not always the methods of meat production) is a relatively uncontentious matter when compared with religious belief and practice, conventional relations between the sexes, or such traditions as arranged marriage, circumcision (of both genders) and the public wearing of the burka by Muslim women. Yet to represent even some of the more controversial imported practices as a *threat* to existing traditions is rarely plausible; co-existence, even if occasionally uneasy, is more common than confrontation. Western women will not start wearing the burka just because some of their Islamic sisters do so. In any case, since toleration and the acceptance of difference are hallmarks of our democratic societies, to object to imported practices that are unfamiliar or disconcerting is to depart from one of our own most prized cultural traditions. Miller remarks that the wish to maintain a sense of kinship with those who have gone before us:

> doesn't rule out cultural change, but . . . it gives a reason for wanting to stay in control of the process – for teaching children to value their cultural herit-age and to regard themselves as having a responsibility to preserve the parts of it that are worth preserving, for example
>
> *(David Miller, 2005: 201).*

This seems broadly right, although it need not (and should not) be taken to imply that guardianship of a particular culture is the proper concern only of those who have grown up in it. The preservation of culture is better seen as a collaborative enterprise. Taking an interest in one another's heritage is one of the best ways by which people from different cultural backgrounds break down any initial barriers between them. (It is reported that some Syrian immigrants in Germany have been appointed by museums in Berlin to explain their Islamic artefacts to visitors.)[1] To stand aloof from the habits and customs, beliefs, religious and moral views, man-ners, art, music, food and pastimes of one's neighbours not only inhibits sociability but loses a precious opportunity to experience and benefit from other ways of living. People who make the effort to understand and appreciate others' cultural traditions will find themselves rewarded for their trouble even if they conclude that certain elements of those other cultures are not for them. What they may have thought was *the* right way to do something they now see to be only one of various possibilities, and not always necessarily the best.

One clearly important question in the management of cultural heritage of all kinds is how immigrant communities can be enabled to relate to the cultural her-itage of the receiving country. But equally, members of established communities need to be encouraged to understand and appreciate the traditions of their immi-grant neighbours. Ideally, people of different communities will themselves reach out to their neighbours. Members of immigrant communities, whether of the first or later generations, are understandably unwilling to jettison all their old traditions when they move to a new land, and they should not be expected to. Yet migrants who discover no sympathy for the customs and ethos of the receiving culture will never feel truly at home in their new surroundings; theirs will remain the mindset of exiles, not of citizens. However, original residents who resent the advent of the newcomers are just as much an obstacle to sociability.

The goal should be for both migrants and original residents to connect with each other's culture while neither cutting nor disvaluing their own cultural roots. Achieving this goal requires *integrative processes that are respectful of difference*, processes that unite rather than divide, invite rather than enforce, look forward rather than backward, and – most importantly – promote the exchange of cultural influences in a two-way direction. And if such processes are not to meet with resentment or resistance, they should be whole-community enterprises, in which migrants play a partnership role in their design and delivery. Some writers argue that this requires in effect a new understanding of what heritage is and can be in contemporary society. For example, Cornelius Holtorf and Graham Fairclough (2013) recently proposed that because heritage in multicultural societies is no longer able to unite citizens by evoking a common origin and historical narrative shared by all citizens, a 'New Heritage' is needed – and already emerging – that provides a range of different societal benefits relating to health and quality of life, belonging and democracy, sustainability and development, and reflection and awareness.

In the wake of the waves of migrants and refugees in recent years, a variety of heritage projects have been developed to assist displaced communities to tell their own stories and make their heritage a reminder of their identity and a signpost to the future. For instance, in the so-called 'Jungle of Calais', the makeshift camp set up by migrants hoping to find their (legal or illegal) way from France into Britain, the occupants displayed their everyday objects on trees in order to tell their stories.[2] Evidently, wherever people gather together, culture and cultural heritage will quickly emerge. Another example which sheds light on the contribution of heritage to meaningful life is that of the UN project with Syrian artist refugees in Jordan.[3] Displaced by the civil war in their own country, these artists were given simple tools to replicate in miniature the heritage monuments of their country. So far, they have chosen to replicate those such as the temple at Palmyra and the Aleppo Minaret that suffered destruction at the hands of DAESH ('Islamic State'). Asked the question why they chose that project, the project coordinator Ahmad Hariri, from Dara'a, responded that 'We chose this project to highlight what is happening in Syria, because many of these sites are under threat or have already been destroyed.' These artworks, he explained, would allow Syrian children of the future to see what these structures looked like before their obliteration in the civil war. He pointed out that 'There are lots of kids living here who have never seen Syria or who have no memory of it. They know more about Jordan than about their own country.' This project may be a possible model for the preservation of cultural heritage (or its memory) in other places too. Future generations of Syrians and likewise those of other countries whose communities have been displaced might be reconnected with their origins via artistic replicas of cultural heritage. While art is no substitute for bread, working with heritage may help refugees to find some relief from the difficulties of their lives in temporary camps and shelters and to retain a sense of who they are.

Cultural integration in an age of mass migration is obviously a huge topic and one that can and needs to be studied from many different disciplinary angles. The scope of the present volume is of necessity limited, its contributing authors having been asked to focus primarily on ethical questions to do with management of the immigrant experience of the material, and especially the archaeological heritage of the countries that receive them. In this context 'archaeological heritage' is understood in a broad sense, to encompass sites and artefacts in the landscape as well as moveable objects held in museum and gallery collections. Although these questions may seem quite narrow when considered in relation to the broader issues adumbrated in the preceding pages, the editors believe that they are not only interesting and important in themselves but very illuminating in regard to those wider issues. Many of the points of discussion of immigration and the archaeological heritage have their close counterparts when other aspects of migration and cultural heritage are the topic of debate. Our method might be termed 'microcosmical', a mode of elucidating the whole by the study of its parts. The individual essays are written by specialists from a variety of disciplinary backgrounds. They present different ethical and political views and the book does not constitute a manifesto for any particular viewpoint or party-line. The choice of authors reflects the editors' conviction that the pooling of the expertise of specialists from different academic backgrounds and from a range of countries produces a volume having an intellectual authority and richness that would not otherwise be obtainable.

There is already a large literature about the archaeological evidence for past migrations and it is not our purpose to add to that. We are concerned, rather, with some of the issues raised by the disciplines of archaeology and heritage studies in the contemporary world of mass migration. What happens when fluid streams of people come into contact with landscapes, sites and objects whose use, analysis, evaluation and presentation are frequently ethically sensitive, particularly where established and immigrant communities differ in their cultural norms and expectations? What material traces and cultural heritage is being brought along or created by migrating people? How do host countries treat the tangible heritage of migrant communities? Are rights to citizenship related to rights to cultural heritage? These issues, although very timely, have not yet attracted as much academic research as they deserve (but see e.g. Ashworth *et al.* 2007, Buciek and Juul 2008, Holtorf 2009, Byrne 2014, Högberg 2016, Hamilakis 2016).

Previously resident and newly arriving communities taking a joint interest in heritage could greatly increase their understanding of and engagement with their shared society; each community may discover that the encounter with the unfamiliar heritage yields considerable intellectual satisfaction as well. Not only archaeologists working in the field but museum curators and directors of preservation bodies (e.g. the National Trust and English Heritage in the UK) who are responsible for the public interpretation and display of archaeological and other historical sites, structures and artefacts must consider how best to do their work in a way that respects the rights, traditions and divergent expectations of all – established communities and newcomers alike (MeLa 2015). Deciding what to research, what to preserve, what to display and what to say about the displayed material are practical questions with a strong ethical dimension. In addition, there are questions about *who* is entitled to make such decisions and *who* is encouraged to pursue the careers that provide the competence necessary for making them.

Migrant communities have legitimate cause for complaint if the only cultural heritage exhibited or celebrated is that of the host country. Because cultural exchange should be a two-way traffic, established communities as well as migrant groups will benefit from the opportunity to become acquainted with other cultural traditions through their material and immaterial products. Thus the exquisite Islamic mosque lamps or the marvellously crafted Benin bronze statuettes now held in the British Museum (albeit in the latter case controversially, these being trophies of imperialist war), while dear to those from whose cultures they emanate, including their descendants now living in Britain, speak eloquently too to people from quite different cultural backgrounds. Encountering objects from many cultures is undoubtedly better than knowing only those from one's own, and supplying the opportunity to do so is a prime aim of such 'encyclopaedic' museums as the British Museum, the Louvre or the Metropolitan Museum, despite their origin in colonial and imperialistic pasts. Yet the museum sector will always face questions about focus, interpretation and the concentration of financial, as well as academic (research), resources. So in a city with an ethnically mixed population and diverse cultural traditions, how should limited museum display-space be used and limited financial resources be allocated to the conserving of objects and the provision of exhibitions and special events; and who should be responsible for the interpretations of a museum's holdings? How should children of established and immigrant communities be brought to engage with a variety of cultural traditions? Do museums have a role here, and, if so, what is it? Is there a danger that well-meaning efforts to keep alive and in the public mind different cultural traditions could have the unwanted effect of fostering social divides, sustaining a sense of 'us' and 'them'? Most generally, how should cultural heritage of different origins be disseminated, preserved and celebrated in our mixed and multicultural societies, so that it brings advantage to all and fosters social integration rather than division?[4]

Questions of this kind are the concern of the authors of the chapters of this book, all of which have been specially written for this volume. The result is a wide-ranging collection which explores, with many case-studies, the place of cultural heritage in the contemporary world of shifting populations. The writers come from a range of disciplinary backgrounds, including philosophy, anthropology, archaeology, political science and cultural studies, and their contributions are informed not only by a rich array of theoretical resources but also, in several cases, by personal experience of working with immigrant communities as they face life in a new land. In pursuing their particular themes, the contributors throw light on fundamental questions about the meaning and importance of cultural heritage, its relationship to citizenship and its role in creating and sustaining community identities, the problems and prospects for cultural integration, the types and viability of 'multiculturalism', the respective cultural rights of 'native' and migrant populations, and the responsibilities of governments and other agencies in managing cultural change. To add that the answers given to these large questions should be seen as tentative suggestions – as prompts to further reflection – rather than definitive conclusions, is to state the obvious without in any way belittling the essays. For discussion of all these issues is a work in progress, for scholars, politicians and ordinary citizens alike.

The contents of the book are divided for convenience into three parts, although these should not be seen as sharply discrete and a number of the papers could have appeared in more than one of them. Following this Introduction by the editors, the papers of Part I, entitled *Things 'r' us: archaeological heritage as a preserver of social identity*, discuss the ways in which culture and social identity are intimately and intricately related in the case of immigrant communities. The chapters of Part II, *Memory, migrants and museums*, focus, with the aid of case-studies, on the potentialities of museums and monuments to support or subvert a people's sense of who they are. Finally, the chapters of Part III, *Cultural heritage as an agent of integration*, look at some of the ways in which cultural heritage has been used to bring together communities containing people of different origins and traditions, yet without erasing or blurring their distinctive and identity-giving cultural features. While the authors of this part do not underestimate the practical difficulties of bringing people of different cultural backgrounds into new relationships that allow them, in Cynthia Dunning Thierstein's words, to feel 'different yet all the same', the successes they report show that the pessimists are wrong to think that societies of mixed origin can only avoid instability or disintegration if they become bland monocultures.

Migration shapes the history of humanity, a fact amply reflected in its cultural heritage. The rich exchange of things and narratives, and the consequent conversations about beliefs, ideals and forms of life, mould heritage and remodel social identities. The present volume acknowledges the relationship between migration and heritage and explores some of the ethical questions which arise from the multiple interactions between people, things, landscapes and knowledge-institutions such as museums. The mass migrations of vulnerable people in the world today rightly call for humanitarian responses from those who are able to help. But contemporary migration should be thought of in terms of prospects as well as of problems. Migration in the twenty-first century provides us with a unique opportunity to redefine and renew our cultural heritage, and to delineate our future epistemic, ethical and political obligations in respect of what we have in common.

Notes

1 See https://ec.europa.eu/epale/en/blog/multaqa-museum-meeting-point-refugees-guides-berlin-museums (Accessed July 2017), www.unhcr.org/uk/news/stories/2016/6/576d29884/berlin-refugee-guides-show-cultural-riches-home.html (accessed July 2017), and www.smb.museum/en/museums-institutions/museum-fuer-islamische-kunst/collection-research/research-cooperation/multaka.html (accessed July 2017).

2 Private communication to Andreas Pantazatos. For further information on cultural activities in the Calais camp, see http://jungle-news.arte.tv/en/2016/10/19/is-the-calais-jungle-an-urban-heritage/ (accessed September 2017).

3 See http://tracks.unhcr.org/2016/01/syrias-landmarks-restored-in-miniature/ (accessed August 2017).

4 The newly founded Migration Museum Project in London (www.migrationmuseum.org) is an effort to address some challenging questions about migrants and their stories in Britain and beyond.

References

Amin, Ash. 2004. 'Multi-ethnicity and the idea of Europe,' *Theory, Culture and Society*, **21**, 1–24.

Ashworth, Gregory J., Brian Graham and J.E. Tunbridge. 2007. *Pluralising Pasts: Heritage, Identity and Place in Multicultural Societies*. London: Pluto Press.

Benhabib, Seyla. 2002. *The Claims of Culture: Equality and Diversity in the Global Era*. Princeton, NJ: Princeton University Press.

Browne, Thomas. 1658. *Pseudodoxia Epidemica: or Enquiries into Very Many Received Tenents, and Commonly Presumed Truths*. London: Edward Dod for Andrew Crouch.

Buciek, Keld and Juul, Kristine. 2008. '"We are here, yet we are not here": the heritage of excluded groups,' in Graham, B. and P. Howard (eds.), *The Ashgate Research Companion to Heritage and Identity*, 105–23. Aldershot: Ashgate.

Byrne, Denis. 2014. 'Counter-mapping and migrancy on the Georges River,' in Schofield, J. (ed.), *Who Needs Experts?*, 77–91. Farnham, UK and Burlington, VT: Ashgate.

Hamilakis, Yannis. (ed.) 2016. 'Forum: Archaeologies of Forced and Undocumented Migration', *Journal of Contemporary Archaeology*, **3(2)**, 121–294.

Högberg, Anders. 2016. 'To renegotiate heritage and citizenship beyond essentialism,' *Archaeological Dialogues*, **23(1)**, 38–48.

Holtorf, Cornelius. 2009. 'A European perspective on indigenous and immigrant archaeologies,' *World Archaeology*, **41(4)**, 672–81.

Holtorf, Cornelius and Fairclough, Graham. 2013. 'The new heritage and re-shapings of the past,' in González-Ruibal, Alfredo (ed.), *Reclaiming Archaeology Beyond the Troops of Modernity*, 197–210. London and New York: Routledge.

Lear, Jonathan. 2006. *Radical Hope: Ethics in the Face of Cultural Devastation*. Cambridge, MA and London: Harvard University Press.

Lindauer, Matthew. 2017. 'Review of David Miller: *Strangers in Our Midst: The Political Philosophy of Immigration*,' *Ethics*, **128(1)**, 269–74.

Lowenthal, David. 1998. *The Heritage Crusade and the Spoils of History*. Cambridge: Cambridge University Press.

MeLa. 2015. *European Museums in an Age of Immigration. MeLa Project Final Brochure*. 90pp. Available via <www.mela-project.polimi.it/publications/1266.htm> (accessed 30 June 2016).

Miller, David. 2005. 'Immigration: the case for limits,' in Cohen, Andrew I., and Wellman, Christopher Heath (eds.), *Contemporary Debates in Applied Ethics*, 193–206. Malden, MA and Oxford: Blackwell.

Miller, David. 2016. *Strangers in Our Midst: The Political Philosophy of Immigration*. Cambridge, MA: Harvard University Press.

Said, Edward. 1978. *Orientalism*. New York: Columbia University Press.

PART I
Things 'r' us
Archaeological heritage as a preserver of social identity

2

CULTURAL HERITAGE, MINORITIES AND SELF-RESPECT

Jonathan Seglow

Introduction

Cultural heritage embraces the significant artworks, rituals, stories, practices, festivals, archaeology, cities, landscapes and sacred places of a people, especially where they are vulnerable or at risk (Harrison, 2013, pp.5–7). It's been argued that culture only becomes 'heritagised' when it is no longer in active use as a tradition (Kockel, 2007). Here I take the opposite view: that those traditions are living ones which practitioners inherit from the past and propel into an indefinite future. Immigrants and other minorities often have a close relationship with a heritage that is vulnerable in the face of social and economic pressures; preserving their intangible heritage is a way of reproducing their cultural identity. Intangible heritage can be a source of ontological security for minorities in a society where other citizens have distinct physical characteristics, cultural beliefs, informal practices, religions and languages. However, that there is some loss when a minority's cultural heritage is eroded does not give us a reason in justice to maintain it; at least not without articulating the legitimate interest which is at stake. My aim here is to explore this interest.

I focus on the intangible cultural heritage (ICH) of (a) ethnic minorities in liberal democratic states, and (b) indigenous peoples who survive in liberal democratic states that were colonised by Europeans centuries ago.[1] Ethnic minorities typically participate in mainstream society, though they may be more or less integrated and often suffer from social and economic disadvantage. Indigenous peoples in settler societies such as Australia and Canada often live relatively isolated from the majority population, and seek to preserve their customs and traditions in the face of modernising pressures. Because my focus is ICH, I elaborate only a little on their situations as such. One could investigate the normative reasons to preserve the ICH of these groups by first examining why we should be concerned about the ICH of the majority, and then extending that answer to minorities. However, we cannot assume that the kinds of reasons to preserve the dominant cultural heritage apply also to minorities, especially as the former can impede the expression of minority heritage or minorities' contribution to the dominant heritage (as we shall see). In what follows, therefore, I examine the distinct reasons to be concerned about the ICH of groups (a) and (b) from the point of view of justice. My argument is that self-respect, as a fundamental and widely shared value, offers a promising basis for securing minorities' ICH, especially for those who are sceptical of the idea of cultural preservation at all.

On intangible cultural heritage

Heritage is defined by the *Council of Europe Framework Convention* (2005) as the resources inherited from the past with which people identify as a reflection and expression of their evolving values, beliefs, knowledge and traditions (cited in Nic Craith 2007, p.3). Heritage is a relatively recent invention. Prior to the nineteenth century, social memories and material heritage were a pervasive part of everyday life, not a subject for commemoration; heritage is a reflexive appropriation of objects and practices considered at risk (in the face of economic, migratory and globalising pressures), and hence worth preserving as social references. Maintaining its heritage provides a community with a sense of identity, meaning and collective continuity. Yet, the values realised *through* safeguarding heritage should not be confused with the value of heritage items in *themselves* – the aesthetic value of a cathedral for example – and it's important to distinguish these two.

From the late 1990s, developing states complained that UNESCO's World Heritage List benefitted Western states with a monumentalist – or more broadly, material – tradition at the expense of those with living, traditional cultures of depth and complexity, and exhibiting diverse relationships to the environment (Munjeri 2009, p.132). Thus was born the 2003 *Convention for Safeguarding Intangible Cultural Heritage*. Article 2.1 of the *Convention* defines ICH very broadly as the 'practices, representations, expressions, knowledge, skills – as well as the instruments objects, artefacts and cultural spaces associated therewith – that communities, groups and in some cases individuals recognise as part of their heritage' (cited in Marrie 2009, p.170). Article 2.2 goes on to clarify that ICH is manifested inter alia in oral traditions, performing arts, rituals and festivals, practices concerning nature and the universe and traditional craftsmanship (cited in Marrie 2009, p.171). While some might baulk that this elides culture and cultural heritage (cf. Kockel (2007)), a case has been made that 'all heritage is intangible, not only because of the values we give to heritage, but because of the cultural work that heritage does in any society' (Smith and Akagawa, 2009, p.6; cf. Smith 2006, pp.53–7).

International Declarations and Charters other than the *Convention* articulate bold aspirations to protect the ICH of indigenous peoples and other minority cultures. UNESCO proclaimed a representative list of masterpieces of oral and intangible heritage in 2001. Article 13 of UNESCO's 2002 *Universal Declaration on Cultural Diversity* states that cultural diversity is an 'ethical imperative, inseparable from respect for human dignity itself'. 'Cultural rights are an integral part of human rights', it states, and 'all persons have the right to participate in the cultural life of their choice and conduct their own cultural practices', especially minorities and indigenous peoples (cited in Langfield et al. 2010, pp.7–8; cf. Harrison 2013, p.160). The 2006 UN *Declaration on the Rights of Indigenous Peoples* similarly claimed that indigenous peoples 'have the right to maintain, control, protect and develop their cultural heritage'; and to practice and revitalise their cultural traditions (Art 31.1, Art 11.1 cited in Marie 2009, p.179).

For indigenous peoples, the landscape is often the central medium through which intangible heritage values are expressed, its inner symbolic meaning the core of their customs and ways of life. '[L]and is seen as a living tradition over which the collectivity holds a communal responsibility and exercises custodianship' (Gilbert, 2010, p.32). Land has trans-generational significance and is the basis for creation stories, religion, spirituality, art, oral traditions, music and myth, besides economic and social imperatives such as hunting, fishing, gathering, exchange and kinship interactions (Magowan 2010, p.158). It's been argued that for the indigenous ontology, culture is omnipresent, destabilising the dualism of intangible and intangible heritage (Lee 2008, p.373). Thus while indigenous territories often appear rugged, remote and ostensibly under-developed, they are also 'cultural landscapes' which unify the inter-dependent natural, material and social worlds, and are imbued with intense symbolic meaning. For example, the Uluru-Kata Tjula National Park in Australia's Northern Territory represents, according to Harrison, 'a coherent landscape-centred ontology' (2013, p.118) that embodies the heroes and ancestors of the Aṉangu people who live there, replete with rules and rituals that govern the delicate ecological relationships between humans, animals, plants and the environment. Control over territory – as the Aṉangu have over Uluru-Kata Tjula – enables indigenous peoples to transmit their ICH to the next generation.

Ethnic minorities, unlike indigenous peoples, are largely imbricated in the institutions and practices of societies to which they or their forebears immigrated. Their cultural heritage is therefore bound up with evolving national cultural story. This is, however, normatively selective; it includes and it excludes. What Laurajane Smith (2006) has called the authorised heritage discourse legitimates certain buildings, places, events and practices as part of 'our' (national) heritage while passing over others. Thus in the UK, English Heritage and the National Trust construct a particular identity and narrative which then merits their stewardship (Smith and Waterton 2009, pp.290–1). Intangible heritage, often central to ethnic minorities' participation in their states of immigration, tends to be relegated by these institutions, even though Smith's earlier ethnographic work concluded that the indigenous British saw heritage as much through intangible categories such as workplace skills, family histories and cultural traditions as through the monumental tradition that was central to the authorised heritage discourse (Smith 2006). Along similar lines, Stuart Hall forcefully argued that, heritage is a discursive practice that *constructs* a collective social memory, foregrounding some events, while foreshortening, or silencing others (Hall, 2008). Nation-building is a process; an ongoing project. Through identifying with certain representations – the battle of Trafalgar, Dunkirk, country houses are some of his examples – we build up a national meaning.

Yet this construction is once again selective, it can silence and disavow those with little power and authority. Hence: 'those who cannot see themselves reflected in its [national heritage's] mirror cannot properly belong' (Hall 2008, p.220). Even institutions which supposedly safeguard the universal, such as the British Museum, are harnessed to the national story. Heritage tends to canonise only certain aspects of an inevitably plural tradition.

The sceptical challenge to cultural heritage

The *Universal Declaration on Cultural Diversity* takes cultural heritage to be a right. But human rights are commonly taken by rights theorists to define the minimum threshold of a decent life, subject to too many inflationary pressures they merely reflect aspirations, not claims of justice. Declarations and conventions are good at symbolically affirming the importance of hitherto unmet interests and crystallising a shared political consciousness; but they say little about the grounds of those interests, nor how to morally evaluate them. To understand why ICH should be a right (if it should) the first step is to investigate the relevant normative interests which might ground it. And we need to remember that their distinct situations – relatively autonomous indigenous cultures as against relatively integrated ethnic groups – means that these two groups' interests may work in quite different ways.

Minority cultural rights are by now a familiar part of the political landscape in multicultural societies, and have been effectively defended philosophically. Such rights include recognition of indigenous people's customary law and their title to historic territories; devolved self-government and political representation in larger democratic institutions; and for ethnic minorities as well as indigenous peoples affirmative action programmes, bilingual education and access to services in their own language, and legal accommodation for distinct cultural identities (for example revising work schedules to fit minorities' religious requirements). (Kymlicka, 2001, p.163). These rights go well beyond mere toleration of minority cultural practices; they involve state-sponsored recognition and promotion of them. Many of them are likely to have positive effects on maintaining a group's cultural heritage. But although, in what follows, I endorse this broad multicultural perspective my narrower aim is articulating the distinct interest in ICH, the assumption being that this requires some defence in itself. I investigate how we might defend the interest in ICH, leaving aside for now the question of whether there is a genuine human right to it.

I earlier distinguished between the value of heritage practices themselves and the values realised through safeguarding them such as identity and collective continuity. A focus on the former is one way of articulating that interest. Charles Taylor's (1994) influential argument for cultural recognition starts with the claim that every culture has a distinct authentic essence which is its unique identity. Members of minority cultures, both ethnic and indigenous, have a duty to express and realise their particular authentic identities as a central part of what is for them to flourish. Recognition of cultural identities, when politically institutionalised, helps realise that interest. This argument is sometimes criticised for its illiberalism. Seyla Benhabib for example cites the case of Canadian First Nations whose traditional practices mean that women lose their legal status by marrying out while men do not (Benhabib, 2002, pp.53-4). If cultural heritage is an interest, it must be balanced against other interests, values and claims. A second criticism is that cultures are internally plural and contested and lack an authentic essence whose expression imposes duties on others. Plainly, there must be space for minority groups to argue and deliberate over what their heritage consists in. A further difficulty for Taylor's argument is that authentic collective identities subjectively valued by their members may not be valuable for third parties; but it is the latter who bear many of the duties to safeguard cultural heritage. Taylor replies that we should presume that cultures which have animated and engaged large numbers of people over many years represent something of value, even if others often lack the moral vocabulary to assess it (1994, pp.66–73). We should engage in inter-cultural dialogue which aims at a fusion of moral horizons. Yet there is no guarantee that this will vindicate cultural value to all parties' reasonable assent. Cultural traditions and practices, after all, embed conflicting normative criteria.

I want to examine a different strategy to articulate the interest in ICH, one which focuses on the extrinsic values its protection realises, for members of those cultures and for third parties who have reason to affirm those values in general. But what are these values? I have mentioned some candidates: identity, meaning, cultural continuity, but there are challenges. First, a sceptical liberal (eg Barry, 2001) might simply deny that these collective values are genuinely valuable, or at least not as valuable as liberal freedom and autonomy. Indeed, the sceptical liberal will point to both members of ethnic minorities and indigenous communities who have rejected their heritage in order to pursue individual life projects of their own. As I said, liberals form part of the constituency of duty-bearers who must bear some of the costs protecting cultural heritage entails. Second, even if these values promote cultural heritage, the connection may still be a contingent, instrumental one. Identity, meaning and cultural continuity have value; they can flower from other sources than one's ethnic or indigenous heritage. Work, family, friendship networks, neighbourhood and community involvement and political participation are all alternatives. This argument about sources of value can be combined with an autonomy argument through the claim that autonomy is exercised through a medium of social practices, most of them not ethnically cultural.

If these points are correct, they point to two challenges. The first is to demonstrate the scope of the relevant extrinsic value. This will show that the interest in ICH, grounded in the extrinsic value, has widespread normative appeal. The second challenge is to show that protecting a community's ICH is peculiarly salient in realising the relevant value; that its flowering is not just a happy accident.

I'll return to the second challenge shortly. In response to the first, I want to examine a distinct candidate value to help ground the interest in ICH: self-respect. Unlike cultural identity, cultural meaning and communal continuity, whose value is disputed by some liberals and cosmopolitans, self-respect commands wide support across the liberal/communitarian divide. Though there is disagreement on its nature and bases, very few would deny that self-respect is valuable and a constitutive component of a flourishing life. Self-respect consists in the moral appraisal of one's own personhood, character, situation, projects, achievements and so on, and it appeals to normative reasons which third parties can in principle share. It is common to distinguish between recognition self-respect and appraisal self-respect (Darwall, 1977). The former consists in the appropriate recognition of one's role, position and membership of particular communities. Appraisal self-respect's domain, by contrast, is an individual's particular character, virtues, achievements and goals. My interest here is recognition self-respect and thus the argument that follows is not subject to objections centred on the contingent value of particular cultures. *Self*-respect is a value and virtue attached to individual persons. My claims are thus intended to satisfy the sceptical liberal. The archetypical liberal John Rawls famously claimed that 'self-respect is perhaps the most primary good' (1999, p.386). As the other primary goods secured by justice include liberty, opportunity, income and wealth, this is a bold claim. A person enjoys Rawlsian self-respect when she appreciates her own value, and has a secure conviction that her aims and goals are worth pursuing, and has confidence in pursuing them. Though this definition makes clear that Rawlsian self-respect is in large part inwardly generated, like other advocates of self-respect Rawls is clear that various modes of respectful treatment from others are also required to secure a person's self-respect. It is these third party sources of self-respect that I investigate here.

Ethnic minorities: fair terms of integration

One general argument for particular citizenship rights directed at ethnic minority immigrants and their descendants is that it offers them fair terms of integration into the society in which they, or their ancestors, have made their home. Will Kymlicka, for example, advances multicultural measures as a way of easing minorities' participation in common liberal democratic institutions which, like other citizens, they need to accept and affirm (Kymlicka, 2001, pp.162-72). But applied to cultural heritage, the fair terms of integration argument does not show why a concern with minorities' ICH in particular is part of those terms. We need to say a little more.

I noted above the view that cultural heritage is a discursive practice, and Smith's notion of an authorised heritage discourse that privileged certain voices at the expense of others. The idea of fair terms of integration can help explain the wrongfulness of an authorised heritage discourse. Ethnic minorities are expected to meet the responsibilities of citizenship such as making a social and economic contribution, practising the virtue of civility towards others and so on. This gives them a set of duties and obligations. Then we have an evolving national heritage – the medley of narratives, practices, places and persons which make up an ongoing national story – that is made by its participants. This is, in a sense, an official representation by society of its own cultural make-up; the story a society tells itself. The wrongfulness obtains when minorities have less input into that representation; their story is relegated by a dominant set of interpretations. That does not mean, of course, that it is not represented in familial and informal social settings. But the notion of an *authoritative* discourse has a certain symbolic imprimatur; the official version commands a certain deference. At the same time minorities as citizens are expected to discharge the responsibilities of citizenship. The wrong involved, then, is not just one of fair representation; but also one of reciprocity. Minority citizens are expected to play their part in the social and economic reproduction of society, but are subordinate as players in its cultural reproduction, a process which helps mark out who belongs.

It might seem strained to call this an injustice. Surely there is a substantial moral difference between a materially exploited worker, for example, and not cataloguing slavery in a museum or omitting South Asian traditions from a music festival? True, there are degrees of injustice and not every omission is an injustice. But the cultural argument needs to be seen against a background in which particular omissions can belong to pervasive, systematic, historic patterns of subordination. Exclusions are pervasive because they reach into multiple areas of social, economic, political and cultural life; they are systematic because they result from structures and institutions, not individual actions; and they are historic because they are rooted in the narrative of national development. Particular exclusions, then, even if ostensibly minor, reverberate within larger institutions and histories. Each exclusion helps feed a general cultural pattern of legitimation, and is an opportunity foregone to forge a counter-narrative. Thus, while lack of diversity in some cultural event may not in itself seem much of an injustice, the net effect of repeated exclusions is substantial, as each one compounds the others and sediments the authorised heritage discourse. The latter feeds in to minority citizens' self-conceptions and identities. This is a subtle form of exclusion; and authoritative exclusion is a very sure route to diminished self-respect.

Axel Honneth's (1995) work provides a theoretically sophisticated way of understanding the moral psychological processes involved here. Honneth's core insight is that individuals require recognition, understood as positive affirmation, from the wider moral community in order to secure their identities. Recognition is a basic need and a matter of justice because agents require it from others in order to live flourishing lives. At the same time those in power very often do not grant others recognition: women, slaves, the working class and religious minorities have been among the under-recognised. Hence, for Honneth, achieving recognition is a struggle, and the central motor of social change. Recognition takes places across several dimensions, among them respect for our rights as citizens, and the esteem that citizens accord each other's values and goals in contemporary societies.

For Honneth, a community of esteem is one in which individuals' contributions to valuable social goals are mutually affirmed.[2] Recognition affirms individuals' particular traits and abilities insofar as they help further these goals; for example, women have historically been under-recognised for their social and economic contribution in raising children. Our focus is the struggles, achievements, setbacks and other stories of minority groups as they contribute to a national story. A more moderate version of Honneth's thesis will say that it is less the precise value of any groups' contribution that is important, nor esteem for their particular abilities, but just the fact that minority groups have had a role in our shared history, as all characters contribute to a drama. There is a strong interest in these roles being acknowledged, and hence an epistemic injustice when minorities' stories are erased or foreshortened by an official heritage discourse. The claim is just that a group's story matters to them, and should matter to all citizens since it is part of their story too.

Cultural recognition fosters self-respect among members of minority communities in a number of ways. First, it guards against the psychologically perilous state of invisibilisation. At its worst, invisibilisation renders certain individuals non-persons, as in slave societies; more commonly it accords a lesser status to certain categories of people by looking through their activities and interests. By contrast, incorporating previously marginalised groups within an authorised heritage discourse, underwrites their agency as individuals with ends and goals they seek to pursue. Recognition of another's agency is a very basic platform for her self-respect. It confirms a person's engagement in the basic human occupation of pursuing projects. Second, incorporation into heritage discourse signals the inclusion of minorities with distinct ethnic, religious or national identities into a larger historical story in which they played a role. This message of inclusion expresses the view that the larger context of people, places and events which realises values of meaning, orientation and continuity among the citizenry is their context too. It thus secures for them the fundamental status of being insiders to a story which is theirs, and to which they are therefore entitled to adopt a cluster of reactive attitudes. Inclusion fosters self-respect through the way it marks out a community of agents who have particular reason to be concerned about one another's interests (above and beyond the basic respect accorded to all). Affirming that another person's history is one's own history too, which one therefore has special reason to acknowledge, will tend once again to augment their self-respect.[3]

I don't want to give the impression of presenting a naively rosy, falsely harmonious picture of national history without its attendant conflicts and grievances. As Honneth clearly sees, mobilising against invisibilisation and exclusion is often a struggle. But where debate about heritage is encouraged and institutionalised in the public sphere, where parties generally acknowledge each other's perspectives and deliberation occurs in a culture of mutual respect then participating in such debate can be a further source of self-respect. Public deliberation of this kind engenders inclusion and mutual respect as participants take seriously and weigh appropriately each other's views.

An example from the UK: in 2003 the then Mayor of London, Ken Livingstone, launched the *Mayor's Commission for African and Asian Heritage*. This sought to recruit ethnic minority communities to a task force to shape the capital's diverse heritage, in particular articulating proposals to integrate Black and Asian histories into mainstream heritage collections, empowering community-based heritage groups and introducing Black and Asian history and heritage into education. The *Commission's* final report in 2009, *Embedding Shared Heritage*, was, according to Clara Arokiasamy, a 'major achievement' in the 'democratisation of London's heritage and the recognition on the Asian and African diaspora communities' cultural rights' (Arokiasamy 2012, p.344). In a modest way, the *Mayor's Commission*, helped incorporate Black and Asian British heritage into the national canon, thus helping prevent its invisibilisation, and encouraged inclusive debate about what that canon should be. It is a good example of the multicultural conception of cultural heritage, championed by Stuart Hall, where minorities can see themselves reflected within it, and are empowered in telling their stories.

At this point we can return to the second challenge about the connection between cultural heritage and self-respect: how far safeguarding the former is necessary for promoting the latter. We can distinguish between a strong thesis which asserts that ICH protection is necessary for self-respect, and a weaker thesis which says that safeguarding ICH has self-respect promoting effects (where it may be promoted in other ways besides). As individual citizens, members of ethnic minorities will no doubt gain self-respect through exercises of first-personal agency: work, family, community involvement, and so on. Our interest is in third-personal sources of self-respect. As I mentioned above in connection with justice, it's hard to sustain the claim that any single cultural event or institution will have significant self-respect promoting effects. But if minorities were wholly excluded and made invisible in a state's cultural reproduction – just effaced from the story – it seems likely this would have a significant effect on their self-respect as citizens with cultural identities. (This, indeed, is a key message of Charles Taylor's argument). State cultural policy has a symbolic authority; it cannot just be left to civil society and the cultural market. So we need to see particular events and institutions as parts of a co-ordinated and systematic programme, advanced by the state, to secure their inclusion and agency. It will be part of a package of measures designed to combat social and economic justice as it affects cultural minorities (and indeed other vulnerable citizens). In some cases where minorities enjoy a fairly stable and secure position in society, then incorporating their history may be less significant for their self-respect. But where, as is common, minorities are more vulnerable and have suffered a history of discrimination, cultural incorporation as a general policy is likely to be peculiarly salient for self-respect even if not strictly necessary.

Indigenous peoples: a community of recognition

Indigenous peoples live in states populated mainly by the descendants of those who colonised them, in contrast to ethnic minorities whose ancestors migrated. They also often differ from ethnic minority cultures by their relatively isolated existence and lack of integration in mainstream society. Many indigenous peoples seek to maintain at least some aspects of their traditional way of life in the face of larger political and economic pressures. This may ground special rights to cultural protection, but at the same time indigenous minorities invariably score lower on the central indices of social and economic well-being. Certainly, this is true of Aboriginal Australians, for example. For some, this counts against perpetuating indigenous people's way of life and relative isolation since combatting their social and economic disadvantages may involve incorporating them into majority-led institutions such as the larger society's labour market.

These considerations map out the difficult context in which debates about the just treatment of indigenous communities take place. But instead of seeking to settle every debate about the fair treatment of indigenous groups, we can restrict ourselves to arguments for preserving their ICH. What role might self-respect play here?

To begin to address this question I want to interpret indigenous cultures in a particular way as communities of recognition, though I do not claim that this is all, or essentially, what they are. On the view I am proposing indigenous cultures are distinguished, not just by the shared values and beliefs of their members, or their common ancestry, but by the collective practices in which their members engage. Enlarging on the dramaturgical perspective of the last Section, my suggestion is that the relationship between members of an indigenous community can be conceptualised processually, as series of social practices and pervasive interactions, a distinct perspective to the spatial metaphors of 'bonds' and 'ties'.[4] In pursuing these practices, members perform their roles and relationships; they keep their cultural community alive as an ongoing concern with which they identify. Though cultural participation is typically role-bound, rule-based and institutionalised; it is still made by its participants who are insiders to their cultural relationship.

Conceptualising cultural identity as something manufactured by its members through their collective interaction helps explain the sense of ownership they feel with respect to their distinctive values and practices. They collectively reproduce the traditions and practices they have inherited, collectively propelling them into the future. This is a form of customary 'ownership'; one owns, in an ideational sense, what one has fabricated. Moreover, members will typically attach agency value to that which they have collectively produced, analogous to the way an artist values her painting through the creative labour she has invested in it. I maintained above that it was implausible to hold that all cultural products and artefacts possessed inherent objective value, but the notion of agency value gives us an alternative perspective on the value-based argument for cultural preservation. The premise is that there is real agency-based value to be found in traditions and practices which are *made*, reflecting the capacity, effort and investment agents put in to their manufacture. The cultural practices of an indigenous community enjoy agency value on account of the ongoing collective investment they involve. In contrast to ethnic minorities' interest in a fair input into an encompassing national story, indigenous communities' relationship with their heritage is more direct.

Adopting this perspective, gives us two routes to self-respect for the members of an indigenous cultural community. The first is through exercising their agency in acting to (re-)produce the intangible aspects of their culture. I identified respect for agency as an important source of self-respect in the last Section. Now we have a sense of agency as a person's recognition that she is investing her practical reason in recreating a heritage with which she values and identifies. The source of self-respect in this sense is the reflexive appreciation that a flourishing cultural heritage is the result of a process of which she is a joint author. A person identifies with what she has produced, its value embodies in part the judgement and labour she has invested to produce it. This diverges from Rawls's notion of self-respect an individual's pursuit of a conception of the good, though I think it's a complementary idea.

The other route to self-respect stems from the fact that members of a community recreate their cultural heritage together as a public good which is enjoyed for them, its members. Music, dance, drama and cultural festivals are quite obviously public goods but even the manufacture of artworks and other craft items contributes to a tradition which is a public good for those whose tradition it is. Fiona Magowan (2010), for example, relates how the singing and dancing of the Garma Festival held by the Yoruba people in Arnhem land (in Australia's Northern Territories) symbolically affirmed their customary land rights over their territory. The collective recreation of cultural heritage fosters the special relationship between the members of an indigenous community, including the sense in which each has *standing* as an insider to the relationship. As I mentioned, this inclusion is a very basic source of self-respect as insiders have tangible reasons to feel that they have been incorporated into the community.

There are countervailing considerations here. For one thing, not all participate or contribute equally to cultural heritage production, and social hierarchies and discriminatory practices can undermine self-respect. Magowan notes how the Garma Festival also served to cement clan leaders' power and authority. By confirming social hierarchies, it may have served to erode the self-respect of subordinate members. The social organisation of the Yoruba community could perhaps be reformed, but not without threatening other values, at least in the short term. Further, practising ICH may keep members of indigenous minorities in the community, whereas given the social and economic deprivation they suffer, there may be good reasons for greater integration in society. This might provide further avenues of self-respect, for example through employment in the larger economy. William Logan shows for example how the Tay Nguyen hill tribe peoples of Vietnam had their musical heritage specially recognised by UNESCO, while paid employment outside the community might better have alleviated the poverty which was their most dire problem (Logan, 2010). These considerations show that promoting self-respect through the collective practice of cultural heritage may have costs, it is not an unmixed good. It is a challenge, and not one I can address here, how cultural and other sources of self-respect can be advanced together, not to mention other rights and interests of justice.

One final route to self-respect through cultural heritage is through empowering local communities to be involved in its management. Since indigenous peoples tend to be territorially concentrated and their relationship with the land is so central, multicultural policies have often involved devolving power to indigenous peoples over territory which is ancestrally theirs. For instance, Australia's 1976 Aboriginal Land Rights Act recognised for the first time Aboriginal claims to land based on customary law, and the result was large tracts of the Northwest Territories leased back to their Aboriginal inhabitants. The Uluru-Kata Tjula National Park I mentioned earlier, is controlled by a Board of Management with a majority Ananga representation. Empowering indigenous communities to manage their own collective cultural resources sends a message of trust and inclusion which is conducive to self-respect. As we noted earlier, involvement in democratic institutions in which one's voice is recognised, enables one to make claims in public deliberation and influence its outcome. There are therefore very good reasons formally to include indigenous citizens' representatives as claims-makers in democratic institutions which make authoritative decisions over their cultural heritage. Of course, these democratic ideals may be far from instantiated in political reality. But promoting localised cultural heritage management is not just independently valuable, making it less hierarchical and elite-driven has positive self-respect effects too.

Conclusion

Though immigrant cultures and indigenous peoples differ in many ways they share the predicament of being minority groups whose distinct cultural practices are often under threat. With immigrant cultures the normative issue is how to engineer their fair integration into a society they or their ancestors have made their home while at the same time preserving a heritage they regard as valuable and distinct. With indigenous peoples the integration issue is more fraught, and arguments for cultural heritage preservation take place against a background where relative separation from mainstream institutions often goes hand in hand with relative deprivation. The various declarations signed in their name focus on the *value* of immigrant and indigenous cultural heritage, but I have suggested that is not a useful strategy given that such value is often contested, and may not be persuasive for philosophical liberals committed to freedom and autonomy. Self-respect, by contrast, is a basic interest of persons and a powerful motive for social change. It is a value that may be endorsed from many different ethical perspectives and which has broad general appeal. Maintaining the cultural heritage of immigrant minorities helps promote self-respect by guarding against invisibilisation and securing their inclusion when minority groups are enrolled into institutional debates on what to preserve, and how it is best interpreted. The self-respect of members of indigenous peoples is secured when institutional conditions allow their ICH to flower in such a way that each can identify their own agency with its production, and regard their own contribution as part of a larger collective enterprise. The argument is more or less robust depending on whether cultural heritage preservation is necessary for or just conducive towards securing self-respect. For indigenous peoples, there is a clearer case that securing cultural heritage is necessary for their self-respect; for some minority citizens, it may only be one means to promote it.

Notes

1 I therefore overlook national minorities such as the Scots and Quebecois in multinational states, linguistic minorities, and minority religions which are not also ethnically differentiated.
2 For Honneth, esteem for one's social contribution fosters self-esteem, whereas having one's legal rights and entitlements respected undergirds self-respect. For reasons of space I leave aside here the complex distinction between self-respect and self-esteem, and the details of how Honneth draws that distinction.
3 A related source of self-respect occurs when injustices committed against the descendent of minority groups are publicly acknowledged as in the recent commemorations of the abolition of slavery in the UK.
4 An excellent account of this processual view of culture can be found in Baumann, 1999, Chapter 7. I defend a related interactionist view of social relationships in Seglow, 2013, Chapter 2.

References

Arokiasamy, Clara. 'Embedding shared heritage: the cultural heritage rights of London's African and Asian diaspora communities,' *International Journal of Heritage Studies* 18/3, 2012, 339–345.

Barry, Brian. *Culture or Equality? An Egalitarian Critique of Multiculturalism*. Cambridge: Polity, 2001.

Baumann, Gerd. *The Multicultural Riddle: Rethinking National, Ethnic and Religious Identities*. London: Routledge, 1999.

Benhabib, Seyla. *The Claims of Culture: Equality and Diversity in the Modern Era*. Princeton: Princeton University Press, 2002.

Darwall, Stephen. 'Two kinds of respect,' *Ethics*, 88, 1977, 36–49.

Fairclough, Graham, Rodney Harrison, John H. Jameson Jnr and John Schofield (eds), *The Heritage Reader*. London and New York: Routledge, 2008.

Gilbert, Jeremy. 'Custodians of the Land: Indigenous people, human rights and cultural integrity' in Langfield et al. (eds) *Cultural Diversity, Heritage and Human Rights*. London: Routledge, 2010

Hall, Stuart. 'Whose Heritage? Unsettling "The Heritage", re-imagining the post-nation,' in Fairclough et al. (eds), *The Heritage Reader*. Abingdon and New York: Routledge, 2008.

Harrison, Rodney. *Heritage: Critical Approaches*. London: Routledge, 2013.

Honneth, Axel. *Struggles for Recognition: The Moral Grammar of Social Conflicts*. Cambridge: Polity, 1995.

Kockel, Ulrich. 'Reflexive Traditions and Heritage Production' in Kockel and Nic Craith (eds), *Cultural Heritages as Reflexive Traditions*. Basingstoke: Palgrave, 2007.

Kockel, Ulrich and Mairead Nic Craith (eds), *Cultural Heritages as Reflexive Traditions*. Basingstoke: Palgrave, 2007.

Kymlicka, Will. *Politics in the Vernacular*. Oxford: Oxford University Press, 2001.

Langfield, Michele, William Logan and Mairead Nic Craith (eds), *Cultural Diversity, Heritage and Human Rights*. London: Routledge, 2010.

Lee, Ellen. 'Cultural Connections to the Land: A Canadian example' in Fairclough et al. (eds.), *The Heritage Reader*. London and New York: Routledge, 2008.

Logan, William. 'Protecting the Tay Ngoyen Gongs: Conflicting rights in Vietnam's central plateau' in Langfield et al. (eds), *Cultural Diversity and Human Rights*. London: Routledge, 2010.

Magowan, Fiona. 'A Sung Heritage: An ecological approach to rights and authority in intangible cultural heritage in Northern Australia' in Langfield et al. (eds) *Cultural Diversity and Human Rights*. London: Routledge, 2010.

Marrie, Henriette. 'The UNESCO Convention for the Safeguarding of the Intangible Cultural Heritage and the Protection and Maintenance of the Cultural Heritage of Indigenous Peoples' in Smith and Akagawa (eds), *Intangible Heritage*. London: Routledge, 2009.

Munjeri, Dawson. 'Following the Length and Breadth of the Roots: Some dimensions of intangible heritage' in Smith and Akagawa (eds), *Intangible Heritage*. London: Routledge, 2009.

Nic Craith, Mairead. 'Cultural Heritages: Process, power, commodification' in Kockel and Nic Craith (eds), *Cultural Heritages as Reflexive Traditions*. Basingstoke: Palgrave, 2007.

Rawls, John. *A Theory of Justice* (revised edn). Cambridge, MA: Harvard University Press, 1999.

Seglow, Jonathan. *Defending Associative Duties*. New York: Routledge, 2013.

Smith, Laurajane. *The Uses of Heritage*. London: Routledge, 2006.

Smith, Laurajane and Natsuko Akagawa (eds), *Intangible Heritage*. London: Routledge, 2009.

Smith, Laurajane and Emma Waterton. 'The Envy of the World: Intangible heritage in England' in Smith and Akagawa (eds.), *Intangible Heritage*. Abingdon and New York: Routledge, 2009.

Taylor, Charles. 'The Politics of Recognition' in Amy Gutmann (ed.) *Multiculturalism: Examining the Politics of Recognition*. Princeton: Princeton University Press, 1994.

3

ANCIENT PLACES, NEW ARRIVALS AND THE ETHICS OF RESIDENCE

Paul Gilbert

Homes and histories

> All over the world people have a seemingly natural interest in their home district. This interest also has a historical dimension: people want to know about the past in the district where they live . . . an interest in the past that is not based on the belief that the home ground contains one's own cultural roots. Instead, the interest is based on an interest in the area itself, the place where you happen to live.[1]

So writes the Swedish archaeologist Mats Burström, who suggests that archaeology can make the world a better place by revealing the cultural diversity of people who have lived at the same place at different times, thus fostering a greater understanding of diversity in the present. I share Burström's sense of the importance that people's interest in their place's past has, and the purpose of this paper is to explore it further. I agree that cultural diversity over time is instructive as to the possibilities of diversity in the present and, in particular, that revealing this diversity may make their new place more congenial to immigrants. I shall have little to add to Burström's compelling account in this regard. However, I hope to extend his case for the ethical function of archaeologists and custodians of heritage in a rather different direction.

A good deal of archaeology has, like much history, been concerned to show people what their home district was like in the past and to encourage them, through exhibiting artefacts, reconstruction drawings and so forth, to imagine what it was like to live then where they live now. People are thereby brought to make connections with their predecessors in this place which may be stronger and more intimate than those involved in imagining earlier people in a different place. Their interest in their place's past is, I suggest, closely related to their ability to make such connections. But what sort of connections are they? It has been tempting to suppose that they are connections between past and present people who are, by some criterion of identity, the same people. Notoriously this is what nationalist historians and archaeologists have claimed about the earlier and later inhabitants of some putative national homeland where there has supposedly been continuous occupation by them. Successive inhabitants are the same in virtue of being members of the same nation. Similar claims or assumptions are sometimes made about past and present people at a more local level. Few would now explicitly assert, as they would have done in the nineteenth and early twentieth centuries, that later people are able to imagine their predecessors' lives because they have the same national or local character. But I suspect that something like this may still be unreflectively assumed, so that a shared identity of this psychological sort is inferred from an attributed ability to make the imagined leap into the past.

I am not for a moment suggesting that sophisticated contemporary archaeologists or historians would consciously entertain similar notions of an independent criterion of identity connecting present occupants with previous ones, especially those in the distant past. Burström's insistence that the past is a foreign country[2] is well appreciated. Nevertheless, it is, I think, often taken for granted that the past is less foreign to some present occupants than to others. Why else should it be presumed that immigrants' distinct cultural identities might be a barrier to their appreciation of the archaeology and heritage of their adopted place of residence, and that this is a problem that needs to be overcome? Certainly there may be aspects of this past, its religious monuments say, which may be more familiar to the natives of a place who have cultural connections with them than to newcomers who do not. But even here it is easy to exaggerate the continuity in what religious observance means to co-religionists over time. The postulation of a shared cultural identity over any considerable stretch of time needs support of a kind that it cannot at all obviously receive.

It might be objected that what makes appreciating the past of a place harder for newcomers to it is simply that the indigenous inhabitants do value it because their own conception of their identity is bound up with the idea, however erroneous, that they and their forerunners come from this place and have been formed by it, so that it is peculiarly their own. This conception of identity at a national level still has its defenders, but whatever its merits or otherwise invoking it at this point is, I believe, irrelevant. For what needs to be shown is something about the relative capacities of indigenous and immigrant inhabitants, not something about their relative inclinations, which is all that the invocation of the former's conception of their identity shows. The question at issue is not whether the natives of a place happen to be more interested in its past than immigrants are, but whether immigrants can be brought to show the same sort of interest as the natives. This is a question about capacities rather than about the inclinations people may have in virtue of their conception of their identity.

Yet why should anyone suppose that there is some shared cultural identity which links the past and present people of a place and thereby distinguishes the present inhabitants from new arrivals in respect of their supposed abilities to take an interest in and to appreciate it? Is it because without such a linkage across generations there is nothing to differentiate a new generation in the place from new arrivals who originate elsewhere? For those born in a place have to learn to find their way about and to adapt to it in just the same way as new arrivals. New generations are, in this respect, new arrivals too. And new generations are born into a place at a time whose cultural assumptions may be as different from those of their parents and grandparents, not to mention remoter ancestors, as are those of people who come from other places, even distant ones.

If we take to heart Burström's contention that the culture of past residents may be at least as different from that of its present indigenous residents as the latter's is from that of immigrant residents, then we should not presume a priori that there is some cultural barrier to immigrants having the same sort of interest in their present place of residents as the natives. Except in the specific and limited ways exemplified earlier by the case of religion, there is no reason to think that either group will be culturally closer to the residents of the past. In some ways, for instance in what appears to present day Europeans to be their moral conservatism, some groups of immigrants may have a greater cultural affinity with earlier residents. But I shall hope to show that all this is quite irrelevant to the qualifications required for someone to take an interest in and to appreciate the past of their present place of residence.

This is not to say that there are not reasons which people may have for an interest in the past of their home district that do spring from the way their cultural identity is constructed in terms of a putative continuing history. Ernest Renan thought that all national identities required 'the possession in common of a rich heritage of memories'.[3] But he notoriously conceded that 'the advance of historical studies is often a danger to nationality'[4] because it can unsettle the supposed memories that are constitutive of identity. It would be wrong, however, to follow Renan in thinking that even all national histories involve history in this way. If that were the case then, as two historians comment, the 'United States would have been in a bad fix, for she had very little history of her own'.[5] Many other counterexamples to Renan's thesis could be cited, not to mention cases of sub-national identities. Avowed urban identities, for instance, may have nothing to do with a town's history by contrast with, say, its present inhabitants' distinctive customs and patterns of speech. These points may lead one to suspect that an interest in one's home district's past is a culturally specific characteristic, contrary to Burström's description of it as 'seemingly natural'. However, I do not think that this is the case for reasons I shall go on to elaborate.

Burström is, I believe, right to describe people's interest in their home district, with its 'historical dimension', as 'seemingly natural' rather than as natural tout court. From the apparent fact that 'all over the world people have a seemingly natural interest in their home district', it would be over hasty to conclude that their interest is natural in the sense of being a biological given. Perhaps something akin to Robert Ardrey's 'territorial imperative'[6] might be invoked to argue for such a natural interest, for people could hardly have a biological drive to defend their territory without some interest in it, (though why the interest should have a historical dimension is unclear). This would be but one species of the possible primordialist accounts of people's interest in the place where they live, all of which would link this interest to an emotional and essentially non-rational attachment to a person's original home to which he or she develops an attachment in early life.

Crucially, primordialist theories regard an attachment to one's home district, and the sort of interest in it which may spring from this, as non-rational. This could mean either that it is not founded upon consideration of reasons or that it is not susceptible of justification by reasons. Maybe the former is true, so that if this is all that primordialists have in mind then the production of justificatory reasons is no argument against them; but I suspect that they would also hold that the interest is non-rational in the latter sense, and it is this that I shall go on to challenge. First, however, I want to examine some of the reasons that explain why someone might have an emotional attachment to their place of residence. I have mentioned birth and upbringing as factors which we regard as likely, other things being equal, to generate the attachment, which is then, because so common, unmysterious. But these factors constitute but one example of a more general condition making for attachment, namely familiarity. One fact that produces familiarity is that it is one's home, in the sense of the place where one resides for a longish period. Such familiarity may explain attachment but it does not justify it, as, say, its scenic beauty might. Let us, though, explore the connection between attachment to and interest in one's home district a bit more closely.

Familiar places

When Burström writes of the 'historical dimension' of people's 'seemingly natural interest in their home district' his words imply that there are other dimensions. One is what we might loosely term 'geographical'. Although people can make their way around their home district unproblematically – a feature we shall say more about shortly – they are quite likely to find maps of it not only instructive in relation to unfamiliar areas but interesting in regard to thoroughly familiar ones. Why should this be so? It is, I suggest, because maps translate the egocentric spatiality in terms of which we negotiate our environment into the public space of objects accessible to anyone whatever their location. In doing so they give us, quite literally, a new picture of our environment, and in giving us this picture they make us, in a novel way, even more familiar with it. Consulting a map can reassure us and justify our confidence even when we were right to be confident on the basis of our pre-geographical familiarity. It is, however, this pre-geographical familiarity which is fundamental to our basic ability to negotiate our home environment.

The spatial ability in question is a manifestation of what Maurice Merleau-Ponty calls our motor intentionality. This is what is involved in the sort of unreflective movements we make in relation to objects in our immediate environment, in which we can include the streets down which we walk in our town or village, making our habitual turns and concentrating upon shop windows or front gardens rather than on the street layout. The object of motor intentionality is, Merleau-Ponty says, 'that highly specific thing towards which we project ourselves, near which we are in anticipation, and which we haunt', rather than its being 'an object represented', so that 'motor intentionality . . . is concealed behind the objective world which it helps to build up'.[7] Motor intentionality is involved in our commerce with the things we encounter in our ordinary everyday activities, which Martin Heidegger terms 'things ready-to-hand',[8] like the pen with which I am writing these words. If I put the pen down and then reach for it again I do not usually conceptualise it as a pen for which I reach. My hand simply goes out for it automatically. Similarly, the large scale things in our environment which we steer ourselves through and around need not be conceptualised in terms of what I must make certain directional movements in response to. Familiar streets, buildings, trees and so on fall into this category. I do not need to think at all of what I am doing as walking down a particular street when I am simply following some habitual route. It is my body that has learnt the route, so to speak, as it is someone's fingers that have learnt a tune on his or her instrument. 'It is,' Merleau-Ponty writes, 'the body which "understands" in the cultivation of habit'.[9]

The foregoing remarks concern the phenomenology of our experience of our local landscape. Some readers will notice that they chime in with Barrett and Ko's observations made in criticism of Christopher Tilley's approach to the phenomenology of landscape.[10] Their criticism is directed against Tilley's claim that 'Being-in-the-world resides in a process of *objectification* in which people *objectify* the world by setting themselves *apart* from it'.[11] This idea, as we have just seen, posits a quite different and less basic relationship to the world than the one in which, in Merleau-Ponty's metaphor, we 'haunt' it. The latter relationship to an environment is one that is possible only through engaging unreflectively in the same sort of activities, the same 'labour'[12] as Barrett and Ko rightly describe it, as others who have been physically involved in that way in the environment. This is not something that strolling around a megalithic landscape today, for example, enables us to do, and thus it cannot reproduce the phenomenological experience of its builders, as Barrett and Ko think Tilley believes it can.

While Barrett and Ko are right to criticise Tilley's ostensible rationale for his phenomenological method, his employment of it seems, at least sometimes, to escape their strictures. It is no doubt too easy to assume that people with the same sort of bodies will have the same sort of experience when traversing the same landscape. Doubtless differences of physique and habitus can affect people's experiences. Yet surely Tilley is right to suppose that there are commonalities in people's experiences of unreflectively following the same familiar route with its characteristic slopes and turns and its natural landmarks. For this would be an example not of a shared objective world but of a shared manifestation of motor intentionality. To question this, risks cutting us off from the experience of past occupants of our environment. For current neighbours too may be different from ourselves as a result of age or origin and yet, as neighbours, share our experience of the everyday negotiation of that environment while occupying what may be, in some respects, different objective worlds. Yet, as archaeologists of inhabitation have claimed about ancient societies, it is in our own society too that routine practices such as walking the same habitual routes relate us together as residents to whom the place we live in is equally familiar. What we have in common with our fellow residents past and present is a shared familiarity based upon similar manifestations of motor intentionality in what is, in many ways relevant to its exercise, the same environment.

The picture I am aiming to draw is of a group of fellow residents who may be separated by cultural differences but who are united in being equally able effortlessly to negotiate their place of residence in virtue of possessing a common capacity to relate to it as only those familiar with a place can. This is not, I want to say, a shared identity, and I want to distinguish a localist identity, as we may call it, from the situation shared by relatively longstanding residents of a place. Unlike a localist identity, the situation of familiarity with a place that they share is a relation which does not require a conceptualisation of that place, since it is a type of relation prior to conceptualisation. Conceptualising the place one lives in as a place of a certain sort is necessary only in special circumstances, such as having to say where one lives, which involves having to contrast one's own home district with others. Having a localist identity based upon one's relation to a place requires just such a conceptualisation.

Someone's identity specifies who he or she is, and providing an identity is how one tells others who one is or is how others identify someone. One may identify someone for certain purposes in terms of where he or she lives, and this will be a collective identity in the sense of being shared by the others who live there. But people may adopt a localist identity not only to say where they live but to indicate in some supposedly deeper way who they are. This requires a richer conceptualisation of their identificatory place, typically one which represents it, on whatever scale, as home, and as a home worthy of attachment by those who share this collective identity. This involves images of the place as a focus of attachment. In the case of a national localist identity this imagery is, notoriously, often rural – the cottage homes of southern England, for example – for the nation needs a single sort of representation that is widely attractive to its members. In the case of identification with a town or village, the imagery will be more specific and will frequently involve particular historic buildings that comprise its 'heritage'. In neither type of case is there any guarantee that the imagery will resonate with those who are newly arrived in the locality. Indeed, they are likely to have their own beguiling images of the different home or homeland from which they have moved away, so that a localist identity associated with their new place of residence is potentially exclusionary.

Here it is worth noting that localist identities, as supposedly deep going aspects of their bearers, are in fact adopted for specific reasons, rather than being universal features of human nature. Typically they result from the insecurity that arises from the fear of homelessness, in the sense of lacking a settled and stable place of residence. This is particularly evident from the prevalence of this type of identity among diaspora peoples. But the mobility of people within a country which results from socioeconomic factors can present a similar threat and lead to the adoption of

localist identities as a comfort and consolation. In all such cases a place is conceptualised in a way that makes it a home, whether it is where people do live, where
they have lived or where they take themselves to have an historic claim to live.[13]

The foregoing discussion allows us to draw a sharp distinction between a localist identity and the role of resident, which may be occupied either by bearers of
this identity or by others. A role is not an identity, for while an identity, in the
sense just discussed, gives who someone is, someone's role gives what he or she
is – that is, what he or she does and is expected to do on a regular basis. Thus,
although an identity is a more or less permanent feature of a person, someone's
role can change radically. I shall say more about the role of resident but here I
want to emphasise that holding this role does not require the sort of conceptualisation of the place that a localist identity focussed upon it does. What acting the
role of resident effectively implies, however, is the sort of subconceptual familiarity
with it which I discussed earlier.

The ethics of residence

Being a resident of a place contrasts with being a visitor – someone not intend-
ing to stay there for long. A place of residence, by contrast, is where people make
their abode, the place where they 'abide' – a word whose etymology of staying or
remaining is the same as that of 'reside'. Making somewhere one's abode, however,
involves taking on a role, and with it accepting the obligations it imposes. These
obligations are, I want to suggest, obligations to the place itself, though the apparent peculiarity of this locution may perhaps be mitigated if we qualify it by saying
that they are obligations to the place as a place of residence, rather than obligations
to it as a place tout court. They include obligations not to spoil the place, but here
that means not to spoil it as a place of residence for people generally and hence for
others – not just for others as neighbours, which duties of neighbourliness might
entail, but also for others who succeed oneself as residents of the place. There is,
I suggest, a general expectation that if one finds oneself somewhere which one
makes one's dwelling place then one should leave it as a place which others can
make theirs. In this way what I characterised as an obligation to a place can be
viewed as an obligation to these others. But it is in virtue of the attitude one has
or, other things being equal, ought to have to the place that one appreciates the
obligation, not in virtue of any thoughts one might have about the residents who
may succeed one.

What is the attitude to a place which, I claim, is normally expected of residents
and why is it expected of them? While it would be unrealistic and sentimental to
say that residents should cherish the place they live in, since they may find it in
many ways unsatisfactory, nevertheless cherishing it may be viewed as the ideal,
connoting, as it does, an attitude of affectionate care. Caring for something implies
protecting and tending it, and therefore not damaging or spoiling it. Something
akin to this attitude is usually needed to enable one to discharge such obligations
without their being a burden. To have this attitude is involved in internalising the

role of resident which carries with it these obligations. Without it they will seem like external impositions rather than as arising naturally from occupation of one's place of residence. The attitude is expected of residents who have had time to acquire it, and a reason for expecting it of them is that it facilitates their discharge of their obligations as residents.

Yet why should people feel such obligations anyway? The answer I shall explore here is that they are, at least in part, obligations of gratitude. Thus political obligations are so conceived on some accounts: 'Obligations of gratitude are intrinsically directed at the past. They stem from favours received'.[14] Socrates' explanation of his obligation to obey the law even when it condemns him to death can be read as exemplifying this kind of account. For it is, he maintains to Athens with its laws that he owes the life he has enjoyed, so that in consequence he owes to the city an obligation to obey them. A similar case might be made for an obligation of gratitude for one's place of residence.

First, it seems reasonable to suppose that people should be thankful to have a place in which to live, in particular a place which they can negotiate in the unreflective and reliable way I have described earlier. This is possible for places of residence as it is not for wildernesses, where continuous changes of vegetation and so on make habitual, unthinking movement around the environment impossible. People should be thankful because this possibility is a benefit bestowed as a result of the work of others. It does not matter that these others may not have been motivated by thoughts of benefitting their successors. One can be grateful for the excellent tuition one received, even from a teacher who despised his students and thought that none would benefit from it. He was, however, acting as his role of teacher required. In the case of the predecessors in one's place of residence, one can assume that in creating and maintaining the place they acted with the analogous sort of impersonality that is implied by their acting as residents. Normally, then, one should be appreciative of the work of those who have created and maintained one's place of residence, and one should be grateful to them as fellow residents past and present.

Now, if we have been done some favour it is natural for us to seek out our benefactor because we are interested in what their motives were in acting in a way that benefits us. If our predecessors in a place were just acting as residents then they will have been acting to constitute and preserve the place we share with them. So it is as previous residents that we beneficiaries of their efforts are interested in them. So, we may notice, it is as such that archaeologists, to some extent by contrast with historians, are interested in their human subjects – not as individuals with personal motives but as people fulfilling certain social roles. It would be fanciful to suggest that archaeologists want to find out about the past inhabitants of a place in order to discover who its current residents' benefactors are. But it may be less fanciful to maintain that what explains these present residents' interest in the archaeologists' discoveries about the place is that they may reveal to whom they are indebted for making it a place fit for habitation. They can quite properly feel a grateful warmth towards them, albeit of a generalised sort, and this is, I think, the sort of emotion that is often felt.

This brings us to the question of how this attitude to our predecessors should be expressed; what obligations does it generate? They are, I suggest, simply the obligations that come with the role of resident; acting otherwise than as complying with these obligations will be ungrateful. Because our predecessors complied with these obligations themselves we will be acting in a way consistent with the spirit in which they acted if we do the same ourselves.

We can compare the foregoing argument with David Miller's claim that a nation is 'a community of obligation' in that:

> because our forebears have toiled and spilt their blood to build and defend the nation, we who are born into it have an obligation to continue their work, which we discharge partly towards our contemporaries and partly towards our descendants.[15]

A rather stronger case, I suggest, can be made for regarding those who share a place of residence as constituting a community of obligation but for analogous reasons. It is stronger partly because it makes no requirement of birth in the place rather than mere receipt of the benefits of residence there, and partly because it is usually much clearer how a shared place of residence is to be determined and what the obligations of residents are than how a nation is to be defined and what national obligations are. It is also stronger, I believe, because it is less open to the objection against Miller that if the history of our nation is a shameful history of aggression and domination then we have no obligation to continue our forebears' efforts in this direction. Of course past residents may have treated the place we live in badly, but then they were not acting as residents should, and so long as past residents were acting rightly our obligations stand. We can make this distinction because being a resident is a role with corresponding obligations. Being a member of a nation, by contrast, is an identity, not a role, so that it carries no determinate role-related obligations. The obligations one has as a member of a nation will derive in part from specific benefits conferred by the acts of former members, and one cannot count their passing on a culture of aggression and domination as a benefit. Thus no general account can be given of what a member of a nation's obligations of gratitude might be, if any.

Accounting for the obligations of residence in terms of a debt of gratitude to one's predecessors in the place one lives begins to provide a justification for an interest in them and, more specifically, in their works. Such an interest is justified, and not simply explained in this way, because it is a proper response to benefactors, whose work the present day inhabitants are continuing, in however small a way, by fulfilling their residential obligations. Thus the fact that the residents of a place are typically more interested in its old buildings and ancient sites than in its narrative history can be explained and justified. For it is in such locations that they actually see and touch monuments to the labour of past residents and grasp how they made the place habitable and gave it the familiar shape it has – labour for which present residents have reason to be grateful in virtue of the way in which it has facilitated a life there. This sort of interest would, incidentally, suggest a reason for conservation rather than the wholesale reconstruction that occurred in many British cities in the post-War period. Destruction of the works of predecessors would, other things being equal, be disrespectful to their memory. But there is also a further, instrumental reason for conservation. It is that the greater the appreciation people have of their predecessors' contribution to making the place they live as suitable for residence as it is, the stronger should be their sense of their residential obligations and the easier it should be to discharge them.

I do not think that the story I am telling of residents' interest in their place should be contentious though linking it to obligations of gratitude which ground the requirements of their role as residents may well be. In its publication *Power of Place* English Heritage suggests that the historic environment matters because it is 'what generations of people have made of the places in which they lived . . . Each generation has made its mark'. The authors go on to say that 'people care about the historic environment. They value its meanings, its beauty, its depth and diversity, its familiarity, its memories, the quality of life it affords, and the opportunities it offers'.[16] No doubt all of this is true, but, unlike the account I am offering, none of it seems to me to show clearly why people should care about their own historic environment. Various reasons are offered associated with what, contingently, they might see in it, but they seem to be instrumental reasons. By contrast my account does not make caring for their historic surroundings an attitude that it is good for people to have just because it fosters a sense of their obligations as residents. Rather, they should care because this is the right attitude to have, given that they owe the benefits of being able to live where they do to predecessors who made it what it is, as expressed particularly in the historic buildings they erected, the old streets and squares they established and, indeed, the very position of the place in the landscape as a place to dwell. Caring about their historic environment is conducive to residents feeling a proper sense of their obligations, but this is not the reason why they should have this attitude.

One should not think of this attitude to the past of a place as an especially intellectual or even a reflective one. People do not need to know much about the past of their place to grasp which parts are old and which are new. Old buildings wear their antiquity upon their weathered faces, old streets declare it in their crooked tracks. The past is directly experienced in such things without the mediation of information and without experiences of it being any more than the unreflective background of our negotiation of the environment around us. And the remains of the past in one's place are commonly experienced with affection, which again need be no more than feelings of warmth in an old part of town, feelings not felt in a newly built one which does not reflect the work of generations of residents. These are feelings akin to those often experienced in relation to aspects of the natural environment – the river that runs through the town, the trees along its banks and so on. Such feelings about one's historic or natural environment may not be explicitly experienced as emotions of gratitude,

gratitude to be able to live in such a place, but it seems to me that such an emotion might readily be cited in making them explicit. They are not, I want to say, simply reactions to beauty, which one might have anywhere, but feelings of gratitude to one's predecessors for choosing and shaping the place one lives in, however shadowy their existence seems, only to be brought to light by archaeological and historical research.

However, I do want to repeat my earlier suggestion of the priority of archaeology over history in focussing residents' attention on the shaping of their place. It is prior because it exhibits the work of predecessors rather than merely describing it. This is a reason why it is easier for residents of a place to constitute a community of obligation founded on gratitude than for people to come together as a nation in this way, as Miller claims they should. For it is harder to exhibit tangible and visually arresting signs of work in which predecessors cooperate to form a nation than it is to show evidence of former residents creating and maintaining a shared place of residence. This does not imply that the idea of a place towards which residents can take up the sort of attitude I have been describing should be thought of as of very limited extent. It is quite natural that they will develop an interest in the wider locality with the system of communications and economic support it provides for a village or town. But none of this builds up into an interest in a nation where this is conceived as involving a shared cultural history. Even if the wider area in which residents become interested is coterminous with national boundaries one can still think of their interests as what might be expected of residents rather than of those who share a national identity.

One model of membership of a state is, indeed, that it is grounded in shared residence. By contrast we may note that the UK citizenship test asks questions about British history like, 'Which landmark is a prehistoric monument which still stands in the county of Wiltshire?' and 'What is the name of the admiral who died in a sea battle in 1805 and has a monument in Trafalgar Square, London?'[17] Such questions presuppose a cultural nationalist model of citizenship and do nothing to relate what is expected of 'new residents', as those taking the test are referred to, to their experience as residents of the places they live in and to the requirements of this role. Similarly it seems to me misguided to attempt to counter feelings of alienation by stressing similarities between earlier indigenous and contemporary immigrant cultures, as in a project described in *Power of Place*[18] in which children of Asian origin from Bradford were invited to find similarities between Whitby Abbey and their own mosque. Not only does this take them out of their home environment but it stresses their distinct cultural identity rather than their shared role as residents. Acquainting immigrants with the archaeology and heritage of their new place of residence would have a very different emphasis, for it is likely to show that they are only the most recent in a succession of newcomers who have contributed to making and maintaining it as a somewhere to live, linking them to fellow residents past and present in a shared project.

Notes

1   Mats Burström, 'Cultural Diversity in the Home: How Archaeology Can Make the World a Better Place' *Current Swedish Archaeology* 7 (1999). p. 25.
2   Ibid. p. 23.
3   'What is a Nation?' In A. Zimmern (ed) *Modern Political Doctrines* (Oxford: Oxford University Press, 1939) p. 203.
4   Ibid. p. 190.
5   A. Nevins and H.S. Commager (eds) *A Pocket History of the United States* (New York: Simon and Schuster, 1981) p. 151.
6   Robert Ardrey, *The Territorial Imperative: A Personal Inquiry into the Animal Origins of Property and Nations* (London: Collins, 1967).
7   Maurice Merleau-Ponty, *The Phenomenology of Perception* (London: Routledge and Kegan Paul, 1962) p. 138 n. 2.
8   *Being and Time* trans. J. Macquarrie and E. Robinson (Oxford: Blackwell, 1973) p. 98.
9   *The Phenomenology of Perception* (London: Routledge and Kegan Paul, 1962) p. 144.
10   John C. Barrett and Ilhong Ko, 'A Phenomenology of Landscape: A Crisis in British Landscape Archaeology?' *Journal of Social Archaeology* 9 (2009).
11   *A Phenomenology of Landscape* (Oxford: Berg, 1994) p. 12.
12   John C. Barrett and Ilhong Ko, 'A Phenomenology of Landscape: A Crisis in British Landscape Archaeology?' *Journal of Social Archaeology* 9 (2009) p. 287.
13   Paul Gilbert, *Cultural Identity and Political Ethics* (Edinburgh: Edinburgh University Press, 2010) pp. 84–87.
14   John Dunn, 'Political Obligation'. In D. Held (ed) *Political Theory Today* (Cambridge: Polity, 1991) p. 41.
15   David Miller, *On Nationality* (Oxford: Clarendon Press, 1995) p. 23.
16   Neil Cossons et al. *Power of Place: The Future of the Historic Environment* (London: English Heritage) p. 4.
17   'Life in the UK: A Guide for New Residents'. Quoted in *The Sunday Times,* 27 January 2013 p. 6.
18   Neil Cossons et al. *Power of Place; The Future of the Historic Environment* (London: English Heritage) p. 24.

4

FOREIGN AND NATIVE SOILS

Migrants and the uses of landscape

Robert Seddon

Introduction

There was land before there was life; though the continents have drifted greatly since their formation. Human beings' involvement with our environment is among our most ancient heritage, and the oldest kind which involves us with things which are not products of human culture: soil, stone, sea, sky and all the ecosystems they support. We can convert earth and stone into artefacts: sculpting with clay we might make a brick, with numerous bricks we could build a house, and now we are in the realm of architecture and civilisation, and have left behind the hole from which the clay was scooped. The land which yielded the clay, however, is not a product of human creation in the same manner, even though human activity has reshaped it.[1]

Part of our long involvement with land is our species' spread across the surface of the globe, moving and expanding from one place to another. Migrants carry their languages, clothes, cuisine, their social hierarchies and their gods with them; but their homelands they have always had to leave behind in order to make new homes in new places. This suggests that land is a different kind of heritage from the items just enumerated. Other kinds are made, developed, transmitted through human thought and interaction; land is discovered and settled.

It might therefore seem that land is particularly open to receiving new modes of involvement from new settlers; for all land was unsettled originally. Many of the longstanding ethical controversies involving cultural heritage concern the ways in which the origins of an artefact ought to determine what may subsequently be done with it: whether the first placing and purposes of the 'Elgin' Marbles mean that they forever belong more in Greece/Athens/the Parthenon than anywhere else. (It is usually the point of creation as an artefact that is identified as the relevant origin: I have seen no suggestions that Stonehenge is in the wrong place because it contains stones from the Preseli Mountains in Wales. However, there was a recent controversy involving coins minted by the Spanish using Peruvian gold (Jones, 2008).) Land may look refreshingly free of any similar point of origin: something shaped by human cultures, but not something that will feature in our ethics as basically another kind of artefact and another sort of heritage object.

Yet sites of many sorts can nonetheless seem artefactual: besides our settlements and the roads that link them (and have made migration an easier prospect than it once was) there are mines and quarries, canals and dams and diverted rivers. Humans plant and harvest crops, and in order to do so divide land into fields: the hedgerow, that unassuming heritage of the English countryside, is a product of continuous human care. Forests can grow of their own accord, but humans have also invented forestry. Humans have even invented the artificial beach,[2] and processes of 'land reclamation' to pile up terrain where nature had seen fit to leave water. Among the historic landmarks of Britain is the earthwork called Offa's Dyke, a ditch and bank along the old border between Mercia and Powys, which can hardly have been constructed as an inducement to migration.

All this might lead us to suspect that when land is heavily settled and reshaped, it can take on a more ambiguous character: perhaps still not an artefact, but not wholly without the characteristics of artefactual heritage. What is certain is that land is not free of controversy. An article by Richard Wilk, for example, describes how the ethnographic history of Toledo District in Belize became a matter of political and legal disputation. The sale of logging rights, and subsequent forest clearances on an industrial scale, led to a dispute over the land which turned in substantial part on what could be uncovered of Toledo District's history of migration and settlement, colonisation, resettlement, expansion and deportation:

> Both the government and the Maya groups have fought much of this battle around the issue of who has the best ancestral claim to the area. The Kekchi and Mopan claim to be descendants of the ancient Maya civilization [. . .]. Some Afro-Caribbean Belizeans cite Afrocentric scholars [. . .] to claim that Africans had colonized Mesoamerica before the rise of Maya civilization. The government's brief [. . .] argues that the Kekchi and Mopan Maya are recent immigrants [and] the true aboriginal inhabitants of the area, the Chol, were wiped out, and replaced only in the last century by immigrants from Guatemala.
>
> *(Wilk, 1999, p. 372)*

Clearly land is not so different from artefacts that it is not subject to disputes about who has 'the best ancestral claim'. While artefacts pass from place to place and from hand to hand, land falls subject to migration, settlement and colonisation. In both cases, evidence of past usage, and the possible interpretations of that evidence, may become points of practical and moral disputation as well as scientific and scholarly enquiry. Yet it remains true that land has no human maker and is not originally a product of any human culture. What then should we make of 'best ancestral claims' to land, particularly land with complicated histories of migration—and where in all this are migrants of the present day, trying to make homes for themselves on lands which might be subject to those ancestral claims?

In the next two sections I survey some of the respects in which landscapes can present themselves to us as cultural heritage. In the first I continue examining the human moulding of landscapes, for this is both the most obvious way in which even a departed population can have left its mark, and the most readily akin to the artefactual 'heritage objects' on whose rightful ownership so much has already been written. Yet the comparison is not straightforward, and I end up emphasising natural (and to some extent rural) landscapes in contrast with the palpably planned and manufactured scenes which comprise so much of architectural and urban heritage.

In the subsequent section I consider how landscapes might act as heritage by attesting to the past and historical migrations evidentially; but the political aspects of landscapes' uses may be more obvious than any moral inferences we might draw from them.

In conclusion I suggest that what little we can say by way of generalisation about people's involvement with their lands as heritage is underdetermined by the archaeological past: scientific enquiry reveals the histories of land as terrain and territory, but an ethics of cultural heritage must deal moreover with normative values of home and home-making, and each successive wave of immigrants in any place makes its home and heritage within the context of environments it finds already there.

Some corner of a foreign field

A people's involvement with a landscape need leave no obvious traces at all. (Indeed, ramblers in the modern countryside are exhorted to 'take only photographs, leave only footprints'.) In the introductory paragraphs I noted some of the more dramatic effects which human settlement may have upon land; and lengthy settlement will leave some mark which archaeology might uncover. Yet a people need not physically alter land as a condition of being involved with it; I do not mean to repeat the error of the notorious legal opinion that Australian Aborigines could not own their land because they did not fence or farm it. Pilgrims at Mount Kailash do not ascend it at all, instead circumambulating the sacred site. What physical alteration can offer is evidence of a landscape's history: it is one of the forms of evidence by which a 'best ancestral claim' might be assessed.

That landscapes can count as a people's heritage is by now a well established thought (Last, 2006, p. 11), and a corresponding conception of landscape has found its way into

> international law and European law. Landscapes are no more considered as portions of territory deserving protection for [concomitant reasons]. They

are considered as the physical daily life context of people, [a] notion summarized using the English expression of surroundings (European Landscape Convention, Article 5 (a)), even if the French expression of *cadre de vie* is perhaps more evocative.

(Lafarge, 2006, p. 40)

This is a conception of the importance of landscape which emphasises its role in a settled human life, whether a native's or a migrant settler's, or possibly that of a nomad transitorily passing through already familiar terrain. It is landscape as the setting of a life and as the home of the person who lives it (a point to which I return in the final section). Emphasis on how such a landscape is *shaped* by human activity is downplayed, but human activity itself is emphasised. It would probably be excessive to infer that natural landscapes, those with which we interfere minimally, are therefore pushed altogether to one side; insofar as there remain natural landscapes, they remain objects of human fascination and often of concerted conservation efforts to keep them in that state (to the extent that some could paradoxically be considered artificially natural). The focus, nevertheless, shifts from soil to settlement.

Of course, we cannot see established populations' relations with their land as static. In the introduction I noted some of the ways in which humans make their mark on landscapes; to these we can add the different significances which landmarks can hold in different times: David Lowenthal notes that landmarks formerly 'demarcated both private and civil boundaries. [. . .] Landowners and local officials committed these landmarks to memory by regularly perambulating the bounds, and preserved such landmarks as irreplaceable evidence of possession.' (1985, pp. 256–7.) He points to the development of sophisticated photographic and cartographic technologies as the reason why such practices died out and the landmarks lapsed into a lesser significance. Those with an ancestral claim to possess land do not necessarily mark that claim as their ancestors did. Similarly to practices handed down as traditions, these claims involve continuity rather than total constancy of form.

While some communities see their lands as an inheritance, others relate places and pasts in different ways. Links between ancestors and ancestral lands may be reflected in 'site specific' religious practices (Coleman, 2013, p. 156). In such practices, land and its resources are understood to be involved in 'a complex web of interrelated spiritual and natural relationships' (Hendrix, 2005, p. 769) which in turn act as a source of moral obligations—and certain sites have a special importance 'as places where visions took place, where spiritual beings can be contacted, and where the human place in the moral order of nature can be understood' (ibid.).

Since there is no single and standard way in which a settled population may understand its relations with the land it inhabits, and with the other generations which have and will, there is also no uniform way in which the position of a settled population may be contrasted with that of the immigrant. Migrants, in any case, are also heterogeneous: the attitudes and practices of colonists in the 'New World' obviously differed from those of displaced Native Americans on the Trail of Tears. (In this respect land is not unlike other things which are placed under the umbrella of heritage: artefacts too may find various and changing uses both within and beyond the cultures of their invention.) David Lowenthal notes the various ways in which migrants develop a sense of identity in relation to both adoptive and (sometimes romanticised) ancestral homelands. Exiles may take the names of the places they knew and bestow them upon new landscapes. Architectural features and street furniture characteristic of one place may start to appear as 'replicas' in another, creating a blend which provides migrants with a sense of familiarity and continuity. (Lowenthal, 1985, p. 42.)

In this limited respect aspects of place, as well as people, can participate in migration. The phenomenon of such 'replicas' gestures at one thing characteristic of human cultures in general: the capacity for replication, for turning an idea into a blueprint or scheme which can be executed multiple times and in multiple places—or even as part of an attempt to replicate places. Modern industrial culture is characterised by the extent to which it has advanced its technological powers of exactly replicating a prototype ('mechanical reproduction', in Walter Benjamin's phrase).[3] This is sometimes reflected in priorities when selecting heritage to be conserved: besides the unique item, or the item made unique by some particular association with people or events, there is the scarce and exemplary object which stands as a surviving instance of what used to be commonplace. Guidance on what might merit the legal protection of 'listing' in the United Kingdom contrasts 'standard survivals' with 'examples of rare materials' (English Heritage, 2011b, pp. 3–4), and advises that 'a sole survivor of a form once typical of the working-class housing of a town should be taken seriously, even if altered' (English Heritage, 2011a, p. 10).

We know how to build 'period-style' houses, but evidently we feel that a really representative building from any period can only be preserved, never truly replaced. If possible we want the tangible link to the past which only the real thing can offer us, while also wanting it to remain as a representative sample of other such artefacts. Yet needs must, and for the migrants noted by Lowenthal, a flagstoned patio in the style of an old homeland or even the name of a hill or river may offer some solace when deployed in new surroundings, evocative of older and earlier and nostalgically remembered things. (Not only migrant heritage involves replica places: a copy of the prehistoric Chauvet cave network was made to benefit a public for which the original cave art is too fragile (Morelle and Denman, 2015).) Such sites are replicas, whether physically or nomenclatorially. They constitute the epitome of places constructed in the manner of artefactual heritage, not because they are physically shaped by settlers (though the flagstones plainly are), but because they are homages and reproductions through which cultural remembrance is achieved. Such places are fated to be ersatz heritage, second-best signifiers of their originals; but they show that humans not only shape places but replicate them along with the other things we make.

So it is with working-class Georgian houses, with flagstones and with toponyms. What of the hills and the plains and rivers themselves: the land upon which human names and borders are imposed? At times the language of conservation applies similar-sounding tropes to ecosystems, be they shrinking rainforests or the patches of ancient woodland where the English bluebell grows. However, hills and plains and rivers are of course not instantiations of some already existing plan or prototype. (In this respect, too, landscapes differ from artworks, though Raffaele Milani (2006) is no doubt correct to note that there can be artistry in humans' involvement with land.) Animal and plant species can themselves migrate or be released into new environments, but natural features of landscapes cannot travel in the same way as an architectural style. Where landscapes do reflect readily recognisable planning and design (golf courses, for example, or canals, or the parklands of Capability Brown), we respond to them as exercises in gardening or agriculture or groundsmanship, rather than as parts of the natural world—until nature 'takes over' if they are ever abandoned to become 'wild' once more.

The case of 'nature' is what chiefly makes it hard to consider land a kind of artefact, since the cultural role of such land is determined by what human hands have *not* done to shape it. Artefacts originate with their human makers, and their conservation involves protection from 'the elements'; whereas earth is one of the classical elements. From this point of view all human impact on landscapes might be seen as migrants' embellishments. The human ability to impose designs upon landscapes, which brings them closest to the museum pieces and other artefacts with which so much thinking about heritage is designed to deal, therefore throws most starkly into relief why it is tricky to apply this artefactual thinking to landscapes wholesale. Human intervention in the shaping of land might be seen less as an act of production from raw materials, and more as the arresting of processes of natural change. Distinctions between originals and replicas have scant meaning in this world of organic growth and decay.

'Nature' and 'wilderness' are of course concepts subject to cultural variation. Even within Western traditions of thought there is ample difference between a forest seen as a source of timber (Martin Heidegger's 'standing reserve'), investigated as a collection of phenomena for scientific study, revered as the handiwork of God, or appreciated aesthetically and mythopoeically as the 'forest primeval. The murmuring pines and the hemlocks, / Bearded with moss, and in garments green, indistinct in the twilight . . .'[4]

Still, the organic realm nowhere cares how our species classifies and divides it, and everywhere streams and plants and animals carry on their business without deigning to consult us. The sciences that ferret out 'nature's secrets' and whisper them around the world also tell us that whole species existed and died out millennia before us—and the land which we treat as property and territory is strewn with their fossils.

Pasts and pastures

Humans' alterations of land are only somewhat akin to making artefacts, then; but we have moved through so many landscapes and depended on them so much that we still have every reason to think them heritage of some kind. What falls under the umbrella of 'heritage' is in some way concerned with the past—with our own past, or with the past which future generations may know better thanks to our efforts at conservation. The language of heritage is never far removed from that of history and ancestry, and the history of peoples is also the history of places where they have lived.

Material traces of movement across and settlement within landscapes both constitute one way in which human cultures are involved with land and attest to it evidentially. In the case of Toledo District described by Wilk, archaeological and other ethnographic evidence was at stake in questions of whether the modern peoples inhabiting the area were earlier inhabitants' descendants who had recently recolonised an ancestral homeland. Land served both as the contested resource in the dispute and as a source of fragmentary evidence of its own history. This evidence, in turn, was invested with moral significance as part of stories supposed to undergird claims to the land.

Changes which humans make to land constitute evidence of its history of use, but they can also damage evidence of earlier uses. A stark example is given in the famous (perhaps notorious) case of 'Kennewick Man', an ancient skeleton found in Washington State and claimed as an ancestor by several Native American peoples living in the region. Whether Kennewick Man attests to their continuous settlement of the area, or to their later immigration and perhaps displacement of earlier inhabitants, is a scientific question not aided by a subsequent transformation of the site where the skeleton was discovered:

> In April 1998, despite the passage of the site preservation bill and despite a report from the Corps' own archeologist advising against it, the Corps [of Engineers] dumped 500 tons of rock and gravel on the site from helicopters [. . .]. Geologist Tom Stafford said of the work that 'the Corps destroyed as much of the site as fast as possible. It's like they hit it with a nuclear bomb.' In this way the federal bureaucracy effectively shut down one line of investigation into America's prehistory.
>
> (Custred, 2000, p. 20)

Whether this was a cynical ploy to preserve cosy ethnic politics from potentially inconvenient science, or a sincere effort to stabilise the shoreline, conducted with the finest military efficiency, is a matter for other authors. As an example of how alterations to a landscape can destroy archaeological evidence or render it inaccessible even as a political and legal dispute over local history and heritage rumbles on, it serves as a warning about the evidentiary role of land. Much as history is written by the victors, land is shaped by its occupiers at each point in history, whose own priorities dictate what they change and which places they choose to preserve unaltered.

Before migrants can move not merely from place to place but across territorial borders, someone must have made a claim to the land whose limits the borders demarcate. The picturesque hedgerows of the English countryside often originated with the 'enclosures' of the common land which turned it into a private agricultural resource for landowners. Britain's colonial regime in India would later use a hedge of dense and thorny shrubs as a customs barrier. Landscapes thus reflect histories of political control; or sometimes history as a tool of political control in the present, for states' shaping of landscapes within their territories reflects the histories they find it advantageous to emphasise. In the Yugoslav republic, for example, landscapes were co-opted by the state's propaganda efforts: the socialist regime dotted the rural landscapes with memorials and the cities with memorial parks, recalling the battles of the Second World War. 'Several generations of young "Yugoslavs" would be bussed to these memorials and steles [and] anyone moving about the countryside would be sure to recall what had happened there, if only because he had seen it in the cinema.' (Kaiser, 2006, p. 28)

This propaganda too has become part of the history of the landscape, contrasting starkly with the ways in which land is used (or underused or disused) in the Bosnia of recent years, following the 'ethnic cleansing' of the 1990s:

> The reconstruction of an Ottoman mosque in a country town without Muslims is a symbolic act that may serve to correct a reading of history; it is not the reconstruction of a society. [. . .] It follows that, when there are returns, as in Bosnia, there is an attempt to recreate the symbols of presence [. . .]. Now building has become a declaration. Some landscapes cannot [. . .] be [. . .] turned into multi- or even mono-cultural landscapes because people do not return.
>
> *(Kaiser, 2006, p. 29)*

Here migration marks a limit of state power over landscapes: power to shape and build on the land does not, especially in a remotely liberal state, entail power to give corresponding shape to its human geography. A historically revised but largely empty landscape may serve well enough as a sort of heritage object, akin to a historic stately home which is preserved, uninhabited by any resident, in order to serve museological functions. Yet instead of evoking the deep roots and enduring presence of a settled population, it speaks of departed ancestries and broken links.

Sometimes displaced people make a return journey when the opportunity arises, undoing an earlier migration to resettle their former homes: evacuees have even slipped back across the borders of the Chernobyl Exclusion Zone. Sometimes they do not, and the dwindling or vanishing of a population can have no less profound implications for a landscape than its settlement. We can look to the archaeology and recorded history of a region to learn what became of its former population, but trying to infer whose heritage the land must predominantly be may seem like consulting temperature records to answer the question 'Mais où sont les neiges d'antan?'

Homes, lands and homelands

People make their marks on the land they inhabit, then, and these marks are traces of their cultures and histories; but no ready moral inferences arise from this, in part because inward migration has always modified land which existed already. For people familiar with the ethical and legal literature on 'cultural property', a temptation exists to reify cultural heritage of any kind: even songs and stories have been treated in this way. Perhaps the heritage of habitation requires some other approach.

His experiences in Toledo made Wilk sceptical of the scientific and the moral utility of notions of cultural continuity. He calls instead for recognition of people's interests in the land they inhabit regardless of whether they can make an ancestral claim to it:

> [M]ore information has just deepened the fundamental contradictions in the idea of cultural continuity being disputed in the courts. Perfect ethnographic knowledge of the 18th Century people of Toledo District, even direct observation with a time machine would not tell us if they were the 'true' cultural ancestors of the modern Kekchi or Mopan. [. . .] Nobody else wanted the land when [the Kekchi] entered the country and nobody else has used it or cared for it as consistently.
>
> *(Wilk, 1999, pp. 372–3)*

This line of thought shifts emphasis away from the evidentiary matter of how land has been shaped by past populations—its role as a record of past inhabitation which archaeological science can uncover—and onto the shaping of land in a different respect: the present population's record of reliably caring for it. Yet that record too, of course, depends upon the available evidence about how land has been treated during an ever-increasing span of years.

Conflicts over artefacts, and in some cases over human remains, often involve demands that an object ought to be 'repatriated' to its country of origin; the underlying supposition is that such an object has 'a "patria", a homeland, a nation to which, and in which, it belongs' (Merryman, 1990, p. 521). Land, however, is supposed to constitute materially, to *be* the patria. Its ownership can be disputed, but it cannot be packed up and sent back anywhere. The only thing to which it could be returned is a semblance (and for the most part only a semblance) of some earlier state of development, cultivation and inhabitation; or, most originally, wilderness and uninhabitation. As the case of Bosnia shows, attempting to return land to people who are gone from it will not always induce them to return to the land.

For some migrant populations, at least, such fussing over material things may seem needless and misplaced. Anny Bakalian writes of the American-born offspring of immigrants from Armenia, for whom

> Armenian identity is a preference and Armenianness is a *state of mind*. [. . .] One can say he or she is an Armenian without speaking Armenian, marrying an Armenian, doing business with Armenians, belonging to an Armenian church, joining Armenian voluntary associations, or participating in the events and activities sponsored by such organizations.
>
> *(Quoted in Nagel, 1994, p. 154; italics in original)*

The 'state of mind' of these second-generation immigrants and their subsequent offspring presumably does not include any deeply nostalgic pining for Armenian soil. (Neither, of course, does it necessarily imply—or exclude—any contrasting reverence for American earth.) Earlier I noted that many forms of cultural heritage, unlike soil, are replicable and therefore boundlessly portable; and its adoption as a pure state of mind is perhaps the ultimate refinement of this approach to constructing and sustaining a sense of identity.

Other populations, of course, have behaved differently. The Zionist movement, drawing upon a lengthy heritage of diaspora, is a case in point. Like artefacts, lands and even homelands can signify different things to different people. There are even people who, presented with archaeological evidence of their origins elsewhere, would rather not endorse it as their own: 'as members of a diaspora, making a bold claim about their cultural heritage would make them outcasts again' when what they wanted was to live quietly in their adopted society and in the surroundings of their adopted homeland. (Pantazatos, 2010, p. 98)

If there is anything which we can say in general terms about these disparate populations and their varied attitudes and interests, it is that all of them find themselves in the basic human situation of making a home somewhere. (Migrant populations, indeed, might be expected to possess a particularly acute sensitivity to the significance of having, making or leaving a home.) This is not an assertion unrelated to ethics. Kirsten Jacobson has argued that it is through having homes, places within which we can feel at home, that we become able to emerge from this private sphere and act publicly as citizens (2010). Her work's main focus is on home in the literally domestic sense of the word, but she recognises that there are other ways, and other places, in which someone can feel at home, citing the example of a nomad on the steppe, at home when in the act of wandering (2009, p. 358).

Our sense of making a home, being at home, having somewhere to come home to, is implicit in notions of a homeland, be it present or ancestral or adoptive. Corresponding thoughts underlie conceptions of landscape as 'surroundings' or '*cadre de vie*', as I quoted earlier. A homeland, a land which is home, is therefore not easily brought under the usual banners of cultural 'property' or 'patrimony'. Certainly, land can have owners, and control and use of land can be contested.

A forest in Toledo cannot be both cleared and preserved, and so disputes naturally arise about whose interests in it count foremost. Yet what is most critically at stake is not a right of ownership: that is merely an instrumental means through which control of the territory can be exercised. For people dwelling in or near the forest, what is at stake, and leads them to care about ownership and control, is the landscape, the surroundings within which they make their home. Even sacred sites, places set aside and emphatically not understood to be fitting domiciles or thoroughfares, belong to such familiar surroundings.

That a population arrived only recently in its present location need not mean that it feels any less strongly the need for home; though migrants' affections may often be split between the new home and the former, with either one potentially receiving the greater share and at any moment looming larger in a person's sense of identity. Still, this does not mean that we can wholly and automatically disregard the question of whether a population is long settled or recently arrived. If we are to take adequate account of the importance of home and homeland, we must acknowledge the importance which they also had for people who occupied a landscape in the past. For settled communities, the ongoing act of settlement and the making of homes may be construed as an intergenerational project, handed down by forebears who tilled the same fields or walked on the same hills or lived and loved and died between the same walls. That these forefathers have passed away does not necessarily erase their presence for their descendants while the places are still there. Earlier I noted some observations about the role of ancestral places in Indigenous religions of North America. For other peoples and in other places, a sense of intergenerational continuity within the setting of a landscape may not be overtly religious or ritualistic, but we should not for that reason discount it. Parentage, ancestry, often runs as deep in us as home, whether or not the fatherland or mother country is the one in which we live.

Janna Thompson has written that the fact 'that people of the past cared about [an] old tree, made an effort to preserve it, and regarded it as an important community landmark, gives their successors a reason to value and preserve it' (2000, p. 250). It may be significant that she writes of 'successors' rather than descendants; at least, if those people of the past were *not* the ancestors of anyone now living nearby, a present population may still be able to find reasons to care about those who have lived in and cared for the same places beforehand. Nonetheless, what we feel for our own ancestors may be among our reasons for acting. If members of a settled (or returned) population do feel that heredity and family history give them a special connection to a place, unavailable to newcomers, we should be hesitant to judge that they are getting something wrong.

These ways in which people involve themselves with the land of a locality, and with its history of such involvement, are on the whole independent of any scientific attitude towards landscapes, or at least underdetermined by it. Archaeology can shed light on past settlements and past migrations, and its findings can be sources of great interest to local people, but for the most part, present practicalities are likely to override any ancestral imperatives which we might suppose we find evidentially embodied in a historic landscape. (The recent referendum campaign for Scottish independence did not make the immigration policies of Hadrian a significant aspect of its arguments, even though one of the most famous ruins in the British landscape is the defensive wall his forces constructed to control the northern border of the Roman province, fixing in the popular mind the image of defiant, unconquered northern tribes.) Even the copious resources of the Yugoslav government, employed in the vigorous memorialisation of battlefields, failed to produce a lasting Yugoslav identity.

Nonetheless, when people do turn to archaeological findings in the course of contestation over land, that the evidential record implies a history of continuous settlement, or that it suggests a history of complex migration and the replacement of populations, may be cited to show either that the present population has unmatchably deep roots in the past of its locality, or that it is the product of one recent wave of migration among others and in no especial position. The Kekchi and Mopan of Toledo may actually manage to be both.

If there is any truly 'best ancestral claim' to a piece of land, however, archaeological or ethnographic research alone will not decisively identify it. Each modification by new waves of migrants is cumulative, so that the first and nearest 'unspoilt' nature may least resemble what the land has lately become; while its current state (especially once touched by urban sprawl or the modern capabilities of heavy industry) may owe little at first glance to the vistas former populations knew, but nonetheless is only the most recent development in a succession of settlements. The history of such a landscape can be traced scientifically, but the elements that have made it any people's home cannot be equivalently prised apart. Such is still the nature of land: however we shape it, whatever we build upon it and whatever battles we fight for control of it, it remains the heritage that goes beyond our artefactual grasp even as it continues to nourish us.

Notes

1 Hypothetically, even an entire planetary surface *could* be made an artefact with technologies of terraforming in some potential future, but we are a long way from the 'green Mars' scenario.
2 These are not necessarily dependent on the seaside. A visitor to the Tropical Islands resort near Berlin describes it in the following cultural terms: 'It's got that Malaysian high concept futurist vibe going, combined with German thoroughness and attention to detail, for an experience that's pretty much what you'd expect if Disneyworld opened a park in Singapore... [A] relaxing tropical beach-side day out in an environment that's barely less artificial than [a] space colony.' (Stross, 2014)
3 Among the ironies of art history is the fate of Marcel Duchamp's 'readymade' *Fountain*, the mass-produced urinal put forward for exhibition as an artwork. The original is lost, but reproductions exist—many specially made, since the production line that manufactured the original has ended. As this indicates, the distinction between an 'authentic' 'original' and a 'mere' 'replica' is not always trivial.
4 From Henry Wadsworth Longfellow's *Evangeline*.

References

Coleman, E.B. (2013) Contesting Religious Claims over Archaeological Sites. In Scarre, G.F. & Coningham, R. (eds.). *Appropriating the Past: Philosophical Perspectives on the Practice of Archaeology.* Cambridge: Cambridge University Press. pp. 156–175.

Custred, G. (2000) The forbidden discovery of Kennewick Man. *Academic Questions.* 13 (3). pp. 12–30.

English Heritage. (2011a) *Designation Listing Selection Guide: Domestic 2, Town Houses.*

English Heritage. (2011b) *Designation Listing Selection Guide: Street Furniture.*

Hendrix, B.A. (2005) Memory in Native American land claims. *Political Theory.* 33. pp. 763–785.

Jacobson, K. (2009) A developed nature: a phenomenological account of the experience of home. *Continental Philosophy Review.* 42 (3). 355–373.

Jacobson, K. (2010) The experience of home and the space of citizenship. *Southern Journal of Philosophy.* 48 (3). pp. 219–245.

Jones, S. (2008) £254m Battle of the Black Swan. *The Guardian.* 24th March 2008. p. 11.

Kaiser, C. (2006) Contentious Landscapes in Bosnia and Herzegovina. In Sassatelli, M. (ed.) *Landscape as Heritage: Negotiating European Cultural Identity.* Fiesole: European University Institute. pp. 27–31.

Lafarge, F. (2006) Landscapes in International Law and European Law. In Sassatelli, M. (ed.) *Landscape as Heritage: Negotiating European Cultural Identity.* Fiesole: European University Institute. pp. 37–44.

Last, K. (2006) Heritage and Identity: The Challenge of Landscapes to the Nature/Culture Dichotomy. In Sassatelli, M. (ed.) *Landscape as Heritage: Negotiating European Cultural Identity.* Fiesole: European University Institute. pp. 9–16.

Lowenthal, D. (1985) *The Past Is a Foreign Country.* Cambridge: Cambridge University Press.

Merryman, J.H. (1990) 'Protection' of the cultural 'heritage'? *American Journal of Comparative Law.* 38 Supplement 'U.S. Law In an Era of Democratization', pp. 513–522.

Milani, R. (2006) The Idea of Landscape and the Perspectives of a Common European Policy. In Sassatelli, M. (ed.) *Landscape as Heritage: Negotiating European Cultural Identity.* Fiesole: European University Institute. pp. 3–8.

Morelle, R. and Denman, S. (2015) *Vast replica recreates prehistoric Chauvet cave.* Available from: www.bbc.co.uk/news/science-environment-32403867 (Accessed: 25th April 2015).

Nagel, J. (1994) Constructing ethnicity: Creating and recreating ethnic identity and culture. *Social Problems.* 41 (1). pp. 152–176.

Pantazatos, A. (2010) Does diaspora test the limits of stewardship? Stewardship and the ethics of care. *Museum International.* 62 (1–2). pp. 96–99.

Stross, C. (2014) *Let's put the future behind us.* Available from: www.antipope.org/charlie/blog-static/2014/11/lets-put-the-future-behind-us-1.html (Accessed: 23rd November 2014).

Thompson, J. (2000) Environment as cultural heritage. *Environmental Ethics.* 22 (3). pp. 241–58.

Wilk, R.R. (1999) Whose forest? Whose land? Whose ruins? Ethics and conservation. *Science and Engineering Ethics.* 5 (3). pp. 367–374.

5

CHANGING DEMOGRAPHICS AND CULTURAL HERITAGE IN NORTHERN EUROPE

Transforming narratives and identifying obstacles: a case study from Oslo, Norway

Christopher Prescott

Introduction

In November 2012 the Norwegian directorate for Cultural Heritage, *Riksantikvaren*, celebrated its 100th anniversary. I participated on a panel assigned with the task of sharing thoughts about the future. Sitting on a raised stage and looking out over a very large audience, it struck me that one would be hard put to find a more ethnically and socially homogeneous audience in contemporary Oslo. This observation fed into previous concerns (Prescott 2013a) that after 45 years of large-scale migration to Norway, recruitment to archaeology and the cultural heritage sector – university programmes and jobs – in no way reflects the country's contemporary population. Recent surveys seem to suggest that important diaspora communities do not use and are not particularly interested in museums, Norwegian heritage or non-ethnic specific culture events.

Does this have something to do with the stories archaeology tells? Norwegian and Scandinavian archaeology was originally an integral part of the national projects. In modern and contemporary times overt nationalism has been critiqued, mainly within the disciplinary discourse. However, the national agenda has largely been replaced by an identity-paradigm based on perceptions of continuous links between ancient inhabitants and contemporary Scandinavian populations. The appeal to identity contains some of the same fundamental ideas that were inherent to traditional national projects. And indeed, the appeal to identity (and its political utility) has been part of the reasons for archaeology's and historical heritage's success in securing recognition, legislation and funding.

However, global migration is conceivably undermining the feasibility of the traditional ethnic identity strategy. Alison Wylie (2003, 16) contended that:

> moral or ethical issues arise when taken-for-granted conventions of practice are disrupted, . . . a rupture occurs, as sociologists sometimes describe it, that

makes it impossible to go on as you've been used to doing, or when you confront a situation where it just is not clear what you should do.

There can be little doubt that immigration is changing Northern Europe. It is reasonable to ask whether globalisation, and resulting global migration, has resulted in just this sort of "rupture" in the ontology and dissemination of archaeology and cultural heritage. Even if it had been possible, it seems politically, ethically and pragmatically untenable to ignore a substantial part of the population, and to continue to maintain identity narratives that are not only inaccurate, but also a priori exclude a substantial part of the population. In line with Wylie's more general observation, it is not immediately clear what strategy should be pursued in the future. Although narratives and their underlying ideological premises need to be reformulated, drawing on previous experiences of incorporating marginalised groups might not offer an appropriate recipe.

Narratives are probably only part of the problem. If a goal is to include and engage diverse groups of the population in heritage issues and archaeology, obstacles are probably not only located in the practices and discourses of cultural heritage institutions and archaeology. There are probably significant structures within various immigrant communities that generate variable practices rooted in socio-cultural structures. In other words, the observed patterns are also a result of structure and practice in the diaspora communities.

Using material from Norway, this chapter first outlines a history of archaeo-logical heritage discourse. The chapter then examines three studies of immigrant attitudes towards heritage, museums and education. Although not an exhaustive analysis, combining main stream society's narratives with studies of immigrant groups' values and practices, it theoretically recognises that "[t]he constitution of agents and structures are not two independently given sets of phenomena, a dual-ism, but represent a duality." (Giddens 1984, 25). Through recognising all parties as knowledgeable actors, with resources and power – a capability to reach outcomes – I hopefully avoid the "derogation of the lay actor" (Giddens 1982, 37f) – a fallacy that in my opinion is inherent to much argument concerning minorities' and institu-tions of main stream society.

Understanding the situation and defining policies are inhibited by limitations in the quality and validity of data concerning immigrant attitudes and practices to material heritage, as the studies below makes apparent. There are, as the reference to Wylie indicates, no clear cut routes of policy and action by which to proceed. Still, the article hopefully illuminates both the need for research and some initial steps to be taken to understand and meet contemporary and future challenges.

Archaeology in the public domain: an ethnic discipline?

Popular perceptions of the value of material heritage and archaeology are largely related to the narratives more or less attached to the material remains – not the material itself. Which narratives that are found to be important by whom are contextually conditioned. For the researcher an obscure object can be immensely important for developing an interpretation. Selling archaeology and cultural heritage to the public or policymakers is often dependent on a readily grasped narrative declaiming relevance for contemporary society (like developing tourist attractions, educational facilities or creating socio-political cohesion) or sub-groups (e.g. identity claims, political agendas). Archaeology in Scandinavia is a case in point.

Scandinavian archaeology is among the prominent international schools within archaeology (Trigger 1989, 73). Given the peripheral position and small size of the Nordic nations, it is rather surprising that they should assume such a prominent position in the history of archaeology. Part of this success can be attributed to generous financial support engendered by comprehensive heritage legislation, and that archaeology has enjoyed a high level of prestige since the 1800's (Trigger 1989, 84f). Archaeology contributed to the consolidation of nation states, and these Nordic states' need to create national narratives both authentic and mythical (Baudou 2004, 112ff, Klindt-Jensen 1975, Prescott 2013b, more generally Díaz-Andreu 2001). As these states lacked substantial written sources for heroic deep-history on which to base national narratives, they turned to archaeology and disciplines like comparative linguistics and ethnology. The national ideals were bound up to a conceptualisation of the populations as homogeneous in terms of genesis, language, culture and ideology.

A decimated Norway entered into a union with Denmark in 1380, and sovereignty was transferred to Copenhagen in 1536. With Denmark's defeat in the Napoleonic wars in 1814, Norway was awarded Sweden. This latter union was dissolved in 1905. In the quest for building a national identity in support of Norwegian autonomy, the historical disciplines had their task cut out:

> Historians everywhere seek to emphasise what can serve to glorify their own nation. For centuries the political situation in Norway has been cause, to a greater extent than for most nations, to see her nationality forgotten, and that the part of [Norway's] history that was part of world events was either ignored or portrayed in an inaccurate light. . . . and the works witness my continuous toil, to the best of my capabilities, for the nation's honour and interests.
>
> *(Munch 1852, v-xiii, transl. by author)*

The tales of government and individuals were not central to this history, as P.A. Munch[1] made clear when he argued that history is about the core of the nation, i.e. the people. The people transcend episodes and ephemeral politics. To this end folklore and comparative linguistics (and much speculation) were prominent sources, but in time archaeology became important, rocketing into centre stage with the Viking Ship finds (from the 1870s to 1903) and the growing appreciation of the Medieval stave churches. At the heart of the ensuing narratives is the idea that culture, people and the land uniquely co-evolved.

The relationship between building national identity, heritage preservation and archaeology has been profitable for all parties. Archaeology has enjoyed political patronage, public interest and an enviable, legislation-generated resource flow. Given the relative homogeneous nature of a country in a struggle to reconstitute its autonomy, the scientific transgressions were perhaps innocuous. Indigenous minorities like the Sami and Kven (peasants of Finnish descent) could have posed a challenge to the national identity narrative. However, these minority groups were initially ignored, assimilated or relegated to insignificance. Later, in the post-colonial atmosphere of the 1970s and on, the Saami struggle for recognition (stoked by the threat of hydro-electric developments) led to an explicit ethnically oriented Saami-archaeology. In many ways the indigenous minorities adopted the familiar strategy of generating ethnic identity narratives as part of a successful national campaign.

Thus, in addition to the goal of generating knowledge about the past, archaeology in Norway (like most countries) also has an ethnic origin. Archaeology resonates with broader political trends in that there are two competing national meta-narratives. First, Norway conceived as *part of Europe* (Shetelig 1925), often propagated by those who identified with the political establishment and cultural elite. In the second narrative Norway conceived as the *other* (conceptually in reference to Baumann 1991), an opposite to *normal* Europe in a dichotomous construction of the continent, Norway being formed by unique environmental and cultural conditions (Brøgger 1925). This latter view has echoed through modern and contemporary national rhetoric of the political right to the political left.

In processual and post-modern Norwegian archaeology, ethnicity and nationalism were criticised and ostensibly abandoned. Still, archaeology had and has a complicated relationship to nationalism. Norway has held two referendums (1972 and 1994) rejecting EU-membership (most intensely opposed by opposite ends of the political scale, the far right and the centre-left). The underlying arguments held a strongly national note. The concurrent political nationalism is found in archaeology's embrace of the cultural exceptionality paradigm, rejection of migration, emphasis on local development and an environmental approach emphasising the connection between natural conditions (perceived as exceptional), culture, society and economy. The ensuing histories are local or regional, avoiding large scale history, and resonating with Baumann's *other* and *norm* (i.e., Norwegian versus European) in the construction of identity.

In appealing to the public, identity narratives that claim a co-evolution of the landscape, the people inhabiting the landscape and the culture used to adapt to the environment have continued to be used. The ensuing histories are often small-scale, discussing regions or national environments (coast, inland valley and the semi-Arctic to Arctic). Archaeology has at times entered contemporary political discourse to prove historical continuity and provide symbols and analogies. Often appealing to the regional, national or ethnically specific, and framed as inclusive localism and environmentalism in opposition to alienating globalism and greed, such campaigns have employed a superficial appreciation of the symbols they lift from prehistory. A case in point is the 1994 campaigns in advance of the second EU-referendum. Opponents used a Bronze Age rock carving motive of a boat. Ironically, these renditions of boats are best perceived as a symbol of European interaction, networks and the power aspirations of the elites.

Identity as a justification for cultural heritage management also saturates the Norwegian 1970/2000 heritage legislation that is still in force:

> Cultural monuments and their environments . . . must be protected, both as part of our cultural heritage and identity . . . .
>
> It is a national responsibility to manage these resources . . . as a source for contemporary and future generations' experience, self-understanding, well-being and activity.
>
> *(in Holme 2005, 24, transl. by author)*

The explication of the legislation not only emphasises scientific material and sources of experience, but that heritage is a "source of values to generate identity and a sense of security", that it is local and "Norway's contribution to world heritage" (Holme 2005, 25–27).

Most archaeologists probably feel uneasy with the identity premise, but as the goals are perceived as benevolent, they have tended to look through their fingers with the scientific shortcomings – in ethical terms a consequentialist approach (Wylie 2003,7). However, identity and attendant concepts of the co-evolution of people, culture and country are also used for ends the archaeological community is less sympathetic to. In the court case against Anders Behring Breivik (the perpetrator of the July 22nd 2011 massacres) he and his supporters referred to Norwegians as an indigenous population that migrated into the country after deglaciation, maintaining that he was defending this indigenous population in the face of colonisation. The historiographical basis for this assertion was laid with the national agenda of mid-1800' history (that aimed to differentiate Norwegians from other Northern Germanic groups), as well as more recent popular rhetoric about the "first Norwegians". A critique of Breivik's assertion is based on the observation that in genetic terms the contemporary population is a result of continuous mobility and migration (though disputed in archaeology). In cultural terms today's population is the outcome of dynamic processes on scales that don't match national borders. In short, even if a contention of Norwegians as an indigenous population had been relevant, there are not strong connections between contemporary populations and the early post-glacial immigrants. Ironically, this critique is equally relevant to a number of more "progressive" uses of the identity paradigm.

When confronted with a need to incorporate new groups into narratives of archaeology, the traditional approach has not been to genuinely question the fundamental ethnic content of the narratives, but to add the identity narratives of new groups – Saami, women, children, elderly and, recently, immigrant groups – to the repertoire of histories, or integrate groups into existing narratives

(Högberg 2013,155ff; 2015,50). But is generating new ethnos-narratives a credible or productive strategy today? Or, does globalising compel us to construct narratives (probably scientifically more honest) that are experienced as relevant and challenging across ethnic lines (Holtorf 2009)?

Demography and agendas

The identity premises can be challenged on empirical and theoretical grounds, and they are ethically dubious. There are also substantial sociological arguments for retiring ethnic identity programmes in their modernist and post-modernist forms. In the course of the last two decades, the population of Norway can no longer be perceived as homogeneously comprised of two ethnic categories with deep histories in the region. According to *Statistics Norway*, in 2013, non-Norwegian immigration was down 14 percent from the year before, but it was still nearly 67,000 – i.e. equating to the size of the Saami population in Norway.

Oslo is one of the fastest growing cities in Europe, a growth fuelled by immigration. In 2014, according to Oslo City's statistics agency, 197,612 of 640,000 inhabitants had an immigrant background. This is nearly 31 percent and up from 22 percent in 2004. Of the immigrant population 41 percent has an Asian origin, 17 percent is of African descent, while Europeans constitute 37 percent. A quarter of those registered as immigrants are born in Norway to two immigrant parents, while the rest are immigrants themselves. Major source nations are Pakistan (22,585), Poland (14,765), Sweden (13,858) and Somalia (13,424), Eritrea, Turkey, The Philippines, Iraq and Vietnam. In 2015, though not processed statistically, Syrians became a significant group of immigrants. *Statistics Norway*, usually conservative in its estimates, predicts that in 2040, 24 percent of the country's and 40–56 percent of Oslo's population will be comprised of immigrants. According to an article from 2011 in the major newspaper *Aftenposten* (Slettholm 2011) the proportion of immigrant pupils in Oslo's schools has increased from 29 percent in 1999 to 40 percent in 2011. A total of 58 of 139 primary schools had a majority of pupils registered as "non-Norwegian speakers" in 2011, 7 percent of the schools had more than 90 percent non-Norwegian speakers.

Statistics of ethnic demography are notoriously difficult to generate, already categories and criteria are subject to heated debates. However, for all their flaws, the statistics demonstrate that the populations of Norway and Oslo are increasingly heterogeneous. Immigration and cultural tensions are contested subjects in Europe, Scandinavia and Norway, but no matter what position one holds on the politics of immigration, the dynamic make-up of the population is a fact. Furthermore, with an increase in immigrant pupils in the schools of one percentage point a year, the immigrant population is young and will increasingly contribute to the shaping of society in the future. Obviously, archaeology and the broader heritage sector have an obligation to strive to be relevant to and involve all major population groups. Such endeavours are also in the discipline's own interest.

Cultural heritage and archaeology, ethnic professions?

The Norwegian Heritage Directorate's (*Riksantikvaren*) 100th anniversary that I mentioned initially, though extreme, is not completely without parallels. The university programs in archaeology (and the humanities in general) do not reflect the ethnic constitution of the population, nor does academic employment in the Cultural Resource Management and heritage sector. The extreme skewing renders statistics superfluous.

There are ethical, pragmatic and political problems with this situation. The immigrant communities are a substantial part of the population, cultural heritage is also managed on behalf of these groups, and cultural heritage narratives should target these groups. It is therefore reasonable to expect a social constitution of the practitioners within archaeology that to some degree reflects the broader population. This is also in the pragmatic interest of archaeology and the heritage sector itself, as not drawing on the talent and labour from a substantial part of the population limits the intellectual and experiential pool in archaeology. As archaeology's success is historically linked to broad political and popular recognition, involving a growing minority to ensure robust legislation is certainly important. Not doing so could readily translate into a reduced resource flow to heritage management, research and training, i.e. jobs.

Though the importance of archaeology in contemporary society tends to be exaggerated by archaeologists, archaeological knowledge can be useful, and archaeology can also make a small contribution to contemporary society in dismantling ethnic barriers by providing long-term perspectives. Archaeology and other heritage disciplines have an obligation to participate in contemporary discourse with insights into the dynamics of migration, culture meetings, and transformations – even if it is naïve to expect these narratives not to contain elements of strife, uncertainty and loss, as well as growth, development and prosperity. The insights to be had from the study of the past are not cotton candy stories about how everyone got along before some arbitrarily chosen institution arose, but they do provide understanding concerning cultural, ethnic and social encounters and transformations.

From producer agendas to user perspectives: two recent museum studies

What should be done (or what is effective) to more strongly involve various immigrant groups in archaeology and the heritage sector is not immediately clear. A starting point is surveying the present situation and identifying analytic strategies. A traditional shortcoming is that approaches have been based on what the sector wants to convey, and its perception of accommodating "them", i.e. immigrant groups (Gran and Vaagen 2010, 7). Is it therefore relevant to investigate initially how archaeology and cultural heritage are experienced by immigrant groups? Methodologically, an ideal starting point would be a three-pronged data-set: quantitative data (e.g. concerning museum visits, impact factors, attitudes among non-users), qualitative data (interviews with various user groups, museum employees, educators, public that is not reached by dissemination etc.) and finally observational data of how people actually respond and act. These data are at best patchy. However, there are surveys concerning immigrants and museums in Oslo and there are studies of educational choices that open the field to initial scrutiny. These are the basis for the following discussion.

Initially, the museum surveys referred to below are used to explore public experiences and expectations. This is followed by a tentative discussion of institutions and structures in immigrant communities that condition actions and priorities. Traditionally there has been a one-way focus on power relations (oppressive majority structures versus minority actors) and categorical dualism where minority–majority populations are concerned. However, all actors draw on resources from institutions and structures that are constraining and enabling, all groups choose actions (though despite intentions, consequences are unpredictable), i.e. a "dialectic of control" (Giddens 1982, 36ff; 1984, 14ff). The practical implication of this sociological position is that it is not sufficient to analyse narratives, public policy or majority behaviour. To pose informed questions one must also draw on the choices generated by resources and constraints located in institutions and structures within immigrant societies. To further complicate things, immigrant societies do not represent a homogeneous entity – there are significant differences in the habitus of urbane Poles compared to people with a background in rural Punjab. The present discussion draws on a study of educational choices in West Asian caste groups. The aim is not to supply definitive answers, but create a platform to define relevant research questions and strategies, not the least in an attempt at replacing dichotomist "dualism" with a dialectic "duality" in the approach to action, structure and institution (Giddens 1982, 36ff).

Two surveys have been conducted in Oslo to explore practices and attitudes in "diverse" museum audiences, *Knowledge about – participation by – public outreach to diverse museumgoers* (Gran & Vaagen 2010) and *Immigrants' use of museums – a survey*[2] (Norsk Folkemuseum/Oslo Museum 2011). Both surveys have a quantitative section based on questionnaires and a qualitative section with interviews of individuals in focus groups. There are significant methodological problems in the data the studies present, and neither study has observational data. However, they are noteworthy for their emphasis on the "reception side", and their attempts at breaking up the heterogeneous "immigrants" category. They tentatively signal a redirection of focus and understanding, as explicitly expressed in the 2010 survey:

> Norwegian cultural policy up to the present has focused on the production side of things when it comes to diversity: it has been about programming (relevant content for "them"), recruiting from minorities (enhancing visibility of diversity) and establishing arenas of dialogue and cooperation with minorities. Politically this has been a question of representation and integration; minority artists and their aesthetics/culture must be represented in

Norwegian cultural institutions. The reception side of things, the audience or culture consumer, has not been absent from the rhetoric of diversity, but in practice has been subordinate to the production side: If one programs relevantly for "them" and/or recruit "their own", the minority audience will turn out. Our data does not support this assumption.

(Gran & Vaagen 2010, 7, transl. by author)

Knowledge about – participation by – public outreach to diverse museumgoers was commissioned by the University of Oslo's Museum of Cultural History. The study targeted immigrant minorities at three college institutions in Oslo. In a wider perspective this group is interesting for several reasons: students are a key target group for cultural institutions. Immigrant students are important as they are well-educated, have a high level of participation in contemporary society, are urbane and balance between modern Norway and their parents' socio-cultural background.

Before shortly presenting and discussing the results, it should be pointed out that there are issues concerning how representative a face-value reading of the quantitative data is. In short, the data conceivably generate a picture that is biased in favour of the museums. The initial survey questionnaires were distributed through 21 societies for minority students at three Oslo colleges, representing 5130 non-western students. With a response rate of 2.7 percent and heavily skewed towards a single student society, the results were deemed invalid. A second campaign used minority interviewers and incentives to attract responses. Out of 1001 students (15.8 percent of the non-western minorities), 32 percent responded after two reminders. Though response rates were low, and despite a number of skewing factors that potentially inflate positive responses, the response rate was deemed adequate. The majority of the respondents were from Africa (23.3 percent) and Asia (65.9 percent). The quantitative survey was followed up by interviews of eight teachers (seven Norwegian and one Romanian, from elementary schools to university summer schools) and six students (from Morocco, Somalia, Pakistan, Vietnam and Iraq). The survey's quantitative data mainly demonstrates that interest in museums is very low. The interviews in the focus groups offer other insights, though representability is not assessable. The interviewed (European) teachers emphasised that exhibitions should reflect cultural heterogeneity, while the (African and Asian) students were more critical of an inclusion practice based on a mechanical extension of the range of ethnic narratives. The students did not call for productions of their "own" culture. Indeed, some respondents were concerned about political agendas at the heart of "ethnic" and "immigrant" productions, and questioned the accuracy of previous exhibitions. Expressing a position outside the dichotomy "Norwegian – immigrant", they encouraged exhibition productions relevant to their experiences, contextualised as part of Norwegian history or in histories of hybridisation. These responses perhaps reflect not so much ethnic or immigrant background, but the experiences of growing up in contemporary Oslo. One might ask if young ethnic Norwegians were part of the same survey, would they have responded along similar lines? In other words, instead of an essentialist ethnicity context, many young people in Oslo experience a dynamic and globalised society as their context and reference (no matter where their parents came from), and explorations of this context's history and content might conceivably engender stronger involvement.

The other survey, *Immigrants' use of museums – a survey*, was commissioned by the Norwegian Folk museum and Oslo Museum. It was based on 411 respondents from four immigrant groups: Poles, Pakistanis, Vietnamese and Somalis. The respondent group encompassed broader age demographics than the University of Oslo's survey, but though it included age groups "31–45" and "older than 46", it was skewed towards the 15–30 age group. There is also a skewing towards people with higher education. As the 15–30 age group has probably visited museums as part of mandatory school trips, and educated people are more inclined to be positive to museums and respond to a survey, the respondent group is conceivably skewed toward people with a positive attitude to museums compared to the immigrant population as a whole. The quantitative data are supplemented by nine interviews.

An interesting feature of this survey is that it encompasses a northern European group, immigrant Poles. Labour immigration from Poland is among the later waves into Norway, and the number of Polish children that have attended and completed school in Norway is probably low. Museum visits in this group are therefore not primarily the result of school excursions. It is noteworthy that nearly 70 percent had visited a museum/cultural event in the course of the last year. A majority of respondents (55–60 percent) from the other groups, mostly with a multi-generational history in Norway, had *not* visited museums at all. As a large segment of the African and Asian population has attended schools in Norway (with the obligatory excursions to museums) this figure is equally remarkable.

The lack of interest in museums among non-European immigrant groups is corroborated by interviews in a focus group. These indicate that work, homework, Quran studies and relaxing with the family are priorities. Some respondents remark that as children they were not encouraged by their parents to visit museums or partake in cultural activities that were not related to their own ethnicity. Though several interviews indicate that the interviewed persons were primarily interested in their "own culture", several younger respondents were concerned about the political agendas of exhibitions, frustrated with being pigeon-holed into socio-ethnic stereotypes and critical of their elders' lack of involvement.

Again, the above surveys have limited quantitative representativeness and suffer methodological shortcomings, and it is difficult to draw detailed conclusions. There are, however, grounds to formulate hypotheses that could guide future research:

- Interest in the museums and cultural heritage is determined by region of origin, and there are substantial differences between immigrant groups. This mirrors patterns observed in educational choices, where variations between immigrant groups is greater than between minority and majority populations (Fekjær 2006, 86f).
- The relevance of the critique of the national and ethnic identity narratives in the first part of this chapter is supported by some of the observations.

The ethnic perspective, whether traditional–national, indigenous or immigrant, is not an adequate base for generating broad interest or perceptions of relevance among youth growing up in Oslo (Prescott 2013a; see Holtorf 2009 for similar argument).

- Productions targeting the experience of globalised genesis in a local place might be experienced as relevant.

Understanding how various social and cultural groups perceive and respond to heritage productions, is not simply a question of supply, narrative and recruitment. The various immigrant communities make active choices based on their broader social context in Norwegian society, but also based on the socio-cultural values and priorities in diaspora communities and their networks that extend to the region of origin. By necessity this impacts success rates for inclusion strategies, and emphasises the need for knowledge of the habitus-specific contexts of the various groups. This is tentatively explored below through a study of educational choices in immigrant societies with roots in caste societies originating in Punjab.

Caste and choice

The above observations suggest that national narratives are but part of the explanation for low immigrant minority involvement in museums and other heritage venues. Values and practices within immigrant communities structure use of museums. However, it would not be accurate to reduce choices in contemporary Norway to solely reflect ethno-cultural values. Choices result from social and economic goals pursued by actors in relation to structural parameters, whether "imported", "indigenous" or generated along the dynamic interface of the two. In-depth studies and qualified interpretative discussions of choices concerning heritage in diaspora communities are limited in Norway, and to my knowledge, otherwise in Scandinavia. However, there are studies of choices within education (e.g. Fekjær 2006, 2007; Moldenhawer 2005), and they can indirectly help understand choices and practices in relation to cultural heritage and archaeology. An underlying premise is that choices concerning cultural heritage are steered by some of the same structural and institutional mechanisms that affect education choices. To generate hypotheses here, I used a 2011 study by Mariann Leirvik entitled: "*To study Art History or Political Science is a luxury not everyone can afford." Do different forms of capital in ethnic communities explain educational outcomes?*[3] This study was based on in-depth interviews of informants from diaspora communities originating from caste societies in Pakistan and India: 23 interviews were conducted between 2006 and 2007 of young women (11) and men (12) from 17 to 29 years of age. They had all grown up in Oslo, half were from India (eight Sikhs, three Hindus) and half were Pakistani (Muslim). The informants were asked about the families' ethnic networks, principles of inequality and how these latter factors influenced their choices of education. In the analysis, Leirvik interprets this data set with reference to Bourdieu's sociology: the forms of capital (Bourdieu 1986) that actors may draw on and the habitus within which they act (Bourdieu 1990).

An important theoretical premise (from Bourdieu) is that society is a multidimensional hierarchy, and that various groups draw on variable forms of capital. Members of the ethnic networks studied in Norway share forms of practice, which can be termed sub-cultures. In Leirvik's study, class is not as important as caste. Though younger cohorts, i.e. second and third generations, are "probably less pre-occupied with these codes [of cultural inequality], they must relate to them" (Leirvik 2012, 197) – and reproduce the sub-cultural habitus. The important reference for the minority networks is not majority society, but values and practices within the sub-cultural networks extending back to the region of origin. Old capital structures are reproduced from the caste-based source countries, but capital may also be converted into new standards of practice and value, especially when interpreted with what Bourdieu termed the "Don Quixote" effect:

> In conjunction with migration one readily experiences that "old" principles of domination lose their meanings when encountering new forms of hierarchisation. . . . though the old principles of dominance do not achieve recognition in the country of reception, they can continue to be of . . . importance in the ethnic network. . . . If the forms of capital in the country of reception . . . gain importance in the family's ethnic network, it will be important to convert old forms of capital.
>
> *(Leirvik 2011, 197, transl. by author)*

Capital conversions are necessary and draw on resources found in Norway, but have values and goals in reference to the socio-ethnic subculture. As practices are internalised in the ethnic subculture through upbringing, they are reproduced.

Caste is thus "transported and transformed", and remains decisive in choices and strategies. According to Leirvik's argument, based on data from her informants, high castes seek to reproduce the hierarchical structures and practices from the caste society of origin. This affects gender practices, reproducing a patriarchal structure, where women are expected to behave and are treated in a traditional fashion, and men gain status through overt displays of power and wealth. From the majority society's perspective, this has a detrimental effect on academic choices – and allows us to generate grounded hypotheses about why certain immigrant groups do not pursue education, or why young men from certain groups are statistically unsuccessful in education (ref. Fekjær 2006) – or why some groups pursue education (and use museums?) more actively than members of the majority society.

Moving to a country with other dominant structural conditions allows new options of choice. Some parents recognise that a conversion of capital to the new context entails changed practices. Despite their high caste background, some parents for example encourage their daughters to pursue education, but primarily within fields that can compete for prestige in the ethnic networks. As society is multi-level, strategies also differ with families' position in the caste system. Lower castes experience problems and discrimination in Norway, but compared to the region of origin this is experienced as a mild problem. Instead, they view the resources, institutions and structures found in Norway as a vehicle for escaping the caste structures to improve their economic and social position. As opposed to trends in the higher castes, this group actively embraces education and a number of the values expounded in the Norwegian part of society.[4] One of Leirvik's high caste female informants ("Ambreen") formulates it like this:

> There are two kinds of Pakistani boys, those who . . . are often lower class, take advanced education and are well integrated in Norwegian society and are preoccupied with equal rights. And then you have the Gujar and Jat caste . . ., I'd say the majority of those in the A- and B-gangs[5] . . . . They're preoccupied with . . . traditional values, segregation of men and women like one finds in the countryside, that they want to show off as chiefs. . . . They brag all the time in Oslo: "In Pakistan our house is so big, we own so much land, and my wife is going to stay home and make children". There is a big difference between . . . [these categories of boys].
>
> *(Leirvik 2011, 203f, transl. by author)*

It is also important that members of mainstream majority society do not have the competence to understand and identify differences in caste systems, treating everyone alike. The lack of relevant competence arguably creates an inefficient platform for policymaking and defining educational (or heritage) involvement strategies.

Good news or bad?

From the above we can surmise that parts of the upper castes that wish to convert out of the traditional capital of the caste system and lower caste groups pursue academic education. For upper caste groups this may represent an attempt to uphold traditional practices and strategies – maintain power and a prestigious position – through capital conversion. Lower castes see the structures of majority Norwegian society as a way of escaping constraints of caste institutions that originate in their home countries.

For those interested in involving immigrant minorities in cultural heritage this could be perceived as good news; at first glance there are substantial groups that could potentially study, work and engage in cultural heritage and archaeology as part of social strategies. However, this hasn't been the case, and again it is probably wise to also look for causes within the community originating from caste societies. The differences between Polish and Asian/African groups identified in the museum studies above, indicates as much.

First of all, there is the common immigrant goal that the next generation should have a better life than the preceding:

> Most of our parents . . . were insecure, they had no job, strictly speaking no future, and they didn't want that for their children . . . it's best to bet on professions that give both status and income, going about studying political science, history and art and stuff like that is a luxury that is not for everyone.
>
> *("Khalid" in Leirvik 2011, 207, transl. by author)*

Moving beyond this virtually universal trait, educational choices are partially determined by the immigrant sub-cultures. Though some of the above groups pursue strategies – education – more in line with mainstream values in Norwegian society, this can be seen as a conversion from traditional caste society values and practices (e.g. overt displays of wealth and power) to more actively drawing on resources in the Norwegian context. However, strong competition in the ethnic sub-group, sending wealth back to the family in India/Pakistan and securing prestigious symbols of success are still active factors. The ethnic sub-culture conditions high academic achievers, but constricts choices to fields that are secure, provide prestige and generate high incomes. The result is what in Norway is called the ALI[6]-syndrome: immigrants apply to studies that generate capital in the ethnic networks and lead to well-paid and prestigious professions – i.e. not the humanities. So, based on Leirvik's studies in disciplines like archaeology and cultural heritage, and jobs within the humanities, museums and CRM are not within the culturally conditioned priorities of the Indian/Pakistani caste communities.

An ethical rupture: connecting the dots

As immigrant communities have grown and matured, they have gained economic and social clout. For example: nearly 30 percent of the permanent seats on the Oslo City Council are held by people with a non-western background. If large sections of the population are indifferent to cultural heritage, or even regard it as a nuisance or waste, the sector risks increased political resistance, weak legislation and cuts in funding. Part of the issues dealt with in this article can be seen from a pragmatic vantage: what serves archaeology best in the competition for minds, recognition and resources?

However, most of the points dealt with have important ethical implications, as well. Ethics are arguments about what we should do. The ethical issues discussed in this article deal with or impact archaeological ontology (particularly Nordic archaeology's stance in relation to migration and concept of cultural evolution), the inaccurate identity narratives that have been reproduced in the public sphere, the obligation for all disciplines to attract the best minds and most diverse perspectives possible and a commitment all disciplines in the humanities should share not to serve narrow instrumentalist purposes, but to generate and disseminate knowledge. For archaeology knowledge is a primary end in itself, and we should further the production of that knowledge. However, there is a social obligation for publicly financed disciplines like archaeology to facilitate the experience of archaeology and cultural heritage for as diverse social groups as possible. A secondary aim, admittedly more based in political philosophy than empirical study, is that critical knowledge helps contemporary citizens better understand their society. From a socio-political angle we also have an obligation to free archaeology from the not completely undeserved perception of it as the luxury pastime of the western middle class.

Returning to Wylie's (2003, 6) claim that ethical issues arise when taken-for-granted conventions of practice are disrupted, it would seem that old practices and narratives are not adequate in a world characterised by global migration, and only time will tell where the rupture will lead us. Contemporary globalisation with conflicts that impact the entire globe, instantaneous communication, global labour markets, global migration and the ensuing cultural and social tensions have ruptured the ethical complacency of post-war archaeology and heritage disciplines that evolved in the nation states of Northern Europe. I would contend that no other force will more strongly challenge established practices in the cultural heritage sector, archaeological ontology and heritage narratives than mass migration. In line with Wylie's argument, it seems that the globalised and dynamic constitution of citizenry in Norway and other nation states of Northern Europe generates the need for new interpretative approaches and narratives, and academic and heritage institutions embedded in new practices. Just what these will be is not yet clear, but to simply continue as before is scientifically dishonest, socially irresponsible (to society and the discipline) and to continue to "programme for them" is elitist.

This article started by outlining the national and ethnic agendas that evolved and served archaeology, cultural heritage and society so well for 150 years, irrespective of their scientific accuracy. It then pointed out that the dominant narratives and practices are increasingly out of step with local societies increasingly impacted by globalising forces, especially migration. The traditional strategies of incorporating new stakeholders into the heritage sector by generating new group-specific narratives has also been attempted in the case of immigrant groups, but with little success (Gran and Vaagen 2010,7).

The two museum surveys referred to in this article suffer from substantial methodological shortcomings in terms of respondent recruitment and frequencies, quantitative significance and lack of observational data of actual behaviour. There is also a lack of repetitive studies that test the validity of the results. However, they suggest not only that the old national or ethnic identity narratives are experienced as irrelevant, but that pigeon-holing a new generation growing up in Norway into immigrant or ethnic stereotypes is unfortunate. Archaeology should be well equipped in the narrative department, because it has always worked with change, culture, innovation, adaptation, materiality and (despite theoretical and political restrictions in its ontology) immigration, information transfers and meetings. In a historical perspective, these narratives should strive not only to be more relevant in contemporary society, but to be more accurate than stories of arbitrary groups within state boundaries. Thus, though acknowledging that historical narratives are a reflection of contemporary society (Durkheim 2005), I would contend that the proposal here doesn't represent politically driven constructivism, nor are new narratives less authentic (Sahlins 1999) than the traditional national or indigenous versions.

There have been attempts to critique the national and ethnic narratives, but these have mainly been from the producer side, often predicated on perspectives of minority exclusion and mainstream dominance. A tentative dialectic appreciation of the audience side of the equation is acutely necessary – as the museum surveys referred to in this article demonstrate. Theoretically this is in accordance with Giddens' "dialectic of power", i.e. not solely incorporating a concept of majority and structural dominance, but also informed choices made by actors leading to unintended consequences, into our analytical strategies.

The surveys and arguments presented in this article do not provide conclusive evidence, but help generate reasonable hypotheses concerning the basis for future strategies of expanding participation in archaeology and cultural heritage. These may be summed up in five points that build on each other. First, the traditional identity narratives are inaccurate and have become unproductive. Second, the dichotomies of "majority/Norwegian: minority/immigrant" are inaccurate. Third, it cannot be taken for granted that all immigrant sub-cultures share the same goals and values. Fourth, the lack of involvement outside traditional, ethnic-specific cultural arenas is a choice generated within the habitus of some diaspora communities and sub-cultures, and reflects priorities in these communities. Fifth, with immigration the habitus of ethnic Norwegians is also transforming. In an increasingly globalised and urban society, youth of Norwegian descent probably do not think in a dichotomy of Norwegian and immigrant. Just like some of the immigrant informants in the museum surveys referred to in this article, they should probably not be pigeonholed into a traditional stereotype.

Changing contemporary patterns is thus not solely a question of top-down politics of accommodation and accessibility. It is also the politics of choice in the diaspora communities themselves. This is probably far more difficult to impact than narratives and politics of access. The tentative observations and arguments in this article primarily serve to generate hypotheses, and are certainly inaccurate in terms of groups and individuals. To better understand what is happening, and to define strategies to expand the demography of future stakeholders in cultural heritage, a body of robust quantitative and qualitative studies is necessary that can throw light on the choices actors are making that impact attitudes to cultural heritage – the constraints and resources they respond to in various subcultures in contemporary society.

Notes

1 P.A. Munch (1810 – 1863) is probably the most prominent member of the generation that created a modern discipline of Norwegian history.
2 *Kunnskap om – medvirkning av – formidling for mangfoldige museumsbrukere* and *Innvandreres bruk av museer – En undersøkelse.*
3 *"Å ta kunsthistorie eller statsvitenskap er en luksus ikke alle kan unne seg." Kan utdanningsatferd forstås ut frå ulike kapitalformer i etniske nettverk?*
4 All education – from elementary school to PhD-level studies – is tuition-free in Norway. All university students qualify for stipends and advantageous government loans to cover living expenses. Tuition for studies abroad is also sponsored by the government.
5 Criminal gangs in Oslo, predominantly Pakistani.
6 ALI: "advokat, lege, ingeniør" = "lawyer, doctor, engineer".

References

Baudou, E. 2004. *Den nordiska arkeologin – historia och tolkningar.* Kungl. Vitterhets Historie och Antikvitets Akademien, Stockholm.

Baumann, Z. 1991. *Modernity and ambivalence.* Cornell University Press, Ithaca.

Bourdieu, P. 1986. The forms of capital. In Richardson (ed.), *Handbook of theory and research for the sociology of education,* 241–258. Greenwood, New York.

Bourdieu, P. 1990. *The logic of practice.* Stanford University Press, Stanford.

Brøgger, A.W. 1925. *Det norske folk i oldtiden.* Aschehoug, Oslo.

Díaz-Andreu, M. 2001. Guest editor's introduction: Nationalism and archaeology. *Nations and nationalism* 7(4), 429–440.

Durkheim, E. 2005. *The evolution of educational thought: lectures on the formation and development of secondary education in France,* Volume 2. Routledge, London.

Fekjær, S.N. 2006. Utdanning hos annengenerasjon etniske minoriteter i Norge. *Tidsskrift for samfunnsforskning* 47(1), 57–93.

Fekjær, S.N. 2007. New differences, old explanations: can educational differences between ethnic groups in Norway be explained by social background? *Ethnicities* 7(3), 367–389.

Giddens, A. 1982. *Profiles and critiques in social theory.* University of California Press, Berkeley.

Giddens, A. 1984. *The constitution of society: outline of a theory of structuration.* Polity Press, Oxford.

Gran, A.-B. & Vaagen, H. 2010. *Kunnskap om – medvirkning av – formidling for mangfoldige museumsbrukere.* Perduco Kultur/Kulturhistorisk museum, Universitetet i Oslo/ Norges Museumforbund. www.museumsforbundet.no/pdf/brukerundersokelse10.pdf

Högberg, A. 2013. *Mångfaldsfrågar i kulturmiljövården. Tankar, kunskaper och processer 2002–2012.* Nordic Academic Press, Lund.

Högberg, A. 2015. The heritage sector in a multicultural society: a discussion from a Swedish perspective. In Biehl, Comer, Prescott & Soderland (eds.), *Identity and heritage: contemporary challenges in a globalized world,* 47–54. Springer, Cham.

Holme, J., 2005. Kapittel I – Formål og virkeområde. In J. Holme (ed.), *Kulturminnevern. Bind II Kulturminneloven med kommentarer,* 10–23. Økokrim, Oslo.

Holtorf, C. 2009. A European perspective on indigenous and immigrant archaeologies. *World archaeology* 41(4), 672–681.

Klindt-Jensen, O. 1975. *A history of Scandinavian archaeology.* Thames and Hudson, London.

Leirvik, M.S. 2011. "Å ta kunsthistorie eller statsvitenskap er en luksus ikke alle kan unne seg". Kan utdanningsatferd forstås ut frå ulike kapitalformer i etniske nettverk? *Tidsskrift for samfunnsforskning* 53(2), 189–216.

Moldenhawer, B. 2005. Transnational migrant communities and education strategies among Pakistani youngsters in Denmark. *Journal of ethnic and migration studies* 31(1), 51–78.

Munch, P.A. 1852. *Det norske Folks Historie.* Chr. Tønsbergs forlag, Christiania.

Norsk Folkemuseum/Oslo Museum/Synovate 2011. *Innvandreres bruk av museer – En undersøkelse.* www.oslomuseum.no/om-oslo-museum/prosjekter/innvandreres-bruk-av-museer

Prescott, C. 2013a. Heritage and the new immigrant minorities: a catalyst of relevance for contemporary archaeology? In Biehl & Prescott (eds.), *Heritage in the context of globalization. Europe and the Americas.* Springer, Cham.

Prescott, C. 2013b. Recurrent themes: Indo-Europeans in Norwegian archaeology. In Begerbrant & Sabatini (eds.), *Counterpoint: essays in archaeology and heritage studies in honour of Professor Kristian Kristansen.* BAR int'nl series 2508, 607–612. Hadrian Books, Oxford.

Sahlins, M. 1999. Two or three things that I know about culture. *The journal of the royal anthropological institute* 5(3), 399–421.

Shetelig, H. 1925. *Norges forhistorie. Problemer og resultater i norsk arkæologi.* Aschehoug, Oslo.

Slettholm, A. 2011. Varsellampene blinker. *Aftenposten* April 19, 2011, 19–22.

Trigger, B. 1989. *A history of archaeological thought.* Cambridge University Press, Cambridge.

Wylie, A. 2003. On Ethics. In Zimmerman, Vitelli & Hollewell-Zimmer (eds.), *Ethical issues in archaeology*, 3–16. Altamira Press, Walnut Creek.

Internet sites, accessed March 2015

Oslo City Statistics: www.oslo.kommune.no/politikk-og-administrasjon/statistikk/befolkning/landbakgrunn/

Sapmi, Allt om Sveriges ursprungsfolk samerna och deras land Sápmi: Bottom of Form: www.samer.se/1536

Statistics Norway: www.ssb.no/en/befolkning/statistikker/flytting/aar/2014-04-28?fane=tabell&sort=nummer&tabell=174053

6

LASTING VALUE?

Engaging with the material traces of America's undocumented migration "problem"

Jason De León and Cameron Gokee

Introduction

> I am appalled that you could even consider publishing an article like The Journey to El Norte. It casts a romantic light on illegal immigration. To compare these criminals to the millions of Europeans who immigrated in the late 19th and early 20th centuries is an insult to their memories and efforts to give their children better lives. My grandparents came to this country legally. They wanted no handouts, learned English, and eventually owned their own company. To document the trash heaps of these current illegal immigrants as artifacts, as if they are sacred, is beyond credibility.
>
> *(Letter to the editor of* Archaeology Magazine *2011)*

> As a class, they [non-Western Europeans] contribute little of lasting value . . . They do not amalgamate. They are here in no small degree for what they can get . . . Such is the type of newer immigration, and its changing and deteriorating character makes restriction justifiable and necessary. No one can stand at Ellis Island and see the physical and mental wrecks who are stopped there, or realize that if the bars were lowered ever so little the infirm and mentally unsound would come literally in hordes, without becoming a firm believer in restriction and admission of only the best . . . Restriction is vitally necessary if our truly American ideals and institutions are to persist, and if our inherited stock of good American manhood is not to be depreciated.
>
> *(Alfred C. Reed, US Public Health Service, Ellis Island 1913:7–9)*

Over the last two decades, both the hidden and more overt politics of archaeology have been slowly excavated from the murky and protective depths of

"Science" and positivism (McGuire 2008), in part through research that interrogates written and oral accounts of the contemporary past to "tell stories in an alternative way" (González-Ruibal 2008:249). Such archaeologies of the contemporary have thrown the discipline into a multitude of difficult conversations about topics including war, poverty, and sovereign power (e.g., González-Ruibal 2007; Zimmerman and Welch 2011; De León et al. 2015). Along these same lines, our research with the Undocumented Migration Project (UMP) employs the mixed anthropological methods of ethnography (De León 2013, 2015), forensic science (Beck et al. 2014), and archaeology (Gokee and De León 2014) to step into heated political debates about the human impact of US border enforcement policies and the experiences and strategies of the many thousands of migrants who cross the Sonoran Desert between northern Mexico and southern Arizona each year.

In using migrant "artifacts" and "sites" to illuminate aspects of clandestine movement across these borderlands, the UMP raises implicit questions about controversial issues of heritage. On the one hand, an archaeological gaze considers the materiality of US/Mexico border crossings as a complex, and oftentimes ambiguous, testament to the interplay between political economic forces and human suffering in the early 21st century. Objects left along the migrant trail, from empty water bottles to worn-out shoes, may be seen as heritage-in-the-making by those sympathetic to Latino border crossers, including humanitarians, artists, and ourselves as archaeologists. On the other hand, when archaeological practice challenges modern political discourse, it can, as the above quotes suggest, ruffle the feathers of those not prepared to see the historical connections between a romanticized past and an ugly present. As with those who believed that European immigrants in the 19th century would "contribute little of lasting value" (see also Brighton 2009) many anti-immigration proponents today consider the material record of border crossing to have no heritage value. The implication is that, much like the Latino migrants who would "inherit" this history of suffering, it must be removed from the landscape and sent straight to the landfill (or back to Mexico). Simply put, the contemporary politics of undocumented migration have long-term consequences for the material record of this social process.

We explore how various forms of identity politics and notions of heritage in the present shape the archaeological record of migration across the US/Mexico border and consider how processes of appropriation and removal work in tandem, and alongside natural processes of decay, to erase migrant sites and artifacts as a tangible heritage-in-the-making. In so doing, we also critically examine the role of our own research with the UMP in both politicizing and transforming the material record of migration in southern Arizona. Rather than engaging in tired and cyclical political arguments about whether undocumented migrants are friend or foe (e.g., see Nevins 2002), we gaze forward to see how these processes shape the material record of clandestine migration, as a form of heritage, now and in the future.

Background

A towering monument of rusted steel unapologetically divides two nations; infrared cameras are perched on giant poles, their glass eyeballs slowly panning left and right like robotic centurions; blinding white orbs shoot down from helicopters to penetrate the darkness in search of intruders. These are the images that the US/Mexico border often conjures up in the public imagination of this geopolitical boundary. In reality, this space is far more ambiguous and mundane. Only 18 percent (351 miles) of the 1,954 miles that make up this frontier has anything resembling a wall (Rosenblum 2012:16) and most of the terrain where these two countries meet is remote, depopulated, rugged, and unsupervised. The dirty little secret of anti-immigrant politicians and lobbyists who use the trope of an unguarded border to generate federal spending is that the construction and maintenance of substantial partitions along most of this political boundary has always been prohibitively costly and an engineering impossibility (see McGuire 2013). Instead, vast portions of the US/Mexico divide are demarcated by three strand barbwire fences, Normandy-style barricades, or nothing at all. The areas of the border that do have significant fencing and other security measures cluster in and around urban ports of entry. These walls and high-tech surveillance cameras abruptly vanish on the outskirts of all official ports of entry.

This discrepancy in security infrastructure between populated areas and uninhabited expanses of wilderness is not just a matter of cost. Leaving large portions of the border relatively open to undocumented migration is part of a United States Border Patrol (USBP) strategy called Prevention Through Deterrence (PTD). Begun in 1993 (Dunn 2009), the logic underlying PTD is that by placing hyper-security measures (e.g., high fencing, motion sensor cameras, ground agents) in unauthorized crossing areas around urban ports of entry "illegal traffic will be deterred, or forced over more hostile terrain, less suited for crossing and more suited for enforcement" (USBP 1994:7). For more than two decades this strategy has funneled millions of migrants towards the Sonoran Desert of Arizona where people seeking illegal entry will walk for long distances (e.g., upwards of 70 miles) while simultaneously negotiating a barren landscape characterized by extreme weather, venomous animals, and other dangers. Mountains, rattlesnakes, and dehydration have been conscripted by federal policy makers to deter migrants (De León 2015). Much to the chagrin of border enforcement agencies, however, 20 years of research has shown that PTD has failed to stop migration (e.g., Cornelius and Salehayan 2007). Unfortunately for migrants, this policy has shaped border crossing into a well-organized, dangerous, and violent social process (De León 2012). Since 2000, over five million undocumented people have traversed the Arizona desert (USBP 2013) and at least 3,199 have lost their lives en route (Derechos Humanos 2018) though this number no doubt undercounts the actual number of deaths (see discussion in Beck et al. 2014). Along the way these migrants have left a trail of empty water bottles, blood-stained clothes, and lost personal possessions.

The UMP is an anthropological research program that seeks to unveil the ways in which technologies of border enforcement and border crossing intersect with the various forms of violence and suffering that migrants experience while

traversing the Sonoran Desert. Addressing these issues through the contemporary archaeological record between the authorized ports of entry at Nogales and
Sasabe in southern Arizona (Figure 6.1), the UMP has documented 341 sites and
more than 30,000 artifacts associated with clandestine migration, border policing,
humanitarian efforts, and narco-trafficking (Gokee and De León 2014). Although
these materials are only a fraction of those deposited since the advent of PTD in the
mid-1990s, they offer a critical complement to those narratives that vilify or dis-
empower migrants, or reduce their suffering into single objects, a point to which
we return in a moment.

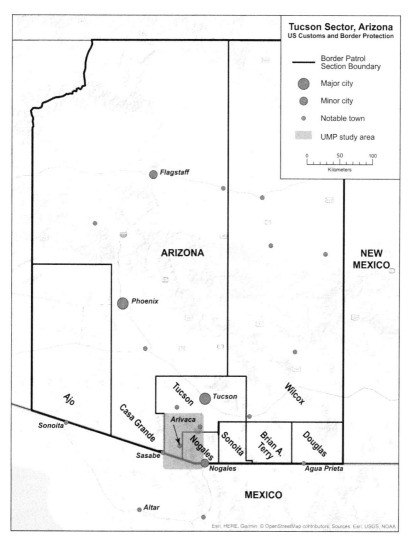

FIGURE 6.1   Map of the Tucson Sector in Arizona showing the UMP study area
between the Nogales and Sasabe ports of entry

The material record of migration is, however, fast disappearing. In contrast to some assertions that plastic water bottles and camouflage backpacks left in the desert will sit on the surface forever (Banks 2009), our data have shown that the material footprint of this process is relatively light and ephemeral. The intense desert sun and other environmental conditions can quickly breakdown most substances, especially plastics, fabric, and non-metal items. The disappearance of this contemporary archaeological record has further been sped up by two decades of systematic attempts by federal agencies, non-profit conservation groups, and local American citizens to collect and dispose of all evidence of migration. As a result, our archaeological work has largely been a salvage operation to recover as much data as possible before the desert or "clean-up" crews can destroy or remove items.

Although many have written about the controversial nature of migrant material culture in southern Arizona (e.g., Sundberg 2008; Squire 2014) and its perceived impact on the environment (Merirotto 2012; Sundberg and Kaserman 2007), much less attention has been paid to its role as the tangible heritage of the clandestine process of border crossing in the early 21st century (although see De León et al. 2015). In what follows, we take up this issue by considering how mutual processes of appropriation and removal have worked over the past two decades to unevenly shape the contemporary archaeological landscape of migration and its future as a heritage resource. By scrutinizing these twin processes we aim for more critical reflection concerning how various individuals and agencies engage with the objects left behind by those people who exist on the margins of American society and what those engagements can tell us about politics, history, and the construction of migrant narratives.

Appropriation

We define appropriation as the diverse pathways through which objects left by migrants in the Sonoran Desert come to have post-depositional lives in contemporary political discourse and activism and the perceived benefits and harm of "taking something produced by members of one culture by members of another" (Young 2005:136). The social actors involved in these processes include, but are not limited to, humanitarians, conservation groups, artists, anti-immigration activists, and archaeologists. Despite the differing motives of these groups, their use of migrant artifacts hinges, we argue, on an often implicit valuing (or devaluing) of these objects as heritage.

Many appropriations of migrant artifacts involve the construction of narratives about suffering. Those who are sympathetic to migrants, especially environmental and social justice activists, often collect items while hiking through the desert that they believe will express the trauma or humanity of the process to both to themselves and especially to others (Mlyn et al. 2014). This leads to the "cherry-picking" of exceptional items that are deeply personal in nature (e.g., photos and letters) or evocative of individual stories and experiences (e.g., baby bottles and bibles). More mundane items such as food wrappers and water bottles, which may actually play the most crucial roles in helping someone survive the desert,

FIGURE 6.2   Discarded plastic bottle

are usually neglected or deemed less valuable (Figure 6.2). These collectors thus select certain objects, and the histories of suffering that accompany them, while at the same time "dehumanizing" the archaeological record of undocumented migration through the selective removal of affective objects, a point to which we return in the next section.

Some migrant artifacts end up in works of art: a religious shrine decorated with a worn-out sneaker and a tattered bible; a bundle of used tooth brushes wrapped in a dirty bandana; a quilt made from sweat stained clothes. While we are sympathetic to the causes that these artists are attempting to raise awareness about—what Young (2005:139) calls appropriation with "social value"—we are also concerned about their use of objects as "stand-ins" for generic suffering and the lack of nuance in the "storytelling" these activities claim to be involved in. For example, the majority of exhibits revolving around migrant artifacts are not only overly sentimental, but also tend to present monolithic narratives about or caricatures of (e.g., Heyd 2003:38) poverty and suffering through isolated objects. More troubling is the glaring absence of the voices of migrants in these installations or the fact that artists themselves claim to be speaking about forms of suffering they are far removed from. This absence of voice becomes especially ironic when media stories focused on these various art projects have headlines such as "Giving Illegal Immigrants a Voice" (Everett-Haynes 2005) and "Artists' Work puts Human Faces on the Complexities of the Border" (Zapor 2013). Neither of these two articles (like most of the artwork they describe) contains interviews with or images of actual migrants. To complicate matters, the bulk of artists in this "migrant" genre are relatively well-to-do white liberals who have taken it upon themselves to be the voice for this disenfranchised group. Because of their precarious sociojuridical status, undocumented people currently lack the power to critique these artistic endeavors. We are left wondering how much traction these art projects would get in the media if the voices of the artists were muted and the complicated narratives of migrants were pushed to the forefront.

As untold migrant artifacts decay beneath the blistering desert sun or disappear to landfills, we worry that the objects in personal collections and art exhibits may come to stand as *the* lasting material heritage of migration in the early 21st century. These few "special" migrant objects have been purposefully and uncritically selected by people who themselves have never experienced the need to migrate without authorization or the terror of the desert. Relatively well-to-do American citizens are deciding what objects should come to stand for the experience of Latino border crossers. In her critique of Holocaust exhibits, Carol Jones (2001) argues that items such as the shoes of concentration camp victims often function as "object survivors" or materials that are burdened to act as both historical proof of an event rendered virtually immaterial and to elicit sympathy in the place of destroyed and absent bodies. Jones' major complaint is that these relics are transformed into aestheticized, traveling tropes that fail to capture the unimaginable and indescribable horrors of the Shoah (Jones 2001:216–217). It is impossible to compare migrant suffering to the atrocities of the Holocaust, but we do see parallels in the ways in which migrant artifacts have been appropriated by artists, activists, and others as a form of generic evidence of what happens in the desert, potentially overshadowing many alternative or more complex narratives irreducible to a few evocative objects.

Partly in reaction to these endeavors, the UMP joined with the Institute for Humanities at the University of Michigan to develop an exhibition in 2013 called "State of Exception" with curator/artist Amanda Krugliak and photographer Richard Barnes. The exhibit included a mix of still photography, video, and artifacts from the Sonoran Desert. The largest element of the installation was a wall covered in hundreds of migrant backpacks (Figure 6.3) that had no explanation or associated text. The goal of the exhibition was to both highlight the work of the UMP and provide a purposefully fragmented and ambiguous narrative about border crossings and the emotionally and ethically complicated nature of our data collection process. In addition, we wanted to point out that migrant objects can be arranged in ways that may appear powerful and overwhelming, while simultaneously remaining opaque and confusing (like the migration process itself). As Krugliak writes in the exhibition brochure: "Stories and objects serve as traces of human experiences. Both have the capacity to be revelatory while at the same time alluding to that which we can never grasp fully as only observers after the fact" (Institute for the Humanities 2013).

In the State of Exception exhibit we wanted to provide a more ambiguous presentation of migrant materials (similar to how we as researchers engage with these disembodied objects in the field and in the lab) and highlight that the stories they "tell" may have more to do with the viewer and less about the border crossing experience, a point that Krugliak also made in the exhibition brochure:

FIGURE 6.3 State of Exception exhibit

> Is a backpack from the desert as affecting as a suitcase from the Holocaust, this exodus as poetic as another? Do the sagging straps and weighty backpacks represent human strife or R.E.I. [Recreational Equipment Incorporated]? Are the barely there remnants of ID cards, bus tickets, and photographs profound or mundane? The overwhelming desire to be sure, to believe in something or someone, has little to do with the Holy Grail, let alone the finding of it.
>
> *(Institute for the Humanities 2013)*

The exhibit attempted to challenge the value of "cherry picked" items by juxtaposing "precious" objects (e.g., a bible and baby bottle) with less evocative materials from the same contexts (e.g., soda cans and plastic snack food wrappers) and also presenting these items with no overarching narrative or explanation. We generally received positive feedback regarding this endeavor. Many, in fact, remarked about the emotional nature of the exhibit despite our purposeful exclusion of migrant photos or narratives in our attempts to see how solitary objects would function in an artistic space. Comments in the exhibition guest book reiterated the idea that for some these artifacts were still able to elicit an emotional response:

> "Makes you feel the pain & realize on a gut level that the undocumented migrants are human beings."
>   "Thank you for giving the forgotten a voice."

Even though some felt emotionally moved by objects, people still wanted more contextual information:

"These objects are powerful and the stories they tell are really though provoking . . . Some more labels would be useful for visitors!"

"I hope to see this exhibition traveling. I like the claustrophobic effect of mounting the backpacks on the wall in such a small space. A bit more contextual info within the space would be great."

In the end, our attempts to provide a counter to the typical ways that migrant objects are presented in other contexts met with some resistance. De León received several critiques of the exhibit that lamented its "lack of a migrant voice", despite the fact that one of the goals was to present these objects as ambiguous objects that couldn't necessarily tell a nuanced migration story. If evocative and mundane migrant artifacts together defy a singular narrative in the present, they will likely be open to reinterpretation as the material heritage of border crossing for generations to come as the politics of the US/Mexico border evolve. Our point has always been that the artifacts recovered in the desert are not adequate stand-ins for actual border crossing stories or human suffering and we should question all attempts to make them "object survivors". Millions of people are still alive today who have crossed the desert and we should be privileging their narratives, not simply relying on objects or their artistic interpretations to speak for the undocumented.

Beyond the work of collectors and artists, the appropriation of migrant artifacts also takes the more politically ambiguous form of commodification. A casual search on eBay (Figure 6.4) shows that some items are selected for their high resale value, especially "drug runner" artifacts. We wonder about the ethics associated with selling artifacts (either in their intact form or as reformulated art pieces) that are intimately associated with someone else's suffering. If we consider this material to be a form of heritage, what does it mean when they end up stockpiled in an artist's garage or put up on the auction block? Who owns these items? Who should be allowed to profit from their sales? Some have suggested that these items could be sold to raise awareness about the issue of clandestine border crossings and perhaps also generate funds that could be funneled back to organizations that assist migrants. We have often found that identity politics and internal organizational struggles about best practices can undermine humanitarian attempts to help border crossers and we worry about where funds would go and how they would be used. For example, De León stopped collecting clothing donations at his university for one migrant shelter in Mexico after he learned that the items were being sold for profit and not being passed on to those in need. Although we are committed to using archaeology to raising awareness about the suffering and violence that migrants experience, attaching monetary value to things that we see as artifacts seems problematic. Given that the materiality of border crossing is only now entering public discourse, the commodification of objects that people leave behind in moments of great duress undermines the capacity of these materials to stand as a cultural and historical heritage open to interpretation now and in the future.

Lastly, we would note that migrant artifacts have sometimes become a tool of anti-immigration activists looking to confirm negative stereotypes of undocumented Latinos crossing into and working in the United States. In an article exploring how

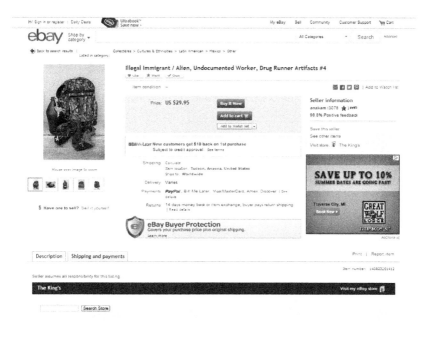

FIGURE 6.4 Migrant material culture sold on eBay

the role of these materials in the cultural construction of the US/Mexico border, Juanita Sundberg (2008:877–878) recounts how activists in southern Arizona in 2003 deposited nearly two dozen bags of water bottles, shoes, clothes, and other objects collected in the desert at the doorstep of their US congressperson—a protest against an "invasion" by Latino migrants seen to be "trashing" the environment and, by extension, US society. Other anti-immigration activists have called attention to trees hung with female undergarments, calling them "rape trees", a move meant to show the vulnerability of women and the base nature of smugglers and Latino men (Wilson 2013:66–95). The appropriation of migrant artifacts as "trash" or "rape trophies" into discourse about Latino border crossers gives these objects a negative valence in contemporary border politics. Or perhaps worse, it implies that they are no heritage at all, and must be removed just like the people who once carried them.

Removal

As the concern for geopolitical boundary enforcement has ratcheted up internationally in the last two decades, so too has the use of deportation. The forcible removal of "aliens" has become a routinized disciplinary strategy that is now key to the maintenance of state sovereignty around the world (De Genova and Peutz 2010:6). This extreme sociojuridical procedure simultaneously functions as a form of discipline (both in practice and as a looming threat) and as relinquishment of accountability by the state (Peutz 2006:220). Similarly, appropriations of migrant artifacts involve their selective removal from sites in the Sonoran Desert—a process which mirrors deportation and at the same time systematically dismantles the contemporary archaeological record. This move implicitly rejects the heritage value of the materiality of border crossing and conveniently erases a controversial chapter in modern American history.

The view that migrant artifacts and sites trash the fragile ecosystem of the Sonoran Desert can be found across the political spectrum from American border militias and anti-immigrant activists on the far right to humanitarian groups and environmentalists on the far left. By devaluing these objects, if not the people who carry them (Sundberg 2008; Squire 2014), this perspective gives rise to conservation efforts to remove all material traces of undocumented migration to landfills. The link between ideology and action is most clearly expressed on the Arizona Border Trash website (Arizona Department of Environmental Quality 2015) set up to encourage and document public clean-ups of migrant sites. On this site, conservation minded people learn how to organize a clean-up and are given tips on educating participants about the dangers possibly encountered at migrant sites, including wild animals, diseases, soiled clothing, hypodermic needles, dust, weapons, drugs, and last, but not least, dead border crossers. This instructional manual works to not-so-subtly reaffirm the racial stereotype that Latinos and their artifacts are "dirty" and "dangerous" (Hill 2006), while at the same time implicitly stressing the need to remove this "hazardous" material from the desert. The website also provides a form where groups can record the location and quantity of "trash" removed in their clean-up efforts; these data can then be publicly viewed on a spreadsheet or an interactive map (Figure 6.4). In this way the Arizona Border Trash website showcases the seemingly vast scale at which migrants are impacting the supposedly pristine desert, while at the same time inciting people to take action through conservation efforts.

With the exception of soiled clothing and the dead bodies and animal-ravaged skeletons of border crossers (see discussion of migrant death in De León 2015), the UMP never encountered any of the "dangerous" materials referenced on the Arizona Border Trash website, suggesting that fears about the "dirty" migrants creating hazards to health are misplaced. These negative characterizations, however, mirror the racist comments thrown at newly arrived immigrants in New York at the turn of the 20th century:

> They are too dirty, ragged, and carry too much vermin about them . . . their homes
> are in the dens and stews of the city, where the thieves, vagabonds, gamblers and

murderers dwell . . . They are familiar with every form of wickedness and crime. As they grow up they swell the ranks of the dangerous classes.

(Smith 1869:208, quoted in Reckner 2002)

Although we do not wish to downplay the potential environmental impact of inorganic materials discarded in the desert, we would note that the emphasis on cleaning up migrant sites has two implications for future heritage. First, the process of conservation works alongside many other natural transformation processes, which already break down artifacts and bodies very quickly (Beck et al. 2014), to "sanitize" the future history of undocumented migration in the early 21st century by eliminating large sites and artifacts that could potentially convey the scale of suffering experienced in the desert. Second, conservation focused on migrant sites implicitly turns our attention away from the environmental impact of other actors in the desert, especially the USBP (Meirotto 2012). The policies of PTD have over the past two decades led to the establishment of a "battlefield" including infrastructure, such as border walls (McGuire 2013), and the cutting of new roadways that damage the Sonoran Desert in ways far exceeding the relatively light material footprint of migrants. Environmental lobbies such as the Sierra Club are well aware of the ways that PTD strategies are harming the desert, but this can be lost on the general public who are often only exposed to popular news media (Banks 2009). Decades from now, when migrant sites have all but disappeared, the segments of border walls and virtual fence stations may endure to imply that undocumented migrants

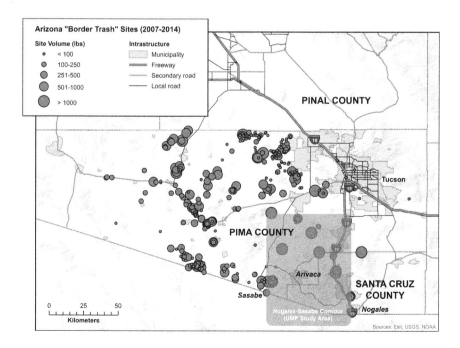

FIGURE 6.5 Map of clean-up efforts

were both a tremendous threat to national security and people whose traumatic personal experiences had no archaeological footprint.

Environmental activists are by no means alone in the removal of the material record of migration. The aforementioned practices of appropriation, of course, all involve the removal of artifacts from their archaeological context. For example, the results of collection by migrant sympathizers are twofold. First, the selection/collection of objects destroys provenience that is vital to archaeological interpretation. A blood-stained shirt discarded high in the vast wilderness of the Tumacacori Mountains conveys a much less hopeful story than one discarded at a migrant pick-up site close to a population center. Second, collection may also work to "de-humanize" archaeological assemblages (and hence the future telling of this history) insofar as they tend to remove more personal or intimate objects. These already account for a small proportion of artifacts in the borderlands, but can be crucial to interpreting the function of a site, or fully understanding the experiences of underrepresented classes of people, particularly women and children. When such objects disappear into someone's collection, they leave a partial story told only through water bottles and torn socks that, while important, makes it more difficult for the general public to access and identify with the experiences of people who have also left photos and other personal items in the desert.

Archaeological curation and heritage

The preceding discussion of the (UMP) participation in the State of Exception exhibit alluded to the ways that our own fieldwork removes migrant artifacts from the archaeological record, though with one goal being to manage and preserve them as a heritage resource. This involves safeguarding objects that can attest to both individual experiences and broader social processes of clandestine migration. Whether as single objects or in whole assemblages, all migrant artifacts have a story to tell when put in productive tension with the ethnographic accounts of the people who bought, used, and discarded them. In practice, however, the quantity and quality of these objects means that decisions about which objects can or should be curated have to be made. These curatorial choices are not beyond critique given that they draw on certain ideologies about the future value of contemporary material remains.

Over the course of four field seasons from 2009 to 2013, the UMP deployed an evolving sampling strategy to record 341 sites and more than 30,000 artifacts associated with clandestine migration and border enforcement in the Sonoran Desert (Gokee and De León 2014). Our decisions about the removal of artifacts for curation varied according to context. All artifacts from religious shrines and humanitarian water drop sites were counted, described, and photographed, but otherwise left in place for ethical reasons—these sites are actively maintained by migrants and humanitarians. Other migrant-related sites were subject to a stratified sampling strategy. During the 2010 field season, we focused on the unbiased sampling of artifacts from 18 sites, including three large camp and pick-up sites, in order to generate a more-or-less complete view of the quantity and diversity of objects discarded by migrants at different points in their journey. The result was the removal of more than 9,000 artifacts for curation at the UMP laboratory at the University of Michigan (these objects were featured in the State of Exception exhibit). Responding in part to the limits of laboratory space, our sampling strategy during the 2012 and 2013 field seasons shifted to record the assemblages of more sites in less detail. We developed a survey protocol to estimate or make an inventory of artifacts by class at each site, then selected a small sample for curation. In some cases, objects were chosen for their unique appearance or biographical richness, not unlike the motivations of collection described previously. In other instances, objects were selected to address specific questions posed by faculty and student researchers with the UMP.

Often our specific research questions entailed the selection of particular artifact classes for analysis. For example, Gokee (2015) is currently looking at the ethnopharmacology and first aid strategies of migrants. We therefore attempted to recover all aid-related artifacts encountered at sites in 2012 and 2013. At the same time, ongoing questions about the experiences of women, children, and non-Mexican migrants led to a persistent emphasis on the recovery of artifacts such as gendered hygiene products, toys for children, and documents of known provenience, such as bus tickets through Guatemala. We sometimes also chose artifacts for curation based on their potential to inform on multiple aspects of the migration process. Notebooks with personalized writing and backpacks with visible use-wear capable of speaking to individual experience and ingenuity (De León 2013) were more likely to be picked up than similar artifacts lacking modification. The results of our curation have been an overall removal of many artifacts from the landscape including some "rare" items.

Our curation of migrant artifacts is motivated by a belief that these objects, and their assemblage into sites in the Sonoran Desert, are tangible future heritage collectively attesting to various aspects of undocumented migration under Prevention Through Deterrence in the early 21st century. We see parallels between these artifacts and those representative of the experience of immigrants in mid and later 19th century America (e.g., Brighton 2009). However, "historical" archaeologists studying migration often have the benefit of chronological distance between the heated political and racial debates that surrounded the people they study. More than 150 years after the Irish Potato Famine, few Americans question the value of preserving the history and material culture associated with the mass exodus to the New World that this phenomenon caused despite the fact this population was discriminated against for decades before being assimilated into white American society. It is only with time and its associated historical amnesia that archaeologists have been able to lend credibility to the study of this once hated ethnic group. Because our work with Latino migrants is happening in real time, we must contend with the modern political debates that directly impact our archaeological work both intellectually and physically.

Conclusion

In this chapter we have argued that the often uncritical removals, appropriations, and destruction of migrant material culture are political projects whose long-term impacts we have yet to fully grasp. Although the forms of removal that impact the archaeological record of undocumented migration are not part of the standard *deportation regime*

(De Genova and Peutz 2010) practiced by the US federal government, many of them are implicated in the larger processes of US boundary enforcement, the political and social marginalization of undocumented people by the state, and revisionist history making that seeks to draw stark divisions between the "Europeans who immigrated in the late 19th and early 20th centuries . . . to give their children better lives" and the desperate people crossing the US/Mexico border at this very moment.

We have sought to outline some productive ways to think about contemporary forms of removal and erasure using some dusty archaeological concepts. The hope has been to find some common language to talk about these contentions and ideologically-driven site formation processes that irreversibly damage future archaeological patrimony. Lynn Meskell points out that "'heritage' occupies a positive and culturally elevated position within many cultures, yet we should recognize that not all individuals, groups or nations share those views, or have the luxury of affluence to indulge these desires" (2002:558). Perhaps rather than just telling different stories about the immediate past and present, archaeology of the contemporary can also help us better understand the privilege and power that underlies notions of heritage so that we can be more critical of "what those creating realms of memory intend for the future" (Holtorf 2000–2008:6.6).

References

Arizona Department of Environmental Quality
2015   Arizona Border Trash. Accessed March 14, 2015 from https://www.azbordertrash.gov/
Beck, Jess, Ian Ostereicher, Greg Sollish, and Jason De León
2014   Scavenging Behavior in the Sonora Desert and Implications for Documenting Border Crosser Fatalities. *Journal of Forensic Sciences*. Volume 60: Supplement S1: S11–S20.
Banks, Leo
2009   "Trashing Arizona: Illegal Immigrants Dump Tons of Waste in the Wilderness Every Day—and it's Devastating the Environment." *Tucson Weekly*. Accessed March 20, 2015 from www.tucsonweekly.com/tucson/trashing-arizona/Content?oid=1168857
Brighton, Stephen A.
2009   Historical Archaeology of the Irish Diaspora: A Transnational Approach. Knoxville: University of Tennessee Press.
Cornelius, Wayne A. and Idean Salehyan
2007   "Does Border Enforcement Deter Unauthorized Immigration? The Case of Mexican Migration to the U.S. of America." *Regulation & Governance* 1(2):139–153.
De Genova, N. and Nathalie Peutz
2010   The Deportation Regime: Sovereignty, Space, and the Freedom of Movement. Durham: Duke University Press.
De León, Jason
2012   "Better To Be Hot Than Caught": Excavating the Conflicting Roles of Migrant Material Culture. *American Anthropologist* 114(3):477–495.
2013   Undocumented Migration, Use-Wear, and the Materiality of Habitual Suffering in the Sonoran Desert. *Journal of Material Culture* 18(4):1–32.
2015   *The Land of Open Graves: Living and Dying on the Migrant Trail*. Berkeley: University of California Press.
De León, Jason, Cameron Gokee, and Ashley Schubert
2015   "By the Time I Get to Arizona": Citizenship, Materiality, and Contested Identities along the US–Mexico Border. *Anthropological Quarterly* 88(2): 487–520.

De León, Jason, Cameron Gokee, and Anna Forringer-Beal
2015   Use Wear, Disruption, and the Materiality of Undocumented Migration in the Southern Arizona Desert. In: Tsuda, T., Baker, B. (eds.) *Migrations and Disruptions: Unifying Themes in Studies of Ancient and Contemporary Migrations*. Gainsville, FL: University of Florida Press, 145–178.

Derechos Humanos
2018   Coalicion de Derechos Humanos. Accessed August 17, 2018 from www.derechoshumanosaz.net

Dunn, T. J.
2009   Blockading the Border and Human Rights: the El Paso Operation that Remade Immigration Enforcement. Austin: University of Texas Press.

Everett-Haynes, La Monica
2005   Giving Illegal Immigrants a Voice. *Tucson Citizen Times*. September 9. Accessed March 14, 2015 from tucsoncitizen.com/morgue2/2005/09/09/24684-giving-illegal-immigrants-a-voice/

Gokee, Cameron and Jason De León
2014   Sites of Contention: Archaeology and Political Discourse in the US–Mexico Borderlands. *Journal of Contemporary Archaeology* 1(1):133–163.

Gokee, Cameron
2015   Pain and Perseverance: An Archaeological Study of the First Aid and Ethnopharmacology of Undocumented Migration. Paper presented at the 48th annual meeting of the Society for Historical Archaeology, Seattle, WA.

González-Ruibal, Alfredo
2007   'Making Things Public': Archaeologies of the Spanish Civil War. *Public Archaeology* 6:203–26.
2008   'Time to Destroy': An Archaeology of Supermodernity. *Current Anthropology* 49(2):247–279.

Heyd, Thomas
2003   Rock Art Aesthetics and Cultural Appropriation. *The Journal of Aesthetics and Art Criticism* 61(1):37–46.

Hill, Sarah
2006   Purity and Danger on the U.S.–Mexico Border, 1990–1994. *South Atlantic Quarterly* 105(4):777–800.

Holtorf, Cornelius
2000–2008   *Monumental Past: The Life-histories of Megalithic Monuments in Mecklenburg-Vorpommem (Germany). Electronic monograph.* University of Toronto: Centre for Instructional Technology Development. Available via hdl.handle.net/1807/245.

Institute for the Humanities
2013   State of Exception: An Exhibition of the Undocumented Migration Project. Exhibit Brochure. University of Michigan.

Jones, Carol
2001   Empty shoes. In: Benstock S., Ferriss S. (eds.) *Footnotes on Shoes*. New Brunswick, NJ: Rutgers University Press, 197–232.

McGuire, Randall H.
2008   *Archaeology as Political Action*. Berkeley: University of California Press.
2013   Steel Walls and Picket Fences: Rematerializing the U.S. - Mexican Border in Ambos Nogales. *American Anthropologist* 115(3):466–481.

Meirotto, Lisa M. 2012
The Blame Game on the Border: Perceptions of Environmental Degradation on the United States–Mexico Border. *Human Organization* 71(1):11–21.

Meskell, Lynn
2002   Negative Heritage and Past Mastering in Archaeology. *Anthropological Quarterly* 75(3):557–574.

Mlyn, Leah, Cameron Gokee, and Jason De León
2014   "Cherry-Picking" the Material Record of Border Crossings: Examining Artifact Selection and Narrative Construction among Non-Migrants. Poster presented at the Society for Applied Anthropology, 74th Annual Meeting (Albuquerque, NM.).

Nevins, Joseph
2002   Operation Gatekeeper: The Rise of the "Illegal Alien" and the Making of the U.S.– Mexico Boundary. New York: Routledge Press.

Peutz, Nathalie
2006   Embarking on an Anthropology of Removal. *Current Anthropology*, 47(2):217–241.

Reckner, Paul
2002   Remembering Gotham: Urban Legends, Public History, and Representations of Poverty, Crime, and Race in New York City. *International Journal of Historical Archaeology* 6(2):95–112.

Reed, Alfred C.
1913   Going Through Ellis Island. *Popular Science Monthly*. Volume 82:5–18.

Rosenblum, M.
2012   Border Security: Immigration Enforcement between Ports of Entry. *Congressional Research Service Report for Congress*.

Squire, Vicki
2014   Desert 'trash': Posthumanism, border struggles, and humanitarian politics. *Political Geography* 38(1):11–21.

Sundberg, Juanita
2008   'Trash-talk' and the Production of Quotidian Geopolitical Boundaries in the USA–Mexico Borderlands. *Social & Cultural Geography* 9(8):871–890.

Sundberg. Juanita and Bonnie Kaserman
2007   Cactus Carvings and Desert Defecations: Embodying Representations of Border Crossings in Protected Areas on the Mexico–US Border. *Environment and Planning D: Society & Space* 25:727–744.

United States Border Patrol
1994   Border Patrol Strategic Plan 1994 and Beyond.
2013   *Southwest Border Sectors: Total Illegal Alien Apprehensions by Fiscal Year* (October 1st through September 30th). Accessed December 22, 2014 from www.cbp.gov/ sites/default/files/documents/U.S.%20Border%20Patrol%20Fiscal%20Year%20 Apprehension%20Statistics%201960-2013.pdf.

Wilson, Jamie A.
2013   The NAFTA Spectacle: Envisioning Borders, Migrants and the U.S.–Mexico Neoliberal Relation in Visual Culture. PhD dissertation, University of Arizona.

Young, James O.
2005   Profound Offense and Cultural Appropriation. *The Journal of Aesthetics and Art Criticism* 63(2):135–146.

Zapor, Patricia
2013   Artists' Work Puts Human Faces on the Complexities of the Border. *Catholic News Service*. July 15. Accessed March 14, 2015 from www.catholicnews.com/data/stories/ cns/1303051.htm

Zimmerman, Larry J. and Jessica Welch
2011   Displaced and Barely Visible: Archaeology and the Material Culture of Homelessness. *Historical Archaeology* 45(1):67–85.

PART II

Memory, migrants and museums

7

CONCORD MIGRATIONS

Ivan Gaskell

Human movement and material things

Human movement concerns at once large numbers of people changing location, whether temporarily or for the long term, and individual transits, alone or aggregated, from one place to another. The movement of people, whether en masse or individually, usually leads to encounters with other people, because for at least 20,000 years few parts of the globe—Antarctica is the exception—have been uninhabited by humans. People who move meet others whose cultures are unfamiliar to them. What follows may be benign mutual incomprehension, or the growth of shared understandings that lead to exchanges of things and people. Alternatively, encounter can lead to conflict, even resulting in the apparent extinction of one people through destruction or cultural absorption.

Most societies craft elaborate material things, whether portable, as in the case of nomads, or immovable, in the form of fixed abodes of varying size and complexity. Few peoples leave no material traces. At the very least they leave fire hearths and middens. All these things, from palaces to dumps, play roles in defining the cultures of the societies that created and in many cases inherited them, whether intact and in continuous, if changing, use, or excavated following abandonment and burial. Insofar as an article of clothing or a building type is distinctive, it is a marker of cultural community permitting identification, and the acceptance or exclusion of those who conform or differ in their usages.

What might be the consequences for relations among social groups of this general observation regarding identification, acceptance and exclusion based on the making and use of material things of many kinds? These are temporal relationships—they take place over time—so are marked by instability, and are properly subjects of history. In this chapter, I shall examine some questions raised by these considerations in the context of a large complex society that has changed through human movement on an enormous scale in a very short period of time: the movement of peoples to North America from Europe and Africa between the sixteenth and nineteenth centuries.[1] I shall do this through the lens of just one settlement in northeast North America, the town of Concord, settled and incorporated by English colonists in 1635 in the Massachusetts Bay Colony, which had been chartered in 1629. This was a relatively late date in the history of human occupation of the grassy plain and low hills at the confluence of what came to be called the Sudbury and Assabet Rivers to form the Concord River. That this was so was only too well known to the Concord native and resident to whose concerns regarding human migration I shall appeal in particular, Henry David Thoreau.

Thoreau, Algonquian peoples, and their things

Thoreau was born in 1817 in Concord, where his father was a pencil manufacturer. He attended Harvard College, graduating in 1837. Thereafter he led a somewhat improvised life, at times teaching, land surveying, and improving processes in his father's pencil works. Encouraged by fellow Concord luminary, Ralph Waldo Emerson, thinking and writing were at the core of his activities. Natural history and the human condition were his major concerns, notably human relationships with the natural world. Although best known for his reflections derived from his sojourn in a one-room cabin he built near Walden Pond, just south of Concord, between 1845 and 1847, *Walden; or Life in the Woods* (1854), the heart of his writing is his journal, which he kept for some twenty-four years until his death from tuberculosis in 1862 at the age of forty-four.

As a white person, Thoreau was a descendant of recent arrivals in that patch of North America its settlers called New England. Although he may have shared at least some of the assumptions regarding the relative standing of various ethnic and cultural groups held by many of his contemporaries, somewhat unusually for a white man he was conscious of the equivocal position he and his fellow settlers occupied. This can be seen, for instance, in his idiosyncratic take on the myth of the Pilgrim Fathers found in his account of his walking tours of Cape Cod, the large peninsular to the south of Massachusetts Bay where the Pilgrims first landed in 1620. They subsequently founded Plymouth Plantation on the mainland opposite Cape Cod, and soon expanded their settlement. Writing of the acquisition of the lands north of the area at the top of the lower cape settled by the inhabitants of Plymouth in 1644 as Eastham, Thoreau expressed his skeptical attitude:

> When the committee from Plymouth had purchased the territory of Eastham of the Indians, "it was demanded, who laid claim to Billingsgate?" which was understood to be all that part of the Cape north of what they had purchased. "The answer was, there was not any who owned it. 'Then,' said the committee, 'that land is ours.' The Indians answered, that it was." This was a remarkable assertion and admission. The Pilgrims appear to have regarded themselves as Not Any's representatives. Perhaps this was the first instance

of that quiet way of "speaking for" a place not yet occupied, or at least not improved as much as it may be, which their descendants have practised, and are still practising so extensively. Not Any seems to have been the sole proprietor of all America before the Yankees. But history says that, when the Pilgrims had held the lands of Billingsgate many years, at length "appeared an Indian, who styled himself Lieutenant Anthony," who laid claim to them, and of him they bought them. Who knows but a Lieutenant Anthony may be knocking at the door of the White House some day? At any rate, I know that if you hold a thing unjustly, there will surely be the devil to pay at last.[2]

The circumstances of the founding of Concord were equally open to question. They were well known to Thoreau, and available to any of his fellow townsfolk in the version told by Boston politician, historian, and publisher, Lemuel Shattuck in his *History of the Town of Concord*, published in 1835.[3] Drawing on sources that include the records of the General Court (the legislative body of the colony), and the journal of the early governor of the colony, John Winthrop (1587/8–1649), Shattuck mentions the devastation of the Indian population by smallpox, the ostensible Indian name of the place, Musketaquid, the allegiance of its inhabitants to the widow of the Massachusett (or Massachuset) sachem, Nanepashemet, and the local sachem, Tahattawan, when the English arrived. "Both assented to the sale of Musketaquid," asserts Shattuck. The sale of some or possibly all of the land took place in 1637, it having been incorporated by act of the General Court in New-Town (Cambridge) in September 1635.[4] These circumstances gave rise to the notion that the new name, Concord, specified in the 1635 act, commemorated its peaceful purchase, though Shattuck doubts this explanation. He plausibly prefers the idea that it refers to the ideal of harmony among the English settlers.[5] Further, he notes how prosperous Musketaquid had been, its lands highly suitable for the agrarian cultivation practiced by the Indigenous inhabitants, as well as hunting and fishing. These advantages clearly made it desirable to the English settlers, too.

Archaeological evidence confirms the prosperity of Indigenous peoples in Musketaquid over a long period. Varied foodstuffs were apparently plentiful over a considerable period of time—from up to about 5,000 years ago onwards—as suggested by bivalve, bone, and turtle remains at sites such as that beside the Sudbury River known as Clamshell Bluff, a place familiar to Shattuck and to Thoreau.[6] Shattuck notes that the principal English negotiators who led the settlement were the religious leader, Peter Bulkely, and the merchant and army officer, Simon Willard. They induced new colonists to leave England for Concord, then the first English settlement beyond tidal waters, and, at the time of the purchase, still entirely surrounded by Indian lands. The major commercial attraction was the availability of beaver pelts, traded by the Indigenous inhabitants for metal, woolen, and linen items.[7]

Shattuck wrote of the continuing Indian presence, though it diminished steadily and, at times, precipitously as a result of English incursions. Ever-increasing numbers of mainly English colonists wanted land. They pressed westwards, creating new settlements. They brought diseases with them to which the Indigenous inhabitants had no resistance, causing devastation. The beaver population was over-hunted and declined wherever Indians trapped these animals and traded their pelts to the colonists. Religious conversion efforts led by the Puritan missionary, John Eliot and others acculturated—at least in part—those Algonquian communities that converted to Christianity and inhabited the towns of so-called "Praying Indians." Most destructive were the wars, notably that between various colonies with their Native allies and the Pequots between 1634 and 1638, and—most far-reaching of all—the mutually devastating conflict known as King Philip's War between 1675 and 1678.[8] The early predominant Algonquian Indian strategy of allying with the various groups of settlers on the New England littoral to support them in their inter-communal hostilities gave way to what turned out to be a climactic fight for survival. The wars led not only to the deaths of many of the Indigenous inhabitants of southern New England, but to the enslavement and deportation to the West Indian colonies of many of the survivors. It is important to state, though, that the Indian presence in Massachusetts, although diminished, was never expunged.

In Shattuck's day, the Indian presence as an independent cultural entity in southern New England, though not entirely absent, was growing increasingly hard to discern. The impact of the European colonists on Native lifeways had been all but overwhelming, at least on the surface. A continuing Indian presence in Massachusetts was limited in the eyes of most settlers to a few small communities. Those Indians who did not move northwards or westwards were to a greater or lesser extent acculturated. A report to the governor of Massachusetts in 1861 recorded that the population of Indians and Indian-descendants was 1,610 persons.[9] Most were members of ten recognized groups with lands, funds, or government support, though not all inhabited Indigenous enclaves. Some lived in or near coastal ports.[10] The settler authorities regarded them as wards of state. In 1869, the Massachusetts Enfranchisement Act extended citizenship to its Indian inhabitants. Although apparently a progressive move, this had a further acculturating consequence, for it led to the sale of most remaining communally owned Indian lands. In the words of the historians who have studied the act and its consequences: "Ironically, the offer of full citizenship carried the price of relinquishing Indian identity—Indian 'peculiarity.'"[11]

Indians in Massachusetts may have seemed to "vanish" in the decades following the 1869 act, but their resurgence in recent decades suggests otherwise. One measure of resurgence is the acquisition by Indigenous communities of federal government recognition as self-governing, sovereign tribal nations by an arduous administrative process. As of February 2015 there are 566 federally recognized tribal governments in the USA.[12] In Massachusetts, the Wampanoag Tribe of Gay Head (Aquinnah) gained federal recognition in 1987, and the Mashpee Wampanoag Tribe acquired federal recognition in 2007. In addition, four further Wampanoag bands and two Nipmuc bands have gained Massachusetts though not federal recognition. There are also organized but governmentally unrecognized groups claiming Massachuset(t) or Praying Indian identity.[13] Casino gambling has seen a huge change in the fortunes of federally recognized sovereign tribal nations in states where gaming is permitted. Although this is not the case in Massachusetts (though it is in the process of limited introduction), casino gambling in neighboring Connecticut has led to the spectacular economic resuscitation of the Mashantucket Pequot Tribal Nation and the Mohegan Indian Tribe thanks to their respective casinos, Foxwoods and Mohegan Sun.

Another measure of resurgence is language recovery, exemplified by the Wôpanâak Language Reclamation Project. Wôpanâak is the language of the Wampanoag peoples of southeastern New England that until recently was dormant. The revival of the spoken as well as written language since 1993 as a result of the work of Mashpee Wampanoag tribal member, Jesse Little Doe Baird, represents a determination not to acquiesce in the submergence of Indigenous cultural identity in that of the dominant society.[14]

Along with resurgence come challenges to white versions of the past. The Mashantucket Pequot have expended considerable resources on revising history through the Mashantucket Pequot Museum and Research Center, challenging white stereotypes and assumptions, especially with regard to Indian survival after the conflicts in the seventeenth century. The example of this institution for research and public education prompts the question of what should become of the plethora of material culture items, many of them archaeological, acquired by generations of settlers and their descendants, large numbers of which are to be found in settler institutions, which include the vast majority of American museums. Among them is the greater part of the collection of Indian artifacts acquired, mostly during his habitual walks in Concord, by Henry David Thoreau.

Thoreau was well aware that the inhabitants of Concord of European descent were newcomers.[15] Referring to land, we have seen him state his belief that "if you hold a thing unjustly, there will surely be the devil to pay at last." In 1835, Shattuck had brought the antiquity of human habitation to his readers' attention with a certain admiration: "Many hatchets, pipes, chisels, arrow-heads, and other rude specimens of their art, curiously wrought from stone, are still frequently discovered near these spots, an evidence of the existence and skill of the original inhabitants."[16] Thoreau, too, was consistently aware of how the land he walked had been inhabited by Indians for many generations. In 1842, echoing Shattuck, he wrote in his journal:

> When I walk in the fields of Concord and meditate on the destiny of this prosperous slip of the Saxon *family*—the unexhausted energies of this new country—I forget that which is now Concord was once Musketaquid and that the *American race* has had its destiny also. Everywhere in the fields—in the corn and grain land—the earth is strewn with the relics of a race which has vanished as completely as if trodden in with the earth.
>
> I find it good to remember the eternity behind me as well as the eternity before. Where ever I go I tread in the tracks of the Indian— I pick up the bolt which he has but just dropped at my feet. And if I consider destiny

I am on his trail. I scatter his hearth stones with my feet, and pick out of the embers of his fire the simple but enduring implements of the wigwam and the chase— In planting my corn in the same furrow which yielded its increase to his support so long—I displace some memorial of him.[17]

Writing of his bean field in *Walden; or Life in the Woods* (1854), he states, "in the course of the summer it appeared by the arrowheads which I turned up in hoeing, that an extinct nation had anciently dwelled here and planted corn and beans ere white men came to clear the land."[18] The writer Nathaniel Hawthorne noted that Thoreau had "a strange faculty of finding what the Indians have left behind them."[19]

Thoreau recorded his observations and reflections on Indian artifacts in his journal. For instance, in his entry for August 22, 1860, he described finding thirty-one pottery shards, some decorated, in a recently washed out section of Clamshell Bluff on the bank of the Sudbury River, plus, in another area of the site, "a delicate stone tool . . . of a soft slate stone," which he sketched.[20] The implement remained in his collection, and is now in the Peabody Museum of Archaeology and Ethnology at Harvard University. (How this, and other Indian items collected by Thoreau, entered the Peabody Museum is described below.) It is a single stone, delicately fashioned so as to consist in what appears to be a gently flaring handle and a wider flat flared blade. Thoreau suspected that it was used for opening clams, and it is currently described in the online collections database of the Peabody Museum as a "clam-shell opener."[21] Thoreau expressed a deep respect for the makers of such implements, and the many stone projectile points he found:

It is a matter of astonishment how the Indians ever made them with no iron or steel tools to work with— And I doubt whether one of our mechanics with all the aids of Yankee ingenuity could soon learn to copy one of the thousands under our feet.[22]

Although most of the Indian artifacts Thoreau gathered were chance surface finds, he knew the value of digging. He conducted no proto-archaeological investigations of the kind made famous by Thomas Jefferson, who reported on his excavation of an Indian burial mound on the south bank of the Rivanna River in his *Notes on the State of Virginia* (1785).[23] However, Thoreau did occasionally dig. His early though not always reliable biographer, Franklin B. Sanborn, reports him finding an Indian hearth site during one of his many expeditions with his students when, between 1838 and 1842, he ran a school in Concord with his brother, John. Drawing on an account told to him many years later by one of the students, Henry Warren, Sanborn relates that the school party had observed a place on the bank of the Concord River from their boat where Thoreau thought Indigenous peoples might have lived. They returned the following week with a spade.

Then, moving inland a little further, and looking carefully about, he [Thoreau] struck his spade several times, without result. Presently, when the boys began to think their young teacher and guide was mistaken, his spade struck a stone. Moving forward a foot or two, he set his spade in again, struck another stone, and began to dig in a circle. He soon uncovered the red, fire-marked stones of the long-disused Indian fireplace; thus proving that he had been right in his conjecture. Having settled the point, he carefully covered up his find and replaced the turf, —not wishing to have the domestic altar of the aborigines profaned by mere curiosity.[24]

The last observation—perhaps stressed by Warren to Sanborn—reveals, if reliable, an attitude on Thoreau's part that is wholly in character. Thoreau was consistently reluctant to be intrusive, whether observing humans, their traces, or the natural world. He would seem to have placed a human value on the ancient Indian hearth, and taken care to see it honored.

Thoreau's curiosity about the long-term inhabitants of New England led him beyond their material remains. He took pains to gather information first-hand from such Indians as he met. One example occurred during a visit to his friend Daniel Ricketson in New Bedford, Massachusetts in June 1856.[25] The two men "heard of, and sought out, the hut of Martha Simons, the only pure-blooded Indian left about New Bedford," as he recorded in his journal.[26] Alluding to his cabin at Walden Pond, where he had lived between 1845 and 1847, he describes in searching detail their visit to her in her "little hut not so big as mine" near the shore. He describes her appearance, and her "peculiarly vacant expression" as she answered their questions "listlessly," though he attributes this not to stupidity, but to cultural habit. He writes a dispassionate account of an elderly woman who has lost her language. He reports that her grandfather, who had lived on the same spot, was the last who could speak the Native tongue, and that she had heard him praying, but could only understand "Jesus Christ." She had gone out to service at the age of seven, and now lived alone with only a "miserable tortoiseshell kitten." However, she identified the specimen of *Aletris* that Thoreau had collected as "husk-root . . . good to put into bitters for a weak stomach," thereby demonstrating her herbal knowledge. This is an unusual description of cross-cultural encounter—from the white point of view only, of course—between an Indigenous person and a third generation immigrant. While Martha Simons's grandfather had come from that very same spot on the south coast of Massachusetts, Thoreau's grandfather, Jean Thoreau, had emigrated to America from the Channel Island of Jersey as recently as 1773.[27] From an Indian perspective, Thoreau, like all whites, was a newcomer.

There are many other instances of Thoreau's questioning of Indians, for instance in the course of his visits to the northern Maine wilderness with Indian guides in 1846, 1853, and 1857, and during a visit to the Dakota peoples in Minnesota in 1861.[28] He compiled a series of twelve manuscript notebooks under the title *Extracts Relating to the Indians*, now in the Morgan Library & Museum, New York, perhaps with a book in mind that he did not live to write.[29] What Thoreau's mature beliefs about the character and future of Indigenous peoples in America might have been is a matter of controversy. However, it seems likely that he shared at least some of the emerging ethnological assumptions that Indians were for the most part unwilling or unable to adjust to the new circumstances that had been introduced by settlers, and were fated to disappear, as he believed they all but had in New England (". . . a race which has vanished as completely as if trodden in with the earth").[30] Yet he clearly valued the Indian artifacts he collected, and the skills they represented.

In the year in which Thoreau died, 1862, the Boston Society for Natural History, of which he had been a member, began building its new museum.[31] Thoreau bequeathed his natural history and Indian artifact collections to the society. Just four years later, in 1866, the London based banker George Peabody donated funds to Harvard College that led to the founding of the Peabody Museum of Archaeology and Ethnology.[32] Jeffries Wyman, Hersey Professor of Anatomy at Harvard since 1847, and president of the Boston Society for Natural History since 1854, chose to become its first curator rather than assume the directorship of the newly built New England Museum of Natural History, founded by the Boston Society of Natural History.[33] The society thereupon divested itself of its archaeological collections, sending them with Wyman to the new Peabody Museum. Among them was Thoreau's collection of Indian artifacts, which entered the museum on its completion in 1869. Its receipt was announced in the third annual report of the museum, where it is described as comprising about nine hundred objects: "over one hundred specimens of axes, pestles, gouges, mortars, chisels, spear points, ornaments, etc, and a larger number of arrow points of very varied patterns and materials."[34] In his description of the galleries published in 1898, the curator, Frederic Ward Putnam, notes that in the north room of the third floor: "The wall cases on each side of the fire-place contain several lots of stone implements from Massachusetts; among them are those picked up by Thoreau in his rambles along the Concord river."[35]

What has been the fate of Thoreau's collection of Indian stone implements? In the twentieth century and beyond, items from the collection have found only occasional use within the museum, whether for research or display. This is largely because, from an archaeological point of view, they are orphans. Thoreau gathered them casually, coming across them by chance during his regular hikes around the Concord countryside, so not many can be definitely associated with a particular site. Only in a few instances can a mention of a find in the journal be associated with a particular item in the collection. The so-called "clam-shell opener," found by Thoreau at Clamshell Bluff on the Sudbury River, described in his journal entry for August 22, 1860, discussed above, is a rare example of the identification of an implement with a site. The collection has not been comprehensively studied to establish the character of each piece beyond basic classification. Their principal scholarly interest is therefore their association with Thoreau. Indeed, his name is inscribed on several items, though presumably Thoreau himself did not do this. For instance, the collection includes an atlatl weight, or bannerstone, made of drilled stone, used as part of a spear-thrower.[36] Some bannerstones, up to six thousand years old, are among the most sophisticatedly fashioned stone implements from ancient North America. Several are displayed in the Metropolitan Museum of Art, New York for their striking aesthetic qualities reminiscent of twentieth century modernist sculpture.[37] The example that once belonged to Thoreau is not so immediately evocative of modernist forms as the New York bannerstones, but its grey stone is streaked with darker parallel bands perpendicular to the drilled hole, so its maker presumably chose it for its visual qualities, and aligned the hole deliberately to accentuate them. Yet Thoreau's name inscribed on this bannerstone in black literally overlays any other significance it may hold.

Items from Thoreau's collection of Indian stone implements have only rarely been exhibited in recent years. A stone pestle with a carved bird's head was included in an exhibition at Harvard about the categorization of material things in museums and elsewhere, *Tangible Things*, in 2011.[38] It was among the very varied items gathered to exemplify the category "archaeology and anthropology," and is discussed briefly and illustrated in the subsequent publication.[39] Three stone projectile points from Thoreau's collection fashioned from rhyolite, a volcanic stone prized by Native Americans, are included in the Peabody Museum exhibition, *The Legacy of Penobscot Canoes: A View from the River* (2014–16), which examines the intercultural significance of birchbark canoes from Maine.[40] Thoreau describes the Penobscot and their canoes in *The Maine Woods* (1864).

In 1990, the US Congress passed the Native American Graves Protection and Repatriation Act. This strong legislation mandates the repatriation on demand from institutions in receipt of federal funds to federally recognized tribal nations of human remains and certain kinds of cultural materials. The items in Thoreau's Indian collection would seem not to be subject to repatriation under its terms. As far as can be ascertained, they are not grave goods, nor would they be used in the practice of Native religion, nor are they objects of cultural patrimony within the meaning of the act. Further, it is doubtful whether a viable federally recognized direct successor community could be identified after a lapse of up to eight thousand years for things found in Musketaquid-Concord. This does not mean that their guardians can treat them casually, though they are not likely to as the scholars at the Peabody Museum have a track record of respect for Indian sensibilities. For instance, the Harvard Yard Archaeology Project, five seasons of excavation in search of traces of Harvard's Indian College in 2005, 2007, 2009, 2011, and 2014, saw the site opened and closed with blessings and invocations by local Indian leaders in recognition of Native moral claims to the land, as well as acknowledgement that the object of research was Harvard College's attempt to educate young Indian men between the opening of the Indian College in 1655 and 1670, when the building was adapted to house the first printing press in the colony.[41] Anthropological scholarship in museums has changed greatly since the entry of Thoreau's Indian collection into the Peabody Museum. This occurred at a time when, as Steven Conn has shown, white American immigrants and their descendants were writing Indians out of history and relocating them within an emerging anthropological schema in which they were described in terms of unchanging ethnicities tied to the natural world.[42] Even Thoreau was not free from the taint of such ethnological racism.

Thoreau, Americans of African ancestry, and their things

If Thoreau was keenly aware not only that "an extinct nation had anciently dwelled here," and that that nation was not entirely extinct, as mentioned above, he was also keenly aware of his own status, and that of all other white people in New England, as relative newcomers. But, as Thoreau acknowledged, not all newcomers were white.

Prior to the Revolutionary War, Massachusetts had been a slave colony. Unlike in the Caribbean and southern plantations, most enslaved people from Africa or of African descent in Massachusetts lived and worked individually in farming or artisanal households.[43] The numerous black slaves kept at his estate in Medford, Massachusetts by Isaac Royall, the wealthiest man in the colony before independence, were an exception, being in this respect a cultural extension of his family's plantation in Antigua.[44] Elise Lemire has given a detailed account of slavery and its aftermath in Concord in her book *Black Walden*.[45] She shows that the end of slavery in Massachusetts was confused and uncertain. It turned on several factors: abandonment by owners (sometimes engineered by slaves themselves), military service in the Patriot cause by slaves, and the interpretation by the Massachusetts Superior Court of the 1780 Massachusetts Constitution. This document did not mention slavery explicitly, and asserted at the beginning of its first article: "All men are born free and equal." Lemire demonstrates how abandoned, self-manumitted and other formerly enslaved blacks and their descendants continued to live in Concord. If slavery in Massachusetts ended during the turbulent times of the Revolutionary War, the plight of those once enslaved did not. "Warning out," by which strangers who might become a charge on the public purse could be expelled from towns to which they tried to move, ensured that many former slaves, unable to leave their own towns, continued to work in much the same way as they had previously. They either endured domestic or farm service little better than the formal slavery that the change of government had tacitly brought to an end, or they lived independently on marginal land that they acquired or on which they squatted with the permission of the owner.

Thoreau was one of many active abolitionists in Concord at a time of rising tension between free soil and slave states in the Union that would lead to the Civil War in 1861, the year before his death. He expressed his anti-slavery stance in published writings, notably *Resistance to Civil Government* (1849)—better known as *Civil Disobedience*—and *Slavery in Massachusetts* (1854). In *Walden*, Thoreau evokes the memory of former slaves: "For human society I was obliged to conjure up the former occupants of these woods."[46] His choice of words, with their associations of ghostly invocation, is quite deliberate. He describes one black woman, who lived independently by making baskets and spinning linen for over forty years in a small hut near to the site of Thoreau's own, in witch-like terms: "One old frequenter of these woods remembers, that as he passed her house one noon he heard her muttering to herself over her gurgling pot, —"Ye are all bones, bones!"[47] Thoreau identifies her as Zilpha, though her name was Zilpah, and, when she was obliged to take a second name, she chose White, probably because of the support she received from John White, Concord's deacon between 1784 and 1830.[48] Thoreau also evokes Brister Freeman and his "hospitable wife, Fenda, who told fortunes, yet pleasantly."[49] Freeman had been the slave of the wealthy John Cuming. Rather than continue in service tantamount to slavery after his military service in the Revolutionary War, Freeman broke away to live independently on a single acre of land near Walden Pond, having chosen his name deliberately when he reenlisted for military service in 1779.[50] Thoreau mentions his obscure grave marker on which he is described, in Thoreau's scathing words, as "'a man of color,' as if he were discolored."[51] A third former slave whom Thoreau mentions who lived nearby was Cato Ingraham, abandoned by his former master, Duncan Ingraham, when in 1795 Cato married Phyllis, the daughter of another former slave.[52]

Lemire surmises that these inhabitants may well have been following African precedents in clustering small dwellings together.[53] By Thoreau's time, few traces of their former existence were extant. He noted that "Cato's half-obliterated cellar hole still remains, though known to few, being concealed from the traveller by a fringe of pines."[54] Brister Freeman's property was marked only by the "apple trees which Brister planted and tended; large old trees now."[55] Thoreau neither explicitly suggests nor denies that by choosing to live in a small cabin on marginal land long associated with impoverished blacks that he was presenting himself as little better, as his fellow townsfolk might believe, than his black predecessors at the site. Yet by conjuring up these former occupants, Thoreau was implicitly identifying as their successor. In doing so he certainly laid himself open to such an accusation by his many suspicious or hostile contemporaries in Concord.

Concord, an almost wholly white and increasingly wealthy town, has largely ignored its African and African American past. I know of no archaeological excavations of sites associated with former slaves and their descendants. Recently, however, the Drinking Gourd Project, a charitable organization dedicated to raising awareness of Concord's African, African American, and anti-slavery history, was able to rescue a house that had been built in the early nineteenth century by another former slave, Caesar Robbins. It had originally stood on marginal land to the north of Concord, but had been moved to another site in the late nineteenth century. In 2009, it was threatened with demolition, but was saved thanks to pressure from the Drinking Gourd Project and others, with the financial support of the Town of Concord Community Preservation Fund. In 2011, the house was moved to a site near the Old North Bridge where it has been restored as the Robbins House Interpretive Center. It now draws the attention of the many visitors to this section of the Minute Man National Historical Park to African American history in Concord.[56] Although scarcely an archaeological undertaking, the rescue of the Caesar Robbins House demonstrates the value of another layer of long-ignored immigrant history in Concord: that of African slaves as involuntary immigrants and their descendants, whose existence—even as "human society" to be "conjured up"—Thoreau was one of the few to acknowledge. Thoreau was among those who drew attention to the African American presence in his town, a presence that, despite considerable local support for abolitionism, was even then being progressively expunged from communal memory and the received historical record.

Thoreau, Americans of Irish ancestry, and their things

If Thoreau was aware of himself and his fellow whites as immigrants and descendants of immigrants in relation to the Algonquian peoples they had for the most part displaced, and of the descendants of African slaves as another category of relative newcomer, he was also well aware of the most recent immigrant group with its own distinctive culture to have arrived in the Boston area from the 1840s onwards, Roman Catholic Irish. While many Irish women worked in domestic service, Irish men found employment in Concord as farm laborers, wood and ice cutters, ditch diggers, and, most notably, as railroad construction workers on the Fitchburg Railroad laid through Concord between 1842 and 1844. Fleeing oppression and starvation in Ireland, they arrived in considerable numbers, prompting hostility on the part of some existing inhabitants that found expression in stereotypes of the Irish as feckless, dirty, illiterate, and prone to excessive drinking. Although Thoreau clearly had sympathetic relationships with several Irish immigrants, Helen Lojek has argued convincingly that he "shared, apparently without thought, most of his society's prevailing anti-Irish sentiments," though more by acquiescing in and repeating accusations of thoughtlessness and squalid living than by active hostility.[57]

In April 1845, when the work on the Fitchburg Railroad had moved on from Concord, Thoreau bought for $4.25 what he describes as the "shanty" that the Irish railroad worker, James Collins, and his family were about to leave behind.[58] Thoreau used it as a source of boards for the cabin he was building on Emerson's wood lot beside Walden Pond. In his description of the hut as inhabited by the Collins family, Thoreau contrasts its "dirt floor for the most part dank, clammy, and aguish" with what he implies were unnecessary luxury possessions within: "a silk parasol, gilt-framed looking glass, and a patent new coffee-mill nailed to an oak sapling."[59] The Collins family took these things with them, so Thoreau's exercise in recycling building materials—or rescue archaeology—was confined to the fabric of the cabin itself. However, he reports being "informed treacherously by a young Patrick" that a neighbor and compatriot of Collins indulged in his own nefarious reclamation work, stealing usable nails from boards from the disassembled cabin while Thoreau was away carting others.[60]

At the end of his residence at Walden Pond, in 1847, Thoreau consigned his cabin to Emerson, who in turn sold it to his gardener, Hugh Whelan, an Irish immigrant. Whelan removed it to the nearby site of Thoreau's bean field, planning to add an extension.[61] In a letter to Emerson, then in England, Thoreau describes Whelan as unable to raise a crop in the sandy soil near the pond. He criticizes Whelan as "Irish-like" for having dug a new cellar for the extension too close to the original cabin, causing one end of it to collapse. Thoreau stated that he had contributed $16 for stone for the cellar.[62] Whelan left Concord, selling the cabin in 1849 when it was moved once again.[63]

Before turning to the rediscovery of the original site of Thoreau's cabin, we should note the circumstances of the publication of what would become Thoreau's best known work, his account of his sojourn in the cabin at Walden Pond, *Walden; or Life in the Woods* in 1854, and the appearance of the article that would subsequently constitute the first chapter of the book, *Cape Cod*, published posthumously in 1865, edited by Ellery Channing and Thoreau's sister, Sophia. Both have a bearing on Irish immigration when that huge movement of people contributed to a radical reshaping of the political landscape of Massachusetts and beyond.

Thoreau's article addressing an Irish tragedy was published with the title "Cape Cod" in *Putnam's Monthly* in June, 1855.[64] Its first section deals directly with the fate of Irish immigrants lost in a shipwreck during a storm just off the coast of Massachusetts on October 7, 1849. When, two days later, Thoreau and Channing visited Cohasset, the coastal town south of Boston near where the disaster had occurred, up to twenty-eight bodies had been recovered. Many anxious Irish relatives of the vessel's passengers were on the same train as Thoreau and Channing, who were bound for Cape Cod. The sea would continue to throw up bodies for weeks afterwards. Some ninety-nine lives were lost, many of passengers from County Galway and County Clare in the west of Ireland. The British brig, *St. John*, which had been bound for Boston from Galway, was a typical so-called "famine vessel," its passengers fleeing from hunger. Many were women, "who probably had intended to go out to service in some American family," as Thoreau surmised when describing one female corpse he saw.[65] His first-hand descriptions of the dead are vivid but all the more affecting for being dispassionate. Of the corpses in makeshift coffins laid on the ground near the beach, he wrote:

> Sometimes there were two or more children, or a parent and child, in the same box, and on the lid would perhaps be written with red chalk, "Bridget such-a-one, and sister's child." The surrounding sward was covered with bits of sails and clothing. I have since heard, from one who lives by this beach, that a woman who had come over before, but had left her infant behind for her sister to bring, came and looked into these boxes, and saw in one, — probably the same whose superscription I have quoted, —her child in her sister's arms, as if the sister had meant to be found thus; and within three days after, the mother died from the effect of that sight.[66]

Thoreau made two particular points: that the dead had

> emigrated to a newer world than ever Columbus dreamed of, yet one of whose existence we believe that there is far more universal and convincing evidence— though it has not yet been discovered by science—than Columbus had of this[67]

and, second, noting that local inhabitants did not scruple to gather the sea-weed cast up by the storm for manure, regardless of the tragedy: "This shipwreck had not produced a visible vibration in the fabric of society."[68]

Yet a great deal happened to engender a visible vibration in the fabric of American society—and notably in Massachusetts—between the loss of the *St. John* in 1849, and the publication of *Walden* in 1854 and "Cape Cod" in 1855. The huge influx of Irish Roman Catholic immigrants had contributed to the sudden growth of what is usually described as nativist sentiment among established settlers: an anti-immigrant wave of hostility on the part of large numbers of American born Protestants. Fraternal societies espousing nativism that were vehemently anti-Catholic as well as anti-slavery sprang up. They maintained strict secrecy, their members being instructed, if questioned, to respond, "I know nothing." These Know Nothings, as they swiftly came to be called, soon organized politically, and in 1854 had their greatest success in Massachusetts where they swept the elections for governor, the commonwealth legislature, and the US House of Representatives winning all eleven electoral districts.[69] It was in these political circumstances that Thoreau's comments on Irish immigrants appeared in print. Indeed, *Putnam's Monthly*, in which Thoreau published his account of the wreck of the *St. John*, took a decidedly anti-Know Nothing line concerning immigration. Associate editor, Parke Godwin published denunciations of Know Nothing hostility to immigrants in the January and May, 1855 issues, the second of which also appeared in his *Political Essays*, published the following year.[70] Nationally, the Know Nothings were to split along sectional lines, North and South, and be overtaken by events as immigration declined dramatically in the second half of the decade, while the issue of slavery came inexorably to the fore.[71]

During this period of rapid and vigorous political and social change even before the yet more tumultuous events of 1861–1865—and Thoreau's death in 1862—Thoreau's cabin at Walden Pond had become no more than a memory. Although local inhabitants led by Bronson Alcott recalled its approximate original location, once the cabin had gone its precise site during Thoreau's stay was lost for the better part of a hundred years. Inspired by the centennial of Thoreau's arrival to live at Walden Pond, a local amateur archaeologist, Roland Wells Robbins, researched the area in the summer and fall of 1945. He discovered the chimney foundation of Thoreau's cabin and other items, establishing its exact location, which is now marked by granite posts and an inscribed stone. Robbins published his findings in 1947 as *Discovery at Walden*, prompting considerable interest.[72] This short book helped to launch Robbins's long career as a historical archaeologist. His subsequent book, written with Evan Jones and first published in 1959, *Hidden America*, brought his pioneering excavation of historical sites in New England and New York to even greater public attention.[73] Historical archaeology, as it came to be known, was then a new practice. Historical archaeology was subsequently established in the US as an academic discipline, championed most conspicuously by James Deetz, author of the hugely influential book, *In Small Things Forgotten: The Archaeology of Early American Life* (1977).[74] In the face of this academic takeover, Robbins lost credibility, though somewhat unfairly. The current prevalence of public and contract archaeology has revived the status of non-academic archaeology, and Robbins's career has recently been positively reevaluated.[75] In this context, though, just as the material culture of the early inhabitants of Musketaquid-Concord underlies the collection of Indian stone artifacts in the Peabody Museum compiled by a third generation immigrant, so the material culture of Thoreau's grandfather's successors as immigrants, the Irish who arrived in Concord in the 1840s, underlies the site of Thoreau's cabin at Walden Pond. And very close to this now celebrated site are others, as yet ignored, that if excavated might furnish much information about another immigrant group, people brought against their will from West Africa, and their descendants.

Some ethical ramifications in Musketaquid-Concord

The United States is often described as a nation of immigrants, but this is only partly the case. The cultural values of the dominant immigrant group—whites of European origin—generally prevail, only selectively accommodating the cultural values of other immigrant groups. Thoreau had recognized this immigrant group—the "prosperous slip of the Saxon *family*"—as having a destiny associated with the "unexhausted energies of this new country," though he stressed that the "*American race*" that it had displaced had had its own destiny too.[76] From the perspective of that "*American race*," though, all those who have arrived from elsewhere since the sixteenth century, whether voluntarily or by compulsion, are recent arrivals. By assembling a large collection of ancient stone implements made by Indigenous peoples in an area recently settled by waves of newcomers—English, other Europeans (such as Thoreau's Channel Islander grandfather), Africans (involuntarily), and Irish (fleeing starvation and oppression)—Thoreau provides a benchmark by which to measure the incidence of human arrival in a part of the world often misperceived as "new."

Migration in the Musketaquid-Concord area and beyond on which Thoreau reflected clearly has ethical implications. As I have observed elsewhere, if to establish grounds for judgment is among the duties of the philosopher, among those of the historian is to ensure that none should be too comfortable in its exercise.[77] I shall look at some ethical ramifications of the cases of Indigenous peoples, Americans of African ancestry, and Americans of Irish ancestry in turn.

The treatment by settler societies over many generations of the Indigenous inhabitants of North America is clearly shameful, and the cause of continuing resentments that have led to occasional violent confrontations.[78] In 2007, the prime minister of Canada, Stephen Harper, formally apologized for the abuse of Indigenous peoples, specifically the abduction of tens of thousands of children for acculturation in residential schools. Justice Murray Sinclair, chair of the Truth and Reconciliation Commission of Canada (TRC) set up to investigate Indian residential schools, called this policy an act of cultural genocide.[79] The TRC issued its final report in December, 2015.[80] Many in Canada believe that more action should follow. The United States has been even more hesitant than Canada to express remorse for its shameful conduct towards Indians and other Indigenous peoples within its borders. In 1993, a joint resolution of the US Congress acknowledged US complicity in the overthrow of the Hawaiian monarchy one hundred years previously, and the unlawful US annexation of the Hawaiian Islands (Nā Mokupuni o Hawaiʻi) in 1898. Buried in the Department of Defense Appropriations Act, 2010, signed into law by President Barack Obama in December, 2009, is the first "apology to Native Peoples of the United States" for "years of official depredations, ill-conceived policies, and the breaking of covenants by the Federal Government regarding Indian tribes," and "for the many instances of violence, maltreatment, and neglect inflicted on Native Peoples by citizens of the United States." However, the text specifically states that this admission is not intended to support any legal claims against the government.[81]

If the ethical state of affairs regarding relations between Indigenous and settler peoples remain at best equivocal in both Canada and the United States, the same can be said of slavery in the United States. The Thirteenth Amendment to the Constitution abolishing slavery may have been ratified in 1865, but the consequences of slavery resonate to the present. The House of Representatives and the Senate passed different resolutions apologizing for slavery in the USA in 2008 and 2009 respectively, but they have not been reconciled and signed by the president. Advocates regularly and prominently make a strong case for reparations.[82] One wonders whether the majority of the people of the United States will ever fully face the ethical implications of their ancestors' actions, or their own individual and communal responsibilities regarding either Indigenous or African American fellow citizens.

The case of the Irish is somewhat different. Although members of the majority US population have discriminated against Roman Catholic Irish immigrants since at least the days of the Know Nothings, most Americans see the United States as a haven to which many oppressed and starving colonial subjects fled. It was not for any US president to apologize to the Irish, but for a British prime minister to do so. In 1997, prime minister Tony Blair expressed regret for Britain's role in the famine that killed over a million people between 1845 and 1852 in a letter to the organizers of an event commemorating its 150th anniversary, but stopped short of apologizing.[83] Commemoration of the famine has grown in US cities in recent years, at times not without controversy. An early example of a memorial is a large Celtic cross dedicated in 1914 to the victims of the *St. John* disaster in Cohasset Central Cemetery by the Ancient Order of Hibernians, a fraternal organization of Roman Catholics of Irish birth or descent. A more recent is the Irish Hunger Memorial, completed in lower Manhattan in 2002, designed by artist Brian Tolle and landscape architect Gail Wittwer-Laird.[84] Entertainments for popular consumption, though, continue to perpetuate the stereotype of Irish immigrant propensity to gang violence and political corruption from the mid-nineteenth century to the present, as can be seen in such American movies as *Gangs of New York* (2002), and *Black Mass* (2015).

All too often, the established members of the settler majority—which includes enculturated members of minorities—perpetuate distrust or outright hostility, whether subtly or crudely, towards Indigenous peoples or other immigrants and their descendants. The cultural values of the settler majority may predominate, but we can appeal to Thoreau's own practices, in particular as a collector and as a manipulator of material things, including his own cabin at Walden Pond, to evoke an alternative view of immigration in Musketaquid-Concord and beyond. If we are not to be too comfortable in the exercise of our ethical judgment with regard to migration we might take notice of the long-term view prompted by a consideration of Thoreau's observation that new immigrants from wherever they may have come, from the seventeenth century onwards, are just that: newcomers to a very old place.[85]

Notes

1   I acknowledge that people moved to North America from Asia and Oceania during this period, but such emigration is beyond the bounds of this study.
2   Henry David Thoreau, *Cape Cod* (New York: Penguin, 1987 [1865]), pp. 49–50.
3   Lemuel Shattuck, *A History of the Town of Concord, Middlesex County, Massachusetts: From its Earliest Settlement to 1832* (Boston: Russell, Ordione, & Co.; Concord: John Stacy, 1835).
4   Shattuck, *Concord*, pp. 4–6.
5   Shattuck, *Concord*, p. 5 n. 1.
6   Shattuck, *Concord*, p. 3; Shirley Blancke, et al., *Clamshell Bluff, Concord, Massachusetts* (*Bulletin of the Massachusetts Archaeological Society* 52, 2, 1995).
7   On early Indigenous uses of European metal objects, see Laurier Turgeon, "The Tale of a Kettle: Odyssey of an Intercultural Object," *Ethnohistory* 44, 1997, pp. 1–29.
8   See, in particular, Alfred A. Cave, *The Pequot War* (Amherst: University of Massachusetts Press, 1996) on the 1636–1637 conflict; and Jill Lepore, *The Name of War: King Philip's War and the Origins of American Identity* (New York: Vintage, 1998).
9   John Milton Earle, "Report to the Governor and Council Concerning the Indians of the Commonwealth under the Act of April 6, 1859" (Boston: William White, Printer to the Senate; Senate Document no. 96, Massachusetts State Library, Special Collections, State House, Boston, MA, 1861), p. lxxviii, cited in Ann Marie Plane and Gregory Button, "The Massachusetts Indian Enfranchisement Act: Ethnic Contest in Historical Context, 1849–1869," *Ethnohistory* 40, 1993, p. 589.
10 Plane and Button 1993, pp. 589–590.
11 Plane and Button 1993, p. 588.
12 National Conference of State Legislatures website: Federal and State Recognized Tribes: www.ncsl.org/research/state-tribal-institute/list-of-federal-and-state-recognized-tribes. aspx (accessed by the author February 9, 2016).
13 These include the Neponsett/Ponkapoag Tribe, and the Praying Indians of Natick and Ponkapoag, both of which maintain websites: www.neponsett.org/ (accessed by the author February 9, 2016); natickprayingindians.org/history.html (accessed by the author February 9, 2016) respectively.
14 See the Wôpanâak Language Reclamation Project website: www.wlrp.org/ (accessed by the author August 27, 2014).
15 Some of what follows on Thoreau's collection of Indian artifacts is derived from my "'Making a World': The impact of Idealism on Museum Formation in Mid-Nineteenth-Century Massachusetts," in *The Impact of Idealism: The Legacy of Post-Kantian German Thought*, gen. ed. Nicholas Boyle, and Liz Disley, vol. 3: *Aesthetics and Literature*, ed. Christoph Jamme and Ian Cooper (Cambridge: Cambridge University Press, 2013), pp. 245–263.
16 Shattuck 1835, p. 3.

17 Journal entry for March 19, 1842: Henry David Thoreau, *Journal*, gen. ed. John C. Broderick, *Volume 1: 1837–1844*, ed. Elizabeth Hall Witherell, William L. Howarth, Robert Sattelmayer, and Thomas Blanding (Princeton: Princeton University Press, 1981), pp. 380–381.

18 Henry David Thoreau, *Walden and Other Writings of Henry David Thoreau*, ed. Brooks Atkinson (New York: Modern Library, 1992), p. 147.

19 Nathaniel Hawthorne, "The Old Manse," *Mosses from an Old Manse*, vol. 1 (Boston: Houghton Mifflin, 1884), p. 19.

20 Journal entry for August 22, 1860: *The Journal of Henry David Thoreau*, ed. Bradford Torrey and Francis H. Allen (Salt Lake City: Gibbs M. Smith, Inc., Peregrine Smith Books, 1984; reprint of Boston: Houghton Mifflin, 1906), vol. 14, pp. 58–60, ill. p. 59.

21 Peabody Museum of Archaeology and Ethnology 69-34-10/2405: pmem.unix.fas. harvard.edu:8080/peabody/view/objects/asitem/search$0040/0?t:state:flow=84096 44f-1efd-4e60-b0d4-cff3bf485b47 (accessed by the author December 31, 2014).

22 Journal entry for October 30, 1842; part of a lengthy consideration of Indian lithic tools: Henry David Thoreau, *Journal*, gen. ed. John C. Broderick, *Volume 2: 1842–1848*, ed. Robert Sattelmayer (Princeton: Princeton University Press, 1984), pp. 58–59.

23 Thomas Jefferson, *Notes on the State of Virginia* (New York: Library of America, 1984 [1785]), pp. 223–226.

24 Franklin B. Sanborn, *The Life of Henry David Thoreau: Including Many Essays Hitherto Unpublished, and Some Account of his Family and Friends* (Boston: Houghton Mifflin, 1917), p. 206.

25 For an account of their friendship, see Earl J. Dias, "Daniel Ricketson and Henry Thoreau," *New England Quarterly* 26, 1953, pp. 388–396.

26 Journal entry for June 26, 1856: *Journal*, ed. Bradford Torrey and Francis H. Allen, vol. 8, pp. 390–392.

27 "Family Tree of Henry David Thoreau (1817–1862)," The Thoreau Society website: www. thoreausociety.org/life-legacy/family-tree (accessed by the author August 28, 2014).

28 See Henry David Thoreau, *The Writings of Henry David Thoreau, III The Maine Woods* (Boston and New York: Houghton, Mifflin & Co., 1906). See also Timothy Troy, "Ktaadn: Thoreau the Anthropologist," *Dialectical Anthropology* 15, 1, 1990, pp. 74–81, and Corinne Hosfeld Smith, *Westward I Go Free: Tracing Thoreau's Last Journey* (Winnipeg, Man. and Sheffield, VT: Green Frigate Books, 2012).

29 See Richard F. Fleck, *The Indians of Thoreau: Selections from the Indian Notebooks* (Albuquerque, NM: Hummingbird Press, 1974); Richard F. Fleck, *Selections from the "Indian Notebooks" (1847–1861) of Henry D. Thoreau* (online edition: Lincoln, Mass.: The Thoreau Institute at Walden Woods, 2007): www.walden.org/documents/file/Library/ Thoreau/writings/Notebooks/IndianNotebooks.pdf (accessed by the author August 28, 2014); Robert F. Sayre, *Thoreau and the American Indians* (Princeton: Princeton University Press, 1977).

30 See n. 14 above; see also Joshua David Bellin, "In the Company of Savagists: Thoreau's Indian Books and Antebellum Ethnology," *The Concord Saunterer*, N.S. 16, 2008, pp. 1–32. Bellin argues that Thoreau shared many of the emerging racist beliefs about the supposed intractability of Indians.

31 Richard I. Johnson, "The Rise and Fall of the Boston Society of Natural History," *Northeastern Naturalist* 11, 1, 2004, pp. 81–108.

32 Franklin Parker, *George Peabody: A Biography* (Nashville, TN: Vanderbilt University Press, 1995). See also Curtis M. Hinsley, "The Museum Origins of Harvard Anthropology, 1866–1915," in *Science at Harvard University: Historical Perspectives*, ed. Clarke A. Elliott and Margaret W. Rossiter (Bethlehem, PA: Lehigh University Press, 1992), pp. 121–145.

33 Toby A. Appel, "A Scientific Career in the Age of Character: Jeffries Wyman and Natural History at Harvard," in *Science at Harvard University: Historical Perspectives*, ed. Clarke A. Elliott and Margaret W. Rossiter (Bethlehem, PA: Lehigh University Press, 1992), pp. 96–120.

34 Jeffries Wyman, "Report of the Curator," in Third Annual Report of the Trustees of the Peabody Museum of American Archaeology and Ethnology, Presented to the President and Fellows of Harvard College, December 1, 1870 (Boston: A.A. Kingman, 1870), pp. 6–7.

35 Frederic Ward Putnam, *Guide to the Peabody Museum of Harvard University, with a Statement Relating to Instruction in Anthropology, Complementary to the American Association for the Advancement of Science, Fiftieth Anniversary* (Cambridge, MA: Peabody Museum, 1898), p. 16.

36 Peabody Museum of Archaeology and Ethnology 69-34-10/2412.

37 The Metropolitan Museum of Art, New York has five bannerstones in its collection, three of which are on view at the time of writing: 1979.206.1129, 2011.154.14, and 2011.154.15.

38 Peabody Museum of Archaeology and Ethnology 69-34-10/2382; included in *Tangible Things*, Collection of Historical Scientific Instruments and other Harvard venues, February–May, 2011, organized by Laurel Thatcher Ulrich and Ivan Gaskell, with Sara Schechner and Sarah Anne Carter.

39 Laurel Thatcher Ulrich, Ivan Gaskell, Sara J. Schechner, and Sarah Anne Carter, with photographs by Samantha van Gerbig, *Tangible Things: Making History through Objects* (Oxford and New York: Oxford University Press, 2015), pp. 25, 79 fig. 65.

40 Three projectile points for spear or arrow fashioned from rhyolite from Mount Kineo or from another of two outcrops of the same rock in Maine, Peabody Museum of Archaeology and Ethnology, 69-34-10/2424.39.3; 69-34-10/2424.39.6; 69-34-10/2424.40.3. Tools up to and over 10,000 years old made by Indians from this Maine rock have been found across New England and beyond, and in Canada.

41 See the Peabody Museum of Archaeology and Ethnology online exhibition *Digging Veritas: The Archaeology and History of the Indian College and Student Life at colonial Harvard*: www.peabody.harvard.edu/DV-online (accessed by the author September 12, 2014).

42 Steven Conn, *History's Shadow: Native Americans and Historical Consciousness in the Nineteenth Century* (Chicago: University of Chicago Press, 2004).

43 See, for example, Joyce Lee Malcolm, *Peter's War: A New England Slave Boy and the American Revolution* (New Haven: Yale University Press, 2009).

44 Alexandra A. Chan, *Slavery in the Age of Reason: Archaeology at a New England Farm* (Knoxville: University of Tennessee Press, 2007); C.S. Manegold, *Ten Hills Farm: The Forgotten History of Slavery in the North* (Princeton: Princeton University Press, 2010).

45 Elise Lemire, *Black Walden: Slavery and its Aftermath in Concord, Massachusetts* (Philadelphia: University of Pennsylvania Press, 2009).

46 Thoreau, *Walden and Other Writings*, p. 241.

47 Thoreau, *Walden and Other Writings*, p. 242. Lemire identifies the "old frequenter" as George Minot (Lemire, *Black Walden*, p. 135).

48 Lemire, *Black Walden*, p. 136.

49 Thoreau, *Walden and Other Writings*, p. 243.

50 Lemire, *Black Walden*, p. 108.

51 Thoreau, *Walden and Other Writings*, p. 243.

52 Lemire, *Black Walden*, pp. 110–111.

53 Lemire, *Black Walden*, pp. 141–142.

54 Thoreau, *Walden and Other Writings*, p. 242.

55 Thoreau, *Walden and Other Writings*, p. 242.

56 Faith Ferguson, "Who was Caesar Robbins and why is his house so special?" Drinking Gourd Project website: drinkinggourdproject.org/blog/who-was-caesar-robbins-and-why-is-his-house-so-special/ (accessed by the author December 31, 2014).

57 Helen Lojek, "Thoreau's Bog People," *New England Quarterly* 67, 1994, p. 280.

58 Thoreau, *Walden and Other Writings*, p. 40.

59 Thoreau, *Walden and Other Writings*, p. 41.

60 Thoreau, *Walden and Other Writings*, p. 42.

61 *The Correspondence of Henry David Thoreau, Volume 1: 1834–1848*, ed. Robert N. Hudspeth (Princeton: Princeton University Press, 2013), p. 320 n. 19.

62 Letter dated January 12, 1848: *Correspondence*, pp. 337–339.

63 The purchaser was James Clark, who moved it to the Carlisle Road: *Correspondence*, p. 335 n. 8.

64 [Henry David Thoreau], "Cape Cod," *Putnam's Monthly: A Magazine of American Literature, Science, and Art 5*, No. 30, June, 1855, pp. 632–640. No contributor was accorded a byline.

65 "Cape Cod," *Putnam's Monthly*, p. 633.

66 "Cape Cod," *Putnam's Monthly*, p. 633.

67 "Cape Cod," *Putnam's Monthly*, p. 635.

68 "Cape Cod," *Putnam's Monthly*, p. 634.

69 There is a considerable literature on the Know Nothings. For a succinct account, see James M. McPherson, *Battle Cry of Freedom: The Civil War Era* (Oxford: Oxford University Press, 1988), pp. 135–144. For the Massachusetts election, see Tyler Anbinder, *Nativism and Slavery: The Northern Know Nothings and the Politics of the 1850s* (Oxford and New York: Oxford University Press, 1992), pp. 87–94.

70 [Parke Godwin], "Secret Societies—the Know Nothings" *Putnam's Monthly: A Magazine of American Literature, Science, and Art* 5, No. 25, January, 1855, pp. 88–97; [Parke Godwin], "America for the Americans," *Putnam's Monthly: A Magazine of American Literature, Science, and Art* 5, No. 29, May, 1855, pp. 533–541; Parke Godwin, *Political Essays* (New York: Dix, Edwards, & Co., 1856), pp. 175–209.

71 The passage of the Kansas–Nebraska Act in 1854 marked the end of the compromise affecting those areas of westward expansion where slavery could or could not be introduced, while the presidential election of 1856 (won by the Democrat James Buchanan) saw the emergence of the new Republican Party, which was to triumph with the election of Abraham Lincoln to the presidency in 1860. This, in turn, precipitated the secession of eleven slave states, the foundation of the Confederate States of America, and the disastrous civil war that ensued. The 13th Amendment to the US Constitution, abolishing slavery, was ratified in December, 1865.

72 Roland Wells Robbins, *Discovery at Walden* (Stoneham, MA: Barnstead & Son, 1947; reprint edition, Lincoln, MA: The Thoreau Society, 1999).

73 Roland Wells Robbins and Evan Jones, *Hidden America* (New York: Knopf, 1959; second edition 1966). He retells the story of his discovery of the Thoreau cabin site, pp. 16–35.

74 James Deetz, *In Small Things Forgotten: The Archaeology of Early American Life* (Garden City, NY: Anchor Press/Doubleday, 1977; revised and expanded edition, 1996).

75 Donald W. Linebaugh, *The Man Who Found Thoreau: Roland W. Robbins and the Rise of Historical Archaeology in America* (Lebanon, NH: University Press of New England/University of New Hampshire Press, 2005).

76 See n. 14 above.

77 Ivan Gaskell, "Historical Distance, Historical Judgment," in *Rethinking Historical Distance*, ed. Mark Salber Phillips, Barbara Caine, and Julia Adeney Thomas (New York and London: Palgrave Macmillan, 2013), p. 34.

78 Among the most widely reported incidents are those at Wounded Knee on the Pine Ridge Indian Reservation (Wazí Aháŋhaŋ Oyáŋke) of the Oglala Lakota in South Dakota in 1973, and the St. Regis Mohawk or Akwesasne Reservation, New York and the Akwesasne Reserve, Ontario and Quebec (an Indian entity that spans the US–Canadian border across the St. Lawrence River) in 1990.

79 *Honouring the Truth, Reconciling for the Future: Summary of the Final Report of the Truth and Reconciliation Commission of Canada*, 2015, pp. 1–3.

80 See www.trc.ca/websites/trcinstitution/index.php?p=890 (accessed by the author, February 16, 2016).

81 John D. McKinnon, "U.S. Offers an Official Apology to Native Americans," *Wall Street Journal*, online edition, December 22, 2009: blogs.wsj.com/washwire/2009/12/22/us-offers-an-official-apology-to-native-americans/ (accessed by the author, February 16, 2016).

82 For example, Ta-Nehisi Coates, "The Case for Reparations," *The Atlantic*, June, 2014, online edition: www.theatlantic.com/magazine/archive/2014/06/the-case-for-reparations/361631/ (accessed by the author, February 16, 2016).

83 Sarah Lyall, "Past as Prologue: Blair Faults Britain in Irish Potato Blight," *New York Times*, June 3, 1997, online edition: www.nytimes.com/1997/06/03/world/past-as-prologue-blair-faults-britain-in-irish-potato-blight.html (accessed by the author, February 16, 2016).

84 Roberta Smith, "Critic's Notebook: A Memorial Remembers the Hungry," *New York Times*, July 16, 2002, online edition: www.nytimes.com/2002/07/16/arts/critic-s-notebook-a-memorial-remembers-the-hungry.html (accessed by the author, February 16, 2016).

85 I am grateful to the director, Jeffrey Quilter, and staff of the Peabody Museum of Archaeology and Ethnology, where I hold an appointment as research associate in North American ethnology, for the opportunity to study items from Thoreau's collection of Indian implements and their records. Writing this chapter has been facilitated by a permanent senior fellowship at the Lichtenberg Kolleg (Advanced Study Institute in the Humanities and Social Sciences) of the Georg-August University of Göttingen. I should like to thank the director, Martin van Gelderen, and his colleagues.

8

AFFILIATIVE RETERRITORIALIZATION

The Manco Capac monument and the Japanese community in Peru

Helaine Silverman

Introduction

Recent studies of urban migration have been enriched by cultural theory as scholars focus on the embodied and tangible placemaking of immigrants that engenders alternative landscapes of meaning in their new residential districts (e.g., Dearborn 2008a, b; Li 2012; Byrne 2017). Attention is directed at how foreign culture-bearers create new moorings in their diasporas – including internal diasporas – generating complex and contingent notions and performances of identity abroad, while still maintaining strong ties to homeland traditions. This perspective reflects the replacement of traditional place-based anthropology's sense of "rooted culture" with an understanding of the world as characterized by transnationalism, globalization, movement, displacement, deterritorialization, marginality, and border crossings (Gupta and Ferguson 1992). Thus, the standard link drawn between identity and place has become more nuanced in recognition that relations and interactions between people socially construct space and place (Lefebvre 1991; Gupta and Ferguson 1992). In this reality "remembered places have often served as symbolic anchors of community for dispersed people . . . memory of places [is used] to construct imaginatively their new lived world" (Gupta and Ferguson 1992:11).

A less commonly recognized phenomenon is what I will call "affiliative reterritorialization" whereby an immigrant group seeks to draw a relationship between itself and its host country and thus assert its participation and place in the nation from a diasporic position of anxiety. Affiliative reterritorialization is not assimilation but rather a strategic engagement with, embrace of and connection drawn to the host country's national identity and character such that the immigrant group can profess itself to be part of the nation while still maintaining its cultural identity. At this time (2015–2017) of heightened interest in and concern in Europe about immigration because of the Syrian refugees and their "cultural baggage" and a Republican candidate for the presidency of the United States (now President) who was similarly troubled by "the Other" – whether from America's southern border or the Middle East – it behooves us to generate a wide array of case studies on immigration and cultural identity for comparative examination.

Affiliative reterritorialization was eagerly sought one hundred years ago in Peru by one of its immigrant communities – the *colonia japonesa* or Japanese colony – which had to negotiate language, customs, economy, and physical and ideological space in its host nation. The liminal position of the Japanese colony in Peruvian society at the beginning of the twentieth century became an intense subject of discussion within the community when the opportunity for generating ideological roots presented itself around the centenary celebration of Peru's independence from Spain (1821–1921). The colony chose to present their new nation with the gift of a great monument portraying the mythic founder of the Inca Empire, Manco Capac (Figure 8.1). That monument implicated not just national identities (Japan, Peru) but also the urban heritage of Lima, Peru's capital city. Gupta and Ferguson have argued that "states play a crucial role in the popular politics of place making and in the creation of naturalized links between places and people" in the advancement of nationalism (1992:12). The Manco Capac monument illustrates the case of an immigrant group, rather than its national host, undertaking those activities.

The Manco Capac monument has played multiple, controversial roles in Peru since its creation. Indeed, applying Nelson and Olin (2003:6, 7), the social and political complications surrounding the monument began even before it was unveiled and reveal competing claims for legitimacy, power, meaning, and place in the nation. Theoretically, the migration issue in this chapter engages the inextricable relationship between cultural heritage, memory, and cultural identity (Graham and Howard 2008; Anheier and Isar 2011). My argument is informed by Perla Innocenti's (2014, 2015) apt construct of *migrating heritage* and Urry's (2007) and Sheller's (Sheller and Urry 2006) *mobilities* paradigm, for as we think of migration and heritage we confront the migration of cultural identities as well. Which identities are maintained, relinquished, reformulated, or heightened in a diaspora are situational arenas in which the dominant culture, political structure, law, and economic opportunities in the host country intervene.

The Japanese colony

Japan's population was about 34 million at the start of the Meiji Restoration. By 1899 it had swelled to 44 million. The modernization of Japan in this era generated tremendous unemployment as small-scale agriculturalists lost their land (Morimoto 1999:40–41). Poverty, unemployment and excess population led the Japanese government to promote a strategy of immigration.

In Japan, the pressure to immigrate coincided with a significant need for labor in Peru. A formal agreement was reached in 1898 between the two countries whereby an orderly, legal immigration was started (Morimoto 1999:47–50). The first shipload of Japanese immigrants arrived in 1899. From field labor on coastal *haciendas* (agrarian estates) with fixed-time contracts of six months to four years

(Morimoto 1999:70) some immigrants rose to become administrators of the *haciendas* and even to acquire their own land (Thorndike 1996:36). Those who left the land immediately following the expiration of their contract, or even prematurely, quickly established themselves in cities. In Lima, it was said that there was nothing more *limeño* (i.e., typical of social life in Lima) than to get a haircut in a Japanese barber shop, so ubiquitous were they (Ramón Joffré 2014:78).

Peru was not unfamiliar with Japan at the time of the mass Japanese immigration. Peru had signed a trade treaty with Japan two decades before, the *Tratado de Paz, Amistad, Comercio y Navegación* (1873 Treaty for Peace, Friendship, Commerce and Navigation). The treaty was replaced in 1885 by a broader one more concerned with economic issues (Morimoto 1999:33). Peru was also the

(A)

(B)

FIGURE 8.1 (A) The Manco Capac monument. (B) Close-up of Manco Capac statue. (Photos: Helaine Silverman)

first Latin American country to establish diplomatic relations with the Japanese imperial court (Ramón Joffré 2014:76). In this era of official Japanese–Peruvian relations some Japanese entered Peru not as contracted labor but as already successful businessmen. They made or already had connections with their established compatriots in the country (Thorndike 1996:34). Within years of their arrival in Peru the Japanese colony had an elite core of successful businessmen, bankers, industrialists, doctors, and other professionals.

By the end of 25 years of immigration, some 18,000 Japanese had arrived. This immigrant group almost uniformly married within (Morimoto 1999:68) and conserved various homeland traditions, for instance by creating Japanese schools and establishing their own newspapers (Gardiner 1975:72–77). Japanese societies proliferated wherever there were Japanese immigrants (Gardiner 1975:73–74). They also adopted some customs of their host country, language most obviously, and religion in some cases. And they hybridized some cultural aspects of Peru and Japan, notably in food since the Peruvian coastal diet was already rich in fish and rice. Some immigrants nationalized and all children born in Peru were Peruvian. Some were given Spanish first names, but the family name remained and children were raised with a strong sense of Japanese community identity.

Of all the foreign communities in Peru at that time the Japanese were the most recent and one of most numerous (Ramón Joffré 2014:78). As a readily identifiable group and a self-identifying group, the early Japanese colony found both welcome and animosity in Peru, occupying an ambiguous place in Peruvian society (see Gardiner 1975). On the *haciendas* where they worked there was often hostility to the immigrant farmers by the Peruvian laborers. And notwithstanding the treaties between Japan and Peru – or because of them – many in Peru regarded the Japanese immigrants as emissaries of the growing Japanese empire (Ramón Joffré 2014:79). Under President Augusto Leguía (1908–1912, 1919–1930), however, they were befriended and respected at the highest level of government, although frequently reviled in the press and on the street. Gardiner's (1975) history of the Japanese in Peru details the pervasiveness of anti-Japanese sentiment in Peru, notwithstanding Leguía. Ambiguity and anxiety, but also ambition to create a space and place for themselves in a new country are the context for understanding the gift of the Japanese colony to the Peruvian nation on the occasion of its centenary celebration of independence from Spain.

The centennial gift

The success of the Japanese community (Gardiner 1975; Thorndike 1996; Morimoto 1999) was well established when Augusto Leguía assumed his second period of office in 1919. He already was well inclined toward the Japanese community, his respect for the immigrants being based, in part, on his admiration for their industriousness as well as Japan's modernization following the Sino-Japanese War of 1894–1895 (Tigner 1978:24). Leguía had served in several cabinet positions at the end of the nineteenth century in which, recognizing Peru's extreme need for labor for its agricultural economy, he facilitated Japanese immigration to Peru as labor for the coastal *haciendas* (Thorndike 1996:29, 38). Once in Peru the Japanese repaid his trust. They were extraordinarily hard-working and apolitical, seeking only to be upstanding members of their new country.

As the centennial approached, the Japanese community was keen to demonstrate its appreciation of their new homeland. For Leguía, the centennial celebration was going to be a highlight of his presidency.

Various "foreign colonies" resident in Peru announced a range of centenary gifts to be located in the public spaces of Lima (or to create them): an ornamental fountain from China and another from the United States, a Moorish arch from Spain, a stadium from England, a statue of Liberty from France, a statue of a longshoreman from Belgium, a clock tower from Germany, the Museum of Italian Art from Italy, and so forth. These gifts changed the urban face of Lima (Hamann Mazuré 2011:282) and fit well with the Peruvian government's interest in urban beautification (*ornato público*) that had begun at the end of the nineteenth century (Najluf 1994).

The written testimony of Ichitaro Morimoto, President of the Sociedad Central Japonesa (Central Japanese Society) indicates that various proposals for a gift were suggested by members of the Society: "a Japanese style tower, a public bath, a stadium, a grove of trees" (Gardiner 1975:78). Other proposals included a Japanese garden or a park (Elguera 1926:68). Federico Elguera Seminario, a former mayor of Lima and President of the Centenary Commission, asserts that he suggested to Mr. Morimoto "a monument to Manco Capac, son of the Sun, founder of the great Inca Empire" (Elguera 1926:68). The Japanese community enthusiastically undertook the Manco Capac project, which would link Peru's indigenous empire with that of Japan: two empires of the sun.

A distinguished Peruvian sculptor, David Lozano won the commission from the Sociedad Central Japonesa to make the monument. They selected another well-known Peruvian artist, Benjamin Mendizábal, to create the iconographic reliefs of the pedestal.

At this time, Lima's urban landscape was marked by just a few monuments: heroes of Peru's struggle for independence and those of later wars, a handful of presidents, Columbus, and a great Italian scholar of Peru (Castrillón Vizcarra 1991; Hamann Mazuré 2011; Ramón Joffré 2014:76). But Incas were nowhere to be seen in the city. Majluf (1994:32) explains the lack of Inca monuments as the result of a new nation iconographically and narratively carving out a new national space that emphasized the recent origin of the nation as well as its modernity. The new nation was legitimizing itself with reference to "universal" values rather than a "savage" ancestry (Majluf 1994:29–33). Hamman Mazuré (2011:159) similarly observes that at that time "Peruvian culture was barely national and it was concentrated on reproducing western canons."

Yet at the end of the nineteenth century and in the early twentieth century there were Incas in Lima, just *not* in monumental form. Incas appeared in the official patriotic canon as seen on currency, postal stamps, and even street names (Ramón Joffré 2014:73–74). And *indigenismo* was on the rise, with intellectuals organizing themselves to recognize the plight of the downtrodden indigenous population of the Andes and advocate for political, economic, and cultural remediation (see Earle 2007:184–190). *Indigenista* art flourished, especially with the creation of the Escuela Nacional de Bellas Artes (National School of Fine Arts) in 1918. Leguía thus had access to a prolific new verbal and visual discourse.

Leguía promulgated several reforms in favor of the Indians, for instance creating an Office for Indigenous Affairs and the new Constitution of 1920, which gave legal recognition to the highland communities. His government also recognized the Comité Central Pro-Derecho Indigena (Central Committee for Indigenous Legal Rights). Moreover, Leguía had decided to create a "national art," explicitly seeking to deploy art to create a new official image in support of the new nationalism he called *Patria Nueva* (New Nation) (Hamman Mazuré 2011:139–140). That image explicitly favored the work of *indigenista* artists, what Gabriel Ramón Joffré (2014) labels "neo-Peruvian," identifying it not just in portable art but also in architecture of Lima. Thus, under Leguía a previously marginalized artistic movement was linked to political power (Hamman Mazuré 2011:161).

When the Sociedad Central Japonesa met to decide upon their centenary gift to the Peruvian nation, Leguía's early, progressive Indian policies were just being formulated and the Japanese were surrounded by the growing wave of *indigenismo*. The Japanese colony proposed their gift at exactly the right time – at the crest of Leguía's turn toward the "Indian problem," as it was widely known (see Klarén 2000:247 on Leguía's "official *indigenismo*"). Their gift was the only one to iconographically and conceptually iterate Leguía's idea of the *Patria Nueva*, with its new interest in "the Indian" (Hamman Mazuré 2011:294). The monument would speak to the "glorious past of the indigenous race", as one magazine stated at the time (cited in Hamman Mazuré 2011:294).

The Sociedad Central Japonesa decided that since the gift was to come from the Japanese colony, all Japanese in Peru should contribute an equal amount to its cost. Easily organized through their networks, the Japanese immigrants – rich and poor – all gave the same modest sum and raised enough money in three months to commission the statue (Thorndike 1996:40). But the Manco Capac monument was not ready in 1921. Rather, it was described at the inaugural ceremony for the laying of the foundation stone in 1922.

At that ceremony Leguía praised the Japanese immigrants who in such a brief time had demonstrated their keen sense of work and initiative and who had engendered so much positive sentiment. He expressed his appreciation for the monument, which would celebrate the momentous centennial and be a symbol of Peru's ancient culture and actual civilization. Amid the bands, dances, parades, presidential cavalry, long line-up of official speakers, invited Japanese and Peruvian guests, and thousands of viewers only two Quechua-speaking, traditionally dressed Indians appeared (Thorndike 1996:47; Ramón Joffré 2014:83). They were an oddity in Lima, to say the least, for there was a complete and prejudicial disconnect between Manco Capac, the great and honored founder of the Inca Empire, and his living descendants, the Indians. As Julian Pitt-Rivers once caustically observed,

> The place of the noble savage is on a pedestal rather than in the market-place where his nobility is soon brought into question, and the less the figure on the pedestal resembles the reality of everyday life, the more convincing his message. Tribute to the pristine forebears must not be permitted to interfere with treatment of their descendants . . . the Indian can only be acclaimed at the level where he does not exist.

(Pitt-Rivers 1965:41).

The discourse that was heard that day was one of mutual congratulations between the Japanese ambassador and the elite of the Japanese colony and the President of Peru. Peru had bet on the value of Japanese immigration and the bet had paid off. Now the Japanese community was saying "thank you." The Japanese ambassador spoke of the friendship between the two countries and their commercial and diplomatic relations (Thorndike 1996:46). The representatives of the Japanese colony affirmed their loyalty, gratitude and affection for their recently adopted country and their desire to keep working cooperatively with the Peruvians. At the same time, they affirmed their respect and veneration for the history of their country of origin, Japan (Thorndike 1996:46).

Due to technical delays in the fabrication of the statue, it was not erected until 1926. The second inauguration was an even larger event than in 1922. Again, effusive mutual praise flowed among the Peruvian President, his highest officials, and the Japanese colony's representatives. This time the government actually brought delegations of Indians from Cuzco (the provincial highland city that had been the capital of the Inca Empire) to the celebration and in his speech Leguía elaborated on his contributions to the wellbeing of the Andean population and his hope that they would be great citizens of the country. There were more speeches honoring Manco Capac (Thorndike 1996:54).

Of course, Manco Capac was not Leguía's heritage nor were the Incas the heritage of the European minority that dominated Peru at that time. And while the *indigenistas* labored for Indian rights, their arguments were made on political and moral grounds, not in an argument of shared national heritage. As Rebecca Earle observes, Peruvian elites viewed "the pre-conquest epoch as part of the nation's past at the same time as they insisted their own ancestry was fundamentally Iberian" (2007:183). Pre-hispanic history was used "to construct national pasts that accorded little place to the contemporary indigenous population" (Earle 2007:183). Like Pitt-Rivers (1965), Earle notes that "pre-conquest Indians were good to build nations with, but contemporary Indians were not" (2007:183). The heritagization of the Incas and their descendants only came to the fore decades later under the revolutionary government of General Juan Velasco Alvarado (1968–1975) and the nascent global regime of UNESCO's 1972 World Heritage Convention.

The discursive space, physical and visual, of monuments

President Leguía enthusiastically took advantage of the centennial to enact a program of urban adornment and beautification (*ornato y embellecimiento*) in Lima, seeking to make it a modern, cosmopolitan capital with plazas, boulevards, and public art. The various gifts of the foreign colonies became part of that goal (Hamann Mazuré 2011). The new monuments of Lima – those given by the foreign colonies and those erected by the government – created their contexts and recursively were nourished by them. A monument could not simply be erected by a diasporic community, however. Physical space had to be obtained. In most cases their locations had not been created with the monuments in mind (Hamann Mazuré 2011:298).

Except for the Manco Capac monument, the gifts of the foreign colonies all followed the traditional western canon in style and subject matter and were installed in prime locations in the heart of Lima, which was then the premier symbolic, cultural, political, and elite space of the city.

The Manco Capac monument, however, was extremely controversial beyond Leguía's circle because of its indigenous theme. After considerable discussion (Hamann Mazuré 2011:295) and difficulty (Ramón Joffré 2014: note 70), the intersection of two principal avenues was designated, a location with high visibility but outside the prestigious center of Lima (see Hamman Mazuré 2011: Fig. 173). The monument was placed at the boundary between Lima and the new working-class district of La Victoria. As Gabriel Ramón Joffré emphasizes, placing an Inca in old Lima, historic Lima, elite Lima, simply was not possible (2014:74, 79, 82, 84). And, to be fair, there had been no Incas in Lima – their homeland was Cuzco, in the mountains way to the southeast. Lima was a hispanic city from its foundation in 1535. Yet as the capital of Peru, a country with a deep pre-hispanic past and a vast living Indian population whose dire situation was unresolved, the Manco Capac monument was appropriate albeit provocative. But controversy was not what the Japanese colony had intended. As Gardiner (1975:79) observes, "However much the Japanese did to ingratiate themselves, the record of Japanese–Peruvian relations at the people-to-people level continued to deteriorate."

The Manco Capac monument was the most important of the foreign colony gifts precisely because of its subject matter and its connection to Leguía's program of *Patria Nueva*. Peruvian art historian Alfonso Castrillón Vizcarra (1991:350) identifies the Manco Capac monument as the first in the country to use Inca motifs. Not only did it feature a monumental statue of an Inca (indeed, at a scale that overwhelms the pedestal), the base was shaped like a (generic) stepped pyramid mound with the representation of Inca stone work and Mendizábal's reliefs portrayed key elements of Inca culture such as collective traditional agriculture and stoneworking as well as religion and great animals of Inca cosmology – the llama, condor, puma, and snake. The monument was a tribute to the indigenous people of the Andes – at least the dead ones.

La Independencia del Perú y la Colonia Japonesa, published in 1926, also contributed to the monument's visual discourse. Produced by the Sociedad Central Japonesa's monument commission, the cover of the volume is decorated with pre-hispanic imagery, albeit it mostly in a generic pre-Inca iconographic assemblage. The typeface of the book's title is very similar to that on the dedicatory plaque of the monument (Figure 8.2). The book expresses the *indigenista* style that was so pervasive at that time.

Finally, the importance of the monument to the standing of the Japanese community and the degree of their success in their new country can be seen in the configuration of the front page of the October 31, 1926 issue of *El Comercio*, Lima's most prestigious newspaper, published six months after the monument's inauguration on April 4, 1926. The monument appears in the center of the page, identified on the left as Manco Capac and on the right as a gift of the Japanese community of Peru. The relationship of the Inca king to his Japanese counterpart

FIGURE 8.2   The dedicatory plaque of the Japanese colony, placed on the monument at the time of its inauguration in 1926. Note the stylised pre-Columbian imagery of the plaque and the *indigenista* style of lettering. (Photo: Helaine Silverman)

is shown by the portraits of Emperor Yoshihito and his wife. Advertisements of prominent Japanese businesses frame the drawings. The dominant narrative of the monument for the Japanese colony was then, as it had been since the inception of the project, a linkage between the two empires of the sun and the desire of the immigrants to be part of their new country – an affiliative reterritorialization.

The relocation

When Leguía was toppled by a military coup in 1930 the Japanese community lost its most important advocate. The anti-Leguía factions, in fact, held Leguía's pro-Japanese stance against him and, among other things, criticized his enthusiasm for the Japanese gift of the Manco Capac monument (Gardiner 1975:48). At this time, Peru was in a deepening economic crisis and Peruvians resented the relative prosperity of the Japanese colony. As they had even during Leguía's presidency, newspapers after Leguía promoted "anti-yellow campaigns" and incited the public against the colony (Gardiner 1975). Armed Peruvians roughed up Japanese–Peruvians, damaged their property and plundered their shops; indeed, there were riots against them (Gardiner 1975:48, 52–53). Relations with Japan itself declined throughout the 1930s.

   In 1938, the government then in power moved the Manco Capac monument several blocks over to an enormous plaza in the heart of La Victoria. I can only guess about the motivation for the relocation, but given that by late 1937 Peruvian dislike of its Japanese community and Japan was raging (Gardiner 1975:71), perhaps the relocation of the monument was a deliberate offense, for although Manco Capac was given a home in a large plaza, in effect the monument had been exiled to a working-class neighborhood. Adding insult to injury, that plaza was near a zone specifically set aside for prostitution (Ramón Joffré 2014:88). An old phrase in Lima, "*el inca indica Huatica*," recovered by Gabriel Ramón Joffré (2014:88), refers to the fact that the upraised arm of Manco Capac pointed to Huatica, the zone of prostitutes. I would suggest, applying DeCesari and Herzfeld to a different context, that the relocation was a manifestation of a "struggle . . . over urban heritage . . . as local actors tr[ied] to regroup . . . [a form of] discriminatory and violent spatial planning" (2015:171).

The new context of the monument

From its inception in 1920, La Victoria has been home to a large immigrant population from the Andean highlands, as well as Italians, Afro-Peruvians, and others. In addition to being working-class, La Victoria has long had the reputation of being an unsavory district. Even though its great plaza is located across the street from the Municipality building and the main church of the district, the plaza was a dangerous place for decades. Thus, the announcement by La Victoria's mayor in 2010 that the Municipality was going to clean up the plaza, push out the delinquents and prostitutes, and create a new, healthy (*sano* in its more social, rehabilitative sense) space – a place of recreation and enjoyment (larepublica.pe, March 21, 2010) – was noteworthy and received significant attention from the press.

For La Victoria, the refurbished plaza is a development project, potentially stimulating business along with tourism. The larger context for the refurbishment of the Plaza Manco Capac is the Municipality of Lima's "Lima Milenaria" campaign with which long abandoned pre-hispanic sites in the city – the *huacas* or pyramid mounds – are being rehabilitated for tourism and a tourist circuit for local and foreign use is being created. Urban memory is being recovered and generated so as to create better public spaces and, in a Foucauldian sense, better citizens.

Moreover, the refurbishment of the plaza is an ideological project for the plaza has been heritagized. It was announced that statues of 14 Inca kings and queens would surround the monument in an open-air museum concept and that there would be a scale model of Lake Titicaca (which, in some Inca myths, was their place of origin), an enormous water fountain, an amphitheater, children's park, and a cafeteria (Perú21.pe, February 2, 2010; larepublica.pe, March 21, 2010). The refurbished plaza would be a "civic place and historic attraction," according to Mayor Alberto Sánchez Aizcorbe. Indeed, the mayor even predicted thousands of visits by national and foreign tourists.

I observed the refurbished plaza on six days in January 2014, January 2015 and June 2015. I was the only tourist regardless of the day of the week (including weekends) and there were few people in the plaza. However, the change from a previous visit I had made in 2004 (accompanied by a husky Peruvian colleague who insisted on protecting me) is remarkable. The plaza is now immaculate, graffiti has been removed from the monument, and municipal guards are on patrol. The project is reported to have cost two million dollars and was financed by the district (20 percent) and central government (80 percent). It has achieved its goal of cleaning up the area.

The plaza was reinaugurated on April 25, 2013 – without all of its announced features but with some new ones. The monument is now surrounded by four walls (approximately 4 meters in height) within which the "museum" will function. The monument has lost some of its visual impact because of the walls (Figure 8.3). Within the walls, I observed just four poorly executed statues of Incas (Figure 8.4); I was unable to obtain information on what the final script will look like. Alongside the exterior side of the walls are rectangular water pools – one on each side. The plaza also has a stage and a screen for outdoor projections. There are pleasant raised seating areas with benches under wood pergolas. Four towering (approximately 9 meters high) cement monoliths of rectangular form stand on one side of the plaza (Figure 8.5). When I visited just after the inauguration full-length banners hung from them: celebrating the inauguration of the plaza, showing a map of the four quarters of the Inca Empire (Tawantinsuyu), announcing the (supposedly) soon to be opened open-air museum, stating the Inca ethical code ("don't steal, don't be lazy, don't lie"), and listing donors. A year later only the Tawantinsuyu and Inca code banners remained.

FIGURE 8.3 The Manco Capac monument is now surrounded by four walls within which there will be an open-air museum. The museum is advertised on the banner, but still had not opened as of June 6, 2015. (Photo: Helaine Silverman)

FIGURE 8.4   Three of the four sculptures of Inca kings and queens. These four were all I had observed as of June 6, 2015. (Photo: Helaine Silverman)

FIGURE 8.5   The four monoliths with their banners. From closest to farthest: map of the Inca Empire; list of donors; announcement of the open-air museum; the Inca ethical code. (Photo: Helaine Silverman)

Most of the articles about the renovation of the plaza did indicate that the monument had been a gift of the Japanese community and some articles gave specific details about its history. But as the proposed refurbishment designs began to appear in the Lima newspapers the project was called, for instance, "an Inca sanctuary in La Victoria" (larepublica.pe, March 21, 2010). The mayor said the project would "give it [the plaza] a new concept with a greater cultural value" and would explain who Manco Capac was and "the value of Tahuantinsuyo [Inca Empire]" (larepublica.pe, March 21, 2010). His discourse reflects the common official fetishization of the Incas in the heritage economy and cultural politics of Peru.

Thus, notwithstanding newspaper stories that identified the monument originally as the gift of the Japanese colony, and the presence of the great nephew of Ichitaro Morimoto at the inauguration of the renovated plaza, and the recollection of La Victoria's mayor that the Japanese–Peruvian community had made the monument possible, the emphasis of the new script is ancient Andean glory: the Manco Capac monument now represents the Incas exclusively (and the eventual museum will iterate that theme). And because the base of the monument is hidden behind the walls of the eventual open-air museum, the dedicatory plaque of the Japanese colony is no longer prominent. As architect Enrique Ciriani Suito, one of the advisors hired by the mayor, said,

> The passer-by will develop a sense of self-esteem, feeling that he belongs to his city, which will therefore manifest a democratic character . . . The space around the statue of Manco Capac should interest, explain and reconcile the Peruvians to their history.
>
> *(Ciriani Suito blog, May 26, 2013).*

That history excludes the Japanese diaspora. Thus, the original link created between the two empires of the sun by the monument is broken.

Although the Japanese colony in Peru is today overwhelmingly prosperous and not living in the working-class district of La Victoria, what is unchanged is La Victoria's connection to immigration. As it was at the time of the monument's construction, La Victoria is still a district predominantly of Peruvians of highland and African descent. It is not without reason that the spectacle provided by the Municipality of La Victoria at the inauguration of the improved plaza featured highland and Afro-Peruvian music and dance.

Conclusion

The choice of an indigenous theme for the gift of the Japanese colony to Peru was most significant in the discourse it engendered on both the Japanese and Peruvian sides concerning "empires of the sun." This chapter has presented the monument in the context of the Japanese diaspora in Peru and the relationship between immigrant, indigenous, mestizo, and elite communities in the construction of Peruvian identity. Following Benedict Anderson, I approached the monument as a type of speech and tried to discern "what is being said [and] why form and content are specifically what they are" (1978:301).

We also have seen that a monument both commemorates and stewards, mediating past and future (see Anderson 1978:301). And monuments create space:

physical, social, and ideological. Therefore, as important as the object is its physical place on a landscape and its social construction of space. These are not confined to the moment of erection but rather continue to reverberate over time. Therefore, this chapter brought the monument up to the present day with consideration of the recent refurbishment of the plaza in which it is located.

While Peru drew on (and still appropriates) the Inca Empire as part of its ideological narrative of nationhood, the descendants of those ancient people – the living Indians of the Andes – were – at the time of the monument's construction – subject to wanton social discrimination and structural forms of outright economic oppression and political disenfranchisement from the Spanish- and other European-descended powerholders. The gift of the Manco Capac monument to Peru at that moment was thus extremely interesting, indeed provocative, although the Japanese colony did not intend it to be so.

That there were debates about the form of the monument and where to locate it should not surprise us. One need only look to the National Mall of the United States to understand the tension between a symbolically charged place and symbolically rich objects (Savage 2009). The Manco Capac monument was, as we have seen, problematical because of its subject matter, its location, and its sponsors. It was, in its inception, a peculiar monument, for the immigrant community that erected it was calling forth a relationship to a national past not their own, but – following Choay (2001:6) – the Japanese were invoking, localizing, and selecting it toward a critical end: the establishment of themselves in a new land, thereby creating an affiliative reterritorialization.

With the remodeling of La Victoria's plaza the Japanese heritage of the Manco Capac monument has been obscured for now the figure of Manco Capac himself comes to the fore as an Andean heritage, an Inca heritage, a national heritage. The statue and the plaza have been rescripted as exclusively Peruvian. As such, city space and architectural landscape work to actively systematize memory (Boyer 2001:137) in which the Japanese colony no longer figures. Indeed, La Victoria's mayor is clearly trying to create a new "vernacular topoi" (Boyer 2001:321) – a landscape whose new sense of place and local customs, through the inaugural spectacle and popular festivals, replace the former dereliction and create a new cultural memory.

The Manco Capac monument in its original location and then for 60-plus years in the eponymous plaza has the quality that Boyer (2001:343) refers to as "rhetorical topoi." From the beginning, the monument has been an official and ceremonial place, "articulated by political and social configurations that a nation [under Leguía] or municipality [under La Victoria's mayor] wants to instill within its public" (Boyer 2001:343). What we see in the monument's history is a significant change in its rhetorical meaning. And at all critical moments of its life, including in its conception, a semiological controversy has surrounded it.

Finally, the Manco Capac monument expresses a mobile heritage that resonates with its immigrant origin. The Japanese colony that created it was mobile, having come to Peru. Decades later the descendants of the Inca Empire who flooded Lima through their migration from the highlands have been mobile and have brought their rich intangible cultural heritage to the city and hybridized it with coastal patterns. The statue itself has been mobile as it moved (was moved) from its original location to the plaza.

The recent urban renewal – itself embedded in a neoliberal economy and global political engagement – has physically diminished the monumentality of the monument and discursively diminished its origin as the product of immigrant sponsors. But the refurbishing of the plaza manifests the political and social mobility of the district of La Victoria. The currently configured plaza generates new understandings of neighborhood and local and national identity among the district's contemporary residents.

Heritage is manifested in identity, landscape, memory, and sense of place. It is expressed in material culture and practices. The case study I have presented enriches perspectives on what may happen to cultural heritage when cultural identities migrate. The Japanese colony did not relinquish its cultural heritage as demonstrated by its numerous Japanese schools, cultural associations, Japanese language newspapers, and Japanese restaurants (etc.) as well as the colony's continued engagement with the homeland. To this day, the post-immigration Japanese colony has a strong cohesion and visibility.

Affiliative reterritorialization is active, situational, and highly adaptive. It has enabled the *colonia japanesa* to negotiate the terrain between assimilation and isolation. Specifically, at the crucial moment of first and second wave Japanese immigration, affiliative reterritorialization was a brilliant strategy for manifesting Japanese appreciation of the new homeland and its heritage, while garnering praise for the heritage of the homeland left behind. It was also quite politically and culturally daring in the 1920s, being enabled by the unique profile of Augusto Leguía who at that very moment was interested in Peru's Andean heritage and its living bearers.

Migrating heritage is about unbounded culture and physical and performative mobility. Migrating heritage has component, interrelated elements in constant movement – dynamic, initiatory, responsive, flexible. Cultural identity is an intrinsic part of that migrating heritage. The Manco Capac monument at its time of creation was a remarkable example of a diaspora using its heritage to generate an ideological link to the originary heritage of its host country, a parallel heritage of commensurate value enabled by the actual political and economic networks that underwrote the migration. The Manco Capac monument today, in the eponymous plaza, reflects a dramatic reorientation of that ideology toward a transnational discourse of tourism and economic development *cum* aestheticized gentrification. The result is the loss of the powerful symbolism of a monument that once marked the physical presence and coming of age of a foreign immigrant community.

References

Anderson, Benedict R. O'G.
1978   Cartoons and monuments: The evolution of political communication under the New Order. In *Political Power and Communications in Indonesia*, edited by Karl D. Jackson and Lucian W. Pye, pp. 282–321. Berkeley: University of California Press.
Anheier, Helmut and Yudhishthir Raj Isar (eds.)
2011   *Heritage, Memory & Identity*. The Culture and Globalization Series, 4. London: Sage.
Boyer, M. Christine
2001   *The City of Collective Memory. Its Historical Imagery and Architectural Entertainments*. Cambridge: The MIT Press.
Byrne, Denis
2017   Encountering migration heritage in a national park. In *Heritage in Action: Making the Past in the Present*, edited by Helaine Silverman, Emma Waterton and Steve Watson, pp. 91–103. New York: Springer.
Castrillón Vizcarra, Alfonso
1991   Escultura monumental y funeraria en Lima. In *Escultura en el Perú*, edited by José Antonio Lavalle, pp. 325–393. Lima: Banco de Crédito del Perú.
Choay, Françoise
2001   *The Invention of the Historic Monument*. Cambridge: Cambridge University Press.
Dearborn, Lynne
2008a   Socio-spatial patterns of acculturation: Examining Hmong habitation in Milwaukee's north-side neighborhoods. *Buildings and Landscapes: Journal of the Vernacular Architecture Forum* 15: 58–77.
2008b   Reconstituting Hmong culture and traditions in Milwaukee, Wisconsin. *Traditional Dwellings and Settlements Review: Journal of the International Association for the Study of Traditional Environments* XIX (2): 37–49.
De Cesari, Chiara and Michael Herzfeld
2015   Urban heritage and social movements. In *Global Heritage. A Reader*, edited by Lynn Meskell, pp. 171–195. Malden: Wiley Blackwell.
Earle, Rebecca
2007   *The Return of the Native. Indians and Myth-Making in Spanish America, 1810–1930*. Durham: Duke University Press.
Elguera, Federico
1926   El monumento a Manco Capac. In *La Independencia del Perú y la Colonia Japonesa*, edited by Comité Organizadora del Monumento a Manco Capac, pp. 67–71. Lima: Imprenta Eduardo Ravago-Zarate.
Gardiner, C. Harvey
1975   *The Japanese and Peru, 1873–1973*. Albuquerque: University of New Mexico Press.
Graham, Brian and Peter Howard (eds.)
2008   *The Ashgate Research Companion to Heritage and Identity*. Farnham: Ashgate.
Gupta, Akhil and James Ferguson
1992   Beyond 'culture': Space, identity and the politics of difference. *Cultural Anthropology* 7(1): 6–23.
Hamann Mazuré, Johanna
2011   Monumentos Públicos en Espacios Urbanos de Lima, 1919–1930. PhD dissertation. Universidad de Barcelona.
Innocenti, Perla (ed.)
2014   *Migrating Heritage. Experiences of Cultural Networks and Cultural Dialogue in Europe*. Farnham: Ashgate.

Innocenti, Perla

2015   *Cultural Networks in Migrating Heritage. Intersecting Theories and Practices across Europe.* Farnham: Ashgate.

Klarén, Peter Findell

2000   *Peru: Society and Nationhood in the Andes.* Oxford: Oxford University Press.

Lefebvre, Henri

1991   *The Production of Space.* Malden: Blackwell.

Li, Chuo

2012   The politics and heritage of race and space in San Francisco's Chinatown. In *On Location: Heritage Cities and Sites,* edited by D. Fairchild Ruggles, pp. 37–59. New York: Springer.

Pitt-Rivers, Julian

1965   Who are the Indians? *Encounter* XXV: 41–49.

Morimoto, Amelia

1999   *Los Japoneses y Sus Descendientes en el Perú.* Lima: Fondo Editorial del Congreso del Perú.

Najluf, Natalia

1994   *Escultura y Espacio Público. Lima 1850–1879.* Documento de Trabajo No. 67. Lima: Instituto de Estudios Peruanos.

Nelson, Robert S. and Margaret Olin

2003   Introduction. In *Monuments and Memory, Made and Unmade,* edited by Robert S. Nelson and Margaret Olin, pp. 1–10. Chicago: University of Chicago Press.

Ramón Joffré, Gabriel

2014   *El Neoperuano 1910–1940. Arqueología, Estilo Nacional y Paisaje Urbano en Lima.* Lima: Municipalidad Metropolitana de Lima y Sequilao Editores.

Savage, Kirk

2009   *Monument Wars. Washington, D.C., the National Mall, and the Transformation of the Memorial Landscape.* Berkeley: University of California Press.

Sheller, Mimi and John Urry

2006   The new mobilities paradigm. *Environment and Planning A* 38: 207–226.

Thorndike, Guillermo

1996   *Los Imperios del Sol. Una Historia de los Japoneses en el Perú.* Lima: Editorial Brasa.

Tigner, James L.

1978   The Ryukyuans in Peru, 1906–1952. *Americas* 35(1): 20–44.

Urry, J.

2007   *Mobilities.* Cambridge: Polity.

9

HERITAGE, PARTICIPANT PERSPECTIVE, EPISTEMIC INJUSTICE, IMMIGRANTS AND IDENTITY FORMATION

Andreas Pantazatos

Introduction: setting the scene

The current waves of immigrants to Europe invigorate the debate about the relationship between cultural heritage and identity, and the immigrants' active participation in the formation of their new identity in the host country. Part of the challenge for the accommodation of new migrants in their host countries is rooted in the fact that the vast majority of European countries are still the products of the long nineteenth century. During that time, the formation of the nation state grounded the collective national identity, which was built on the idea of the nation's great heritage and its continuity via collective memory. The states of Greece and Italy are prime examples in this era. Because cultural heritage played a role in the creation of the new national identity, any newcomer who carries her/his own heritage can be perceived as a threat to the *status quo* of the nation state. Although there has been pressure for immigrants to integrate into their new countries, their own national identity which has been shaped by their cultural heritage can still be an obstacle in this regard.[1]

If one accepts that cultural heritage is important for both the host country and the incoming migrants, one might expect to be able to resolve any possible conflicts by employing Article 4 of the Faro 2005 Convention on the Value of Cultural Heritage to Society.[2] Article 4 assumes that everyone alone or collectively is a participant in heritage. However, the new migration within Europe challenges traditional unified understandings of heritage in the European context. If Europeans understand themselves as participants in heritage, there is a set of old questions we need to re-address in the context of contemporary migration: 'whose heritage?', 'who are the heritage participants?', 'how is participation in heritage made possible?', and 'how does participation in heritage affect identity formation?'

In this chapter, I will sketch a framework for the relationship between epistemic injustice and identity formation. I start my argument from the premise that heritage is related to knowledge, broadly construed. There is a kind of injustice, namely epistemic injustice, which occurs when people are excluded as informants from the economy of knowledge because they are wrongly judged to be unreliable source of information or their testimonies not deemed credible.[3] Alternatively, they are taken to lack the hermeneutical toolkit to understand and provide relevant information. For instance, I understand that many Indigenous peoples would like to exercise both testimonial and hermeneutical roles: they will not testify about their cultural heritage unless they are also allowed to ensure that it is interpreted in the right ways.[4] As I have argued elsewhere (Pantazatos 2017) there is a kind of epistemic injustice which is specifically related to heritage, namely participant perspective epistemic injustice, according to which human beings do not merely contribute to the exchange of knowledge as informants but also as participants. Participant perspective epistemic injustice highlights a broader issue.[5] One may find oneself excluded as a participant if one is judged for the wrong reasons to be incompetent or ill-placed to contribute to a debate or a topic of discussion. One is therefore excluded from shaping the future of the debate or topic under discussion.

Similarly, migrants can suffer from participant perspective epistemic injustice because they are not provided with the space and/or are not encouraged to make contributions about their own heritage and its possible associations with the heritage of the host country. They are excluded and thus marginalised in virtue of their status as migrants. Participant perspective epistemic injustice can undermine the new identity formation which is central for the establishment and the well-being of migrants in their new country. In developing the discussion further, I employ Anthony Appiah's proposal of the three stages of identity formation.[6]

Heritage and knowledge

Heritage, broadly construed, is what we inherit from the past. This includes material traces such as ruins, objects, structures and buildings serving different purposes (e.g. religious, military, civic, domestic), monuments and landscapes. We also inherit intangible things from the past, such as values, beliefs, traditions and social structures. Heritage has many different sorts of value: cultural, epistemic, historic, financial and religious, to mention just a few. Heritage is valuable in part because it is a major source of knowledge. Heritage can provide knowledge about forms of past lives, civilisations and life styles around the globe which are highly relevant for us who live in the present. It is often assumed, rightly or wrongly, that all human beings have an interest in heritage and, more generally, in the past because they help us to understand who we are today and how we got here. In addition, attempting to connect with the distant past has the potential to help us to connect with very different cultures in the present. Heritage is what we inherit from the past, but its significance is relevant for both present and future people. Heritage is multifaceted and dynamic: what is understood as heritage today might be altered tomorrow (and heritage anyway continues to accumulate over time). It is open to interpretation and the different associations people develop with it add new layers to its meaning. Hence, heritage does not convey 'frozen' knowledge and merely information about what took place in the past. Rather, it sets in motion, via our interactions with what we have inherited from the past, a set of questions about our self-understanding, our engagement with others and our understanding of the world. Given that our interaction with what we have inherited is central to the epistemic role of heritage, constraints that obstruct this interaction undermine the epistemic role of different stakeholders of heritage.

A common thread of argument in the ethics and politics of heritage is that communities – such as migrants – whose own histories are excluded or not represented in the official interpretation of heritage are marginalised and that their silencing might lead to alienation from their own heritage.[7] As a result, social injustices might occur which are rooted in the abuse of rights over place and misrepresentation of the identity of marginalised communities. The core of the argument is that communities in one way or another are not provided with space to tell their own story and supply their own interpretation of heritage, and this excludes them from the economy of knowledge. Sometimes, for instance, museums that purport to tell the story of migrant communities have even been known to fail to include the voices of those whose story they claim to be telling! For an inspirational example of a museum that has avoided this pitfall, I refer to the Digital Museum of Smyrna and New Smyrna, which provides ample space for Smyrnian refugees to share their own story with the rest of the world.[8]

The Digital Museum of Smyrna and New Smyrna

In April 2016, the President of the Greek State opened the Digital Museum of Smyrna and New Smyrna in Athens.[9] This is the first digital museum in the country. The museum is the outcome of a long-standing effort by the residents of the area of New Smyrna in Athens. One of the main features of the first Digital Museum is that it is a collaborative and participatory endeavour. Local residents of New Smyrna with a refugee background were invited to bring any available testimonials from their families. One of the principal curators of the museum digitised the testimonials, which were then returned to their owners. Additionally, living refugees or their descendants were invited to share their stories, which were digitised and which are going to be presented in the museum space as the museum develops.[10] The vast majority of the residents of New Smyrna are refugees or descendants of refugees. The residents of New Smyrna were expelled from their homeland in Smyrna (modern Izmir in Turkey) during the revolution of Young Turks in 1922. According to contemporary testimonies, Smyrna was one of the greatest urban centres of the nineteenth century in the Levant, a successful merchant centre and a city famous for its good life.[11] Greeks used to be one of the most prominent communities in the city, and to some extent they were perceived as the rulers of the city. The quality of life of Greeks in Smyrna was almost legendary and

Smyrnian refugees have suffered not only the loss of their beloved city but also loss of their whole way of living, which is now manifested in the form of a perpetual nostalgia for their homeland. One would expect that refugees from Smyrna would be welcomed in mainland Greece, given that they were Greeks and shared the same language and same religion with the people of mainland Greece. By contrast, they were perceived as intruders and it took a goodly amount of time for them to integrate with their compatriot Greeks. Although Greek refugees are celebrated by national Greek history as those who contributed the most to the development of the New Greek State, their own heritage and their distinct identity were never given space in the national narrative of Greek heritage. The Digital Museum of Smyrna and New Smyrna is the first museum that provides a space for Smyrnian refugees not only to share their story but also to share with other Greeks what has contributed to the formation of their new identity in Athens and far away from the eternal place of nostalgia: Smyrna. The museum provides an accurate and detailed narrative of the life of Smyrnians in Smyrna and describes how all their original customs and habits were re-established in the new area they were allocated in Athens, 'New Smyrna' as it came to be called, through the painful process of their migration from the one side of the Aegean to the other. The museum does not focus on the burning of the city of Smyrna in 1922 and the disaster which followed. The details of Smyrna's disaster are included in the museum narrative *as part of* the heritage of the Smyrnians who were trying to form a new identity in a new place without abandoning their heritage. That heritage is twofold. It includes their past lives in Smyrna and their present lives as refugees and strangers in a new home. One could argue that more or less all migrants carry a similar twofold heritage.

The Digital Museum of Smyrna and New Smyrna is interesting for my purpose here because it provides some food for thought about the role of heritage in identity formation. The museum 'presents' the new identity of the Smyrnians, an identity which was established because Smyrnians were able to become participants in their own heritage.[12] However, it took more than 60 years for this to happen. The example of the Digital Museum of Smyrna and New Smyrna invites the following questions: 'how are we to understand the idea of being a participant in relation to heritage and knowledge?' and 'what are the implications for epistemic injustice?' I will address both questions by providing a brief discussion of the relationship between heritage and epistemic injustice.

Heritage and epistemic injustice

According to Miranda Fricker (2007: 28), "Testimonial injustice occurs when the testimony of an individual or collective is perceived as less credible owing to an identity prejudice". For instance, one's capacity to provide testimony is undermined on the basis of being a woman or being a foreigner in a country. Hermeneutical injustice occurs when an agent's assertions 'are not given attention because of a lack of the requisite conceptual and other resources that are required for formulating important problems or for addressing them systematically (Fricker 2007: 30).'

snobbishness?

The main difference between the two kinds of injustice is that for testimonial injustice the agent is treated as someone who cannot be a credible informant in exchanges of knowledge, whereas for hermeneutical injustice the agent is taken to lack the conceptual resources to contribute to the understanding of certain claims and thus as incapable of making them. Both kinds, however, highlight the role of the agent as an informant. Her capacity to provide information in obtaining and transmitting knowledge is what is undermined when the agent suffers testimonial or hermeneutical injustice. While Fricker primarily focuses on the lack of self-knowledge as the main harm of hermeneutical injustice, we can also note that this lack of self-knowledge is necessarily accompanied by an inability to transmit the knowledge one lacks, making it similar to testimonial injustice in this way: in both cases epistemic agents are hindered in their capacity to transmit knowledge.[13] For Fricker, victims of epistemic injustice are not merely insulted by not being listened to. I suggest that there is also a stronger point she aims to communicate. By being disregarded, victims of epistemic injustice cannot benefit from that fruits that would flow were they to be more 'integrated' member of an epistemic community. These fruits remain at a constant distance from victims of epistemic injustice because they do not only experience marginalisation, but also their epistemic confidence is undermined when they are judged to be unfit for epistemic transactions.

There is, though, a third kind of epistemic injustice which is not captured by Fricker's discussion. Christopher Hookway (2010) puts forward what he terms 'participant perspective epistemic injustice'. Hookway points out that there are different epistemic roles which one can take in the economy of knowledge. He distinguishes between being an informant and being a participant. For Hookway, those who act as participants do not exchange information as informants do, rather they contribute to knowledge by asking questions. In making suggestions relevant to the debate, they participate, they consider alternative possibilities for the topics they discuss and they put forward alternative possibilities for consideration. Although Hookway stipulates that obtaining and transmitting knowledge as an informant can be understood as participation and it is thus difficult to draw sharp distinctions between participants and informants, he claims that being a participant has a broader scope than being merely an informant.

Hookway starts from the significance of testimonial credibility and the hermeneutical aptness of informants, stressing that to participate in the exchange of knowledge is not and cannot be limited to information exchange. Participation encompasses both the exchange of information and the exercise of hermeneutical skills. However, it pushes the boundaries of knowledge exchange beyond credibility checks and availability of hermeneutical tools, because it focuses on any contribution which can expand and further the matter of a debate without responding merely to questions requesting information. Informants are no doubt participants, but not all participants are necessarily and merely informants. Let us consider the following hypothetical scenario. Suppose that a number of immigrants have moved successfully from their home land to a new host country. After their agonising journey they still carry with them some artefacts and an abundance of intangible things which are significant for how they understand and identify themselves. Also, they happened to gather some artefacts during their journey which they acknowledge as important, given that they have accompanied their journey to the new land. The host country invites immigrants to a round-table debate about their own heritage and what can be done about the tangible and the intangible things which immigrants have carried with them. Immigrants can contribute in this debate by providing information about the artefacts they carried with them and those objects which they happened to acquire in the course of their journey. They are considered credible informants because they can provide testimony and interpretation concerning these objects. Given that they are welcomed and encouraged to exchange this kind of knowledge, one would claim that they have not been silenced and that their voices have been heard. This is, however, only one mode of participation. An interesting challenge arises if immigrants are not encouraged to get involved beyond this preliminary exchange of information. While they may ask questions about the future treatment of their artefacts and the sustaining of their practices and traditions, their questions are dismissed as irrelevant to the host community's predominant concerns. Or, if immigrants try to articulate proposals for sustaining their cultural practices within the host country, their contributions are not take seriously and they are given little or no space to influence future planning.

It is the latter form of participation in epistemic activities which Hookway focuses on in relation to epistemic injustice. It is the perspective as *participants* in the development of knowledge which is not given credit, rather than the capacity for conveying credible information. Participant perspective epistemic injustice results in a phenomenon that can undermine knowledge transmission. Silencing agents under participant perspective epistemic injustice entails that their questions or contributions broadly speaking are not used as pillars for the furtherance of knowledge (and this may lead to a failure of epistemic confidence on their part). More importantly, it undermines their capacity to shape the future of the debate and inform the possible priorities it may select. Agents who suffer participant perspective epistemic injustice are deprived of the possibilities to direct the debate in ways that will be fruitful for themselves and future generations. In being rendered powerless in the present, such agents become irrelevant in the future also. Recall the scenario above. The immigrants are able to respond as informants providing credible information and that way contribute to a body of knowledge about their objects and cultural practices. But their contributions as participants in the future are disallowed or disregarded. Although they have contributed as informants about their things and practices, they have been excluded from shaping their future. To respond to questions with credible information is one thing, to contribute to a body of knowledge and shaping the alternative possibilities of its future quite another. Hence it is Hookway's variety of epistemic injustice (2010), I suggest, that is often the more dangerous, insidious and overlooked (see Figure 9.1).

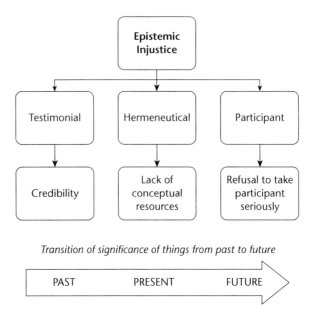

FIGURE 9.1 The relationship between epistemic injustice and heritage

I have argued elsewhere (Pantazatos 2016) that museums are in a unique position to manage the transit of things between past and future in such a way as to secure the transfer of their significance, broadly construed. By 'transit', I mean that museums not only convey the physical objects in their collections, but they are also conveyors of the things from one stage of their lives to the next. Given that this is the *modus operandi* for museums, the duty of care they bear requires attention to how the transit from past to future is accomplished.

In museums what is in transit from past to future is more than just the physical things themselves. What can also be transmitted includes also their significance – their meanings, associations and allusions, and these have been shaped in the different stages of their lives by their relationships with communities. A wide variety of participants who are related to a thing may be entitled to participate in determining its significance, which stage(s) of its life is (are) most important, and what reasons recommend its secure transfer to the future. For instance, the digital photo of the cheque instalments the refugees of Smyrna had to pay back to the Greek State for their housing in the area of New Smyrna in Athens reveals details of what Smyrnians went through to get their own house in a new country (see Figure 9.2). The photo is more than a testimony to the past lives of Smyrnians. The photo highlights what is considered as significant for the future life of Smyrnians and it adds a layer of meaning to their lives at the area they live in.

What is inherited from the past and what is in transit from past to the future is under constant interpretation and negotiation. Heritage is in continuous flux.

FIGURE 9.2 Digital exhibit of a receipt for the money which was paid by Smyrnian refugees to the Greek State towards the help they received for their housing in the city of Athens, from the Digital Museum of Smyrna and New Smyrna, Athens, Greece. (Photo: author's own)

What is inherited and at the same time is in transit from past to future is shaped by the contributions of different stakeholders who have developed associations with it. These stakeholders can act both as informants and as participants (following the distinction proposed by Hookway). Stakeholders can offer testimony about what they know about an object, thus enabling their conceptual resources to contribute to how it may be understood in the present. Hence, heritage stakeholders can be victims of testimonial or hermeneutical injustice when they are not epistemically involved in the transit of an object and its significance from past to present to future. Non-expert stakeholders are usually victims of epistemic injustice because they are charged by experts with lack of the knowledge or conceptual resources to provide adequate interpretations of what is in transit.[14] Given that heritage is a dynamic process and it is open to interpretation, expertise is one of the ways in which one can become epistemically involved with heritage. Stakeholders who are not experts might have developed associations and thus different kinds of knowledge from experts but their information is likewise highly relevant to heritage and plays a role in how things from the past can be understood. On a similar note, Indigenous communities have frequently been victims of testimonial injustice because their epistemic contributions to what has been inherited from the past and its significance have been prejudicially judged to lack credibility because of ideas and stereotypes rooted in racial attitudes. Let me pause for a moment and recall Article 4 of the Faro 2005 Convention on the Value of Cultural Heritage to Society.[15]

Article 4: rights and responsibilities relating to cultural heritage

a.   everyone, alone or collectively, has the right to benefit from the cultural heritage and to contribute towards its enrichment;

b.   everyone, alone or collectively, has the responsibility to respect the cultural heritage of others as much as their own heritage, and consequently the common heritage of Europe;

c.   exercise of the right to cultural heritage may be subject only to those restrictions which are necessary in a democratic society for the protection of the public interest and the rights and freedoms of others.

According to Article 4, non-expert stakeholders are considered participants in heritage unconditionally. If we understand the term 'participant' in the Faro convention according to Hookway, epistemic access for heritage participants is to play a role in the future shaping of heritage. This is to say that their contributions and their consideration of alternative possibilities should not be dismissed as irrelevant because, as I have said earlier, this constrains their epistemic confidence and can possibly lead to alienation from their heritage and their identity (as I will show in the next section). For instance, stakeholders (e.g. local people or Buddhists) who consider alternative possibilities for the reconstruction of the Bamiyan Buddhas, destroyed by the Taliban in Afghanistan in 2002, may lack the expert knowledge of art historians or archaeologists but should have their views taken into account. Participation, however, as central to the economy of knowledge and with regard to heritage is successful only if it is *sustained* and *maintained*. Sustaining and maintaining guarantee that participation takes place beyond norms of etiquette and compliance. To go through the motions of taking into consideration the proposals of such 'non-expert' stakeholders, for example by inviting them to a one-off meeting, does not amount to successful participation. It takes both time and effort for such stakeholders to build confidence so they can contribute to the future of their heritage making. By sustaining and maintaining stakeholder participation we negotiate the boundaries of participation. From the moment participation begins to be positively encouraged and supported, it can be further developed over an extended period of time. Since wide participation enhances fruitful debate, sustaining and maintaining it militates against epistemic silencing and exclusion.

Let me trace my steps for a moment. I argued that participant perspective epistemic injustice is particularly relevant to heritage. And I have shown that marginalised communities such as immigrants which suffer participant perspective epistemic injustice may well be alienated from their heritage through not being allowed space to shape the future of their own heritage. In what follows, I will take my argument for participant perspective epistemic injustice and heritage a step further. If cultural heritage plays a role in the formation of identity, and if participant perspective epistemic injustice alienates immigrants from their heritage, then this kind of injustice sets certain constrains on how immigrants may determine their new identity in the host country.

Participant perspective epistemic injustice and formation of identity

My identity as I conceive it shapes the way I live my life, providing a standpoint from which my being and my actions are rendered intelligible. For instance, I consider that there is 'an appropriate way of acting' for a scholar, a European, a citizen and so on. The labels I choose confer an identity which frames the obligations I have towards myself and others. Of course, constructing my identity (or rather, the complex of components that constitute it) is not a process that is independent of others. Identity construction is a process of dialogue between how I perceive myself and how others perceive me. The dialogical process acquires its own dynamic which influences the multiple identities that one shapes during one's life. Our actions to some extent can be explained and justified by the different identities we have crafted during our life, such as race, gender, nationality, religion, profession. These identities yield different obligations although this does not mean that they are necessarily in conflict. Different identities entail different priorities during one's everyday routine and one's life as a whole. What factors contribute to the formation of our identities? Saying that identity formation is a dialogical process between ourselves and others hardly portrays the full picture. In this chapter I have space to talk about only one of the factors involved in identity formation, and that is cultural heritage. The objects, practices, traditions and beliefs I inherit from the past help to give shape to my present and influence what I shall be in the future. For instance, if I happen to be born in a state in which higher education is highly respected and provided free to its citizens, then I may form an ambition to go to university which I would not have had if I had lived in a different state in which higher education was not so valued.[16] My decision concerning whether or not to study is thus heavily influenced by the cultural milieu in which I find myself. Importantly, heritage is not limited to the formation of national identity but to individual identity too, and its social and practical implications can be profound.

To investigate the role of heritage in identity formation, Anthony Appiah's (2007: 62–113) proposal for identity formation is a good starting point. According to Appiah, we can distinguish, roughly, three stages in identity formation. Let me start with the first of these. For one to ascribe oneself a social identity, there should be some criteria or qualifying conditions available in public discourse, mutually known, which, if one fulfils, one can then recognise oneself to be part of the social group. These criteria are usually organised around stereotypes and beliefs about how certain members of a social group behave and how they may be distinguished from those who do not share this identity. For immigrants, these criteria might include socialising together with peers from the same nationality, using the language of their home country in preference to the local language or wearing distinctive dress – all factors that may make their communication with locals difficult.[17] If immigrants happen to be refugees they might appear unconfident and traumatised by the long journey they have made, and unsure how to tackle the difficulties of making a new a life in a strange land. Immigrants may share customs and cultural practices which demand certain types of clothing and/or certain work timetables and periods for prayer. The criteria which can be used to define what might be typical for an immigrant are by no means final and predetermined. Their boundaries are negotiable and might differ from place to place. The thread behind them is that they are used, by the immigrants and others, to ascribe membership to a social group. Immigrants in a new country might acknowledge themselves as immigrants according to such criteria as I have sketched, but they also need to be able to use and adapt the cultural heritage they bring with them to smooth their passage into the life of the host country. Identity formation, remember, is a dialogical process between how we perceive ourselves and we are perceived by others in society. This requires that they should maintain a strong self-consciousness of who they already are while they adjust their identity to fit new circumstances.

Part of this process is to communicate what they have inherited from the past. Immigrants are not just a bunch of people who have travelled to a new place for a new life. They come with a certain set of established features. For example, prominent in the heritage of Smyrnian refugees is their characteristic success in running merchant shops and trading in a variety of commodities. This part of their heritage can shape their new life in a particular way, making them much more than merely war refugees (a commonly held belief among Greeks). The memory of successful trading and merchandising can be a guide for their future lives. If they were acknowledged as successful traders in the past, there is hope that they can be successful traders in the future. The memory of the past awakens aspirations which affect positively their new identity and their well-being in the host country. However, a question invites itself here. What happens in cases where immigrants are not in position to recover this part of their heritage, and thus not in a position to import this aspect of their past to their new conditions?[18]

Recall my proposal for the relationship between heritage and participant perspective epistemic injustice. I said earlier that those whose contributions to their own heritage are not taken on board tend to be alienated from their heritage. One of the results of this alienation is to render them effectively absent from the future shaping of their own heritage. This might lead to loss of memory so that applications and uses of their heritage might not be available for future generations of the group. It is the latter that matters for identity formation. If immigrants are not provided with space to retell their story and consider the alternative possibilities offered by their heritage, they lose an important measure of control over the formation of their identity in the new land. Their (re)formation of identity is now severely constrained. For Smyrnians, their traditional role as competent merchants eased their integration and gave them a recognised position in the new society which was forming at the start of the twentieth century in Greece. It is not by accident that the Digital Museum of Smyrna and New Smyrna provides insights into these early Smyrnians' organisation of their social life. Their festivals, their magazine publications of poetry and literature and their own recorded words reveal what comes from their preserved identity as successful merchants (see Figure 9.3). The museum with the active participation of the Smyrna refugee families exhibits for a first time this aspect of their identity as a part of their heritage which made a vital contribution to their well-being.

The consequences of participant perspective epistemic injustice for heritage and identity formation are not limited to the criteria of identity. They extend to the process of internalisation of these criteria, which is the second stage of identity formation. One can identify oneself with a group by thinking of oneself as a member of this group 'in a way that makes a difference'. To think as a member of a particular group one may experience feelings of pride whenever the group or one of its members achieves something important. And one can recognise that being a member of this group means having to fulfil certain obligations which members of this group understand that they owe to each other. For example, acknowledging oneself to be a member of a nation involves acknowledging one has an obligation to behave in a way that does not discredit the nation and its members. There are also obligations of loyalty and solidarity towards members of one's nation.

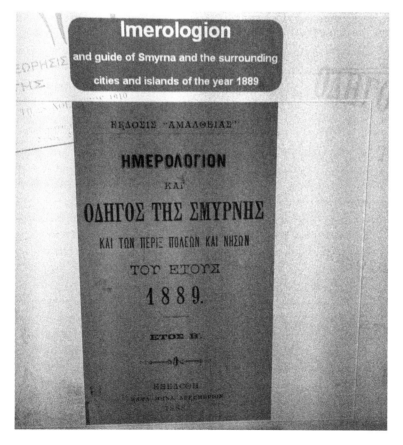

FIGURE 9.3   Digital exhibit of a diary and guide to Smyrna from the Digital Museum of Smyrna and New Smyrna, Athens, Greece. (Photo: author's own)

The internalisation of the conditions of group membership and the patterns of behaviour which are normal to it situate one's personal narrative in regard to the larger stories of the society or the nation. Given that heritage provides continuity between generations, it is not difficult to see how heritage advances the internalisation of such criteria of identity.[19] Immigrants who share the same heritage can acknowledge themselves as people with shared roots and can therefore feel pride or shame for achievements or misdeeds of members their heritage community.

For example, the fact that a member of their social or national group manages to establish a great business endeavour induces pride in being a member of that group. Their common heritage is not only what brings them together but also shapes the patterns of their everyday behaviour. They see their individual life-narratives within a larger narrative of the group. Hence the immigrant who achieves a great business success is not only someone who makes his or her own dream come true but at the same is a source of pride to the whole group. Heritage helps to define the parameters of the larger narratives within which we can identify our own as component parts, but this requires that our participation is not constrained.

Hookway proposed that participants in the exchange of knowledge should ask relevant questions and consider alternative possibilities. The nature, the mode and the tone of questions have an impact on the development of heritage and the selection of possibilities to be considered conditions what is handed down to future generations. If no questions are asked about how immigrants have understood their move from their homeland to the new land, this part of their heritage will probably be forgotten or at least liable to misinterpretation. If heritage contributes to identity formation in the way I explained above, then participation in heritage affects which parts of heritage are the ones which provide reasons for one to be proud of being a member of certain group. Not everything from what is inherited from the past can provide a good basis for the larger narrative to fit one's life. If participation in heritage is not encouraged or is even obstructed, then what counts as one's heritage is defined by others. Furthermore, it may be that the roots of one's identity are obscured. To repeat, the process of identification is a dialogical process. If participation in this dialogue is lacking or impeded, then this process becomes a monologue spoken by others.

Because the museum of Smyrna has been founded on the principle of participation by the Smyrnian refugees, Smyrnians have become very active in its running. Through it, they show clearly what they believe their heritage to be and how it has evolved since they were removed from their beloved city of Smyrna. Another part of their heritage that they have kept alive since that removal is their habit of getting together during certain festivals, a prominent marker of their cultural identity which would certainly not have survived in the absence of their own active participation in keeping that culture alive. More generally, recognising that certain criteria are pertinent to identifying members of a certain group needs to be complemented by patterns of action, including certain patterns of behaviour towards other members of the group. A potential downside of this is that members of an immigrant community may manifest characteristic forms of action that mark them off clearly as immigrants in the eyes of others. Appiah

(2007: 65–70) rightly points out that patterns of behaviour towards others with certain identities are commonly rooted in stereotypes and discrimination. The more they preserve their own identity, the more that identity serves to marginalise them and evokes certain stock responses in other people. This, however, need not always be negative. For instance, if someone identifies you as a member of a religious group, they may respect your piety and loyalty to your faith even though they do not share it.

Once again, those who are encouraged to be participants in their heritage and become actively involved in determining what has been significant within that heritage and how it could develop in the future, also help to steer how they should regarded and consequently treated by others. The Smyrna museum provides an excellent example of how the framework I have just described can work. For their museum, the Smyrnians have chosen to tell the story of two cities. One is the city which was left behind and the other is the new one in which they finally and after long struggles found themselves. The narrative of their heritage acknowledges the painful movement and the nostalgia for the old city; it takes notice of the difficulties the refugees faced in the new land but sees these as themselves being important elements of their heritage; this is what makes them Smyrnians now. Thus, Smyrnians want to be treated according to the new identity they have crafted. They reject the identity of 'no-man's land people', but embrace their sense of being a people who changed their lives by moving from one place to another successfully. This development in their self-conception has been greatly assisted by the museum which has provided them with the space to participate in their heritage, and therefore to tell the story of their new identity. Without being participants in their heritage, the Smyrnians of Athens would have been first and foremost refugees with an identity chosen by others who wanted merely to see and treat them as such.

Notes

1 For a similar point see Miller, David 2016. *Strangers in Our Midst: The Political Philosophy of Immigration.* Oxford: Oxford University Press.
2 See www.coe.int/en/web/culture-and-heritage/faro-convention (Accessed on the 29th of November 2016).
3 See Fricker, Miranda, 2007. *Epistemic Injustice: Power and the Ethics of Knowing.* Oxford: Oxford University Press.
4 For this claim see Cooper, David E. 2006. 'Truthfulness and "Inclusion" in Archaeology', in Chris Scarre and Geoffrey Scarre (eds.) *The Ethics of Archaeology: Philosophical Perspectives on Archaeological Practice.* Cambridge. Cambridge University Press, 131–145.
5 Hookway, Christopher 2010. 'Some Varieties of Epistemic Injustice: Reflections on Fricker, *Episteme* 7: 151–163.
6 Appiah, Anthony 2007. *The Ethics of Identity.* Princeton, NJ: Princeton University Press.
7 Smith's point about the Authorised Heritage Discourse (AHD) shows successfully how expert perception and interpretation of heritage lead to the exclusion of communities from their own heritage. Here, building upon Smith's AHD framework, I highlight the nuances behind the formation of Authorised Heritage Discourse. See Smith, Laurajane 2006. *Uses of Heritage.* London: Routledge.

8 For the relationship between museums, migration and identities see Whitehead, Christopher, Lloyd, Katherine, Eckersley, Susannah and Mason, Rhianon (eds.) 2015. *Museums, Migration and Identity in Europe: Peoples, Places and Identities*. Abington: Ashgate.

9 The title of the museum guide booklet is *Panorama de Smyrne, Digital Museum of Smyrna and New Smyrna.*

10 For more see: www.smyrnimuseum.gr (Accessed on the 16th of December 2016).

11 For an informed account of Smyrna's fascinating life see Mansel, Philip 2012. *Levant: Splendour and Catastrophe on the Mediterranean.* Yale: Yale University Press.

12 I would like to remind the reader here that my purpose is not to present an argument for the role of museums in the formation of migrants' new identity or the role of museums in the construction of memory and the distribution of knowledge. My purpose is to argue for the relation between participant perspective epistemic injustice and the formation of migrants' new identity in relation to cultural heritage.

13 For the victims of hermeneutical injustice self-knowledge is at risk because they are not aware that they lack these conceptual resources. For instance, if one lacks the concept of exploitation, one is maybe unable to communicate when and for how long one has been exploited in cases where one is asked if one has been a victim of exploitation. So, one cannot provide any information about whether one is exploited or not because one lacks the understanding of what it means to be exploited.

14 David Cooper (2006) explains sufficiently this occurrence of epistemic injustice arguing that it is not without difficulties to accept non-experts accounts for the interpretation of the past.

15 www.coe.int/en/web/culture-and-heritage/faro-convention (Accessed on the 29th of November 2016).

16 Annette Baier discusses how future generations inherit social structures such as higher education from past generations. See Baier, Annette 2009. *Reflections on How We Live.* Oxford: Oxford University Press. 1–16.

17 A stereotype rooted in the use of local knowledge can be that newcomers are not competent to talk our language and this can always lead to trouble.

18 One should bear in mind that not all characteristic of 'a people' should be recovered given that there are aspects of identity which are related to what might be perceived as dissonant heritage. For instance, if you are a German and you happen to think of German heritage of running effectively concentration camps in the time of the Holocaust, then to sustain this aspect of your heritage as part of your identity is not tantamount to an ethical outlook. I am grateful to my co-editor Cornelius Holtorf for this example.

19 For example, a commonly held belief among Greeks is that they are good at enduring difficult times and they proudly refer to parts of their heritage such as their struggles for freedom and prosperity over the years. One of their characteristics which is shaped by their heritage is that they have developed an attitude of persistence and resistance against difficulties.

References

Appiah, Anthony. 2007. *The Ethics of Identity*. Princeton, NJ: Princeton University Press.

Baier, Annete. 2009. *Reflections on How We Live*. Oxford: Oxford University Press, 1–16.

Cooper, David E. 2006. 'Truthfulness and "Inclusion" in Archaeology', in Chris Scarre and Geoffrey Scarre (eds.) *The Ethics of Archaeology: Philosophical Perspectives on Archaeological Practice*. Cambridge. Cambridge University Press, 131–145.

Fricker, Miranda. 2007. *Epistemic Injustice: Power and the Ethics of Knowing*. Oxford: Oxford University Press.

Hookway, Christopher. 2010. 'Some Varieties of Epistemic Injustice: Reflections on Fricker', *Episteme* 7: 151–163.

Miller, David. 2016. *Strangers in Our Midst: The Political Philosophy of Immigration*. Oxford: Oxford University Press.

Smith, Laurajane. 2006. *Uses of Heritage*. London: Routledge.

Pantazatos, Andreas. 2017. 'Epistemic Injustice in Archaeology and Cultural Heritage', in I.J. Kidd, J. Medina, and G. Pollhaus (eds.) *Routledge Handbook to Epistemic Injustice* (London and New York: Routledge).

Pantazatos, Andreas. 2016. 'The Ethics of Trusteeship and the Biography of Objects' in *Philosophy* supp. 79: 179–198.

Whitehead, Christopher, Lloyd, Katherine, Eckersley, Susannah and Mason, Rhianon (eds.) 2015. *Museums, Migration and Identity in Europe: Peoples, Places and Identities*. Abingdon, UK: Ashgate.

PART III

Cultural heritage as an agent of integration

10

WHAT IS CROSS-CULTURAL HERITAGE?

Challenges in identifying the heritage of globalized citizens

Laia Colomer and Cornelius Holtorf

Introduction: heritage in a globalized world

Cultural heritage has long been linked to an essentializing notion of culture which bundles together ethnicity, collective identity, territory and the idea of a common origin and shared past. In this framework, which has been dominating mainstream heritage discourses since their emergence in the 19th century, cultural heritage is the visible manifestation of a shared cultural history and common collective identity which the members in a given ethnic group or nation ascribe to themselves. When members of such tightly connected cultural groups get dispersed from their land of origin their cultural identity can nevertheless stay alive. In the diaspora, the culture of the homeland, including movable parts of its heritage, can survive even though the location is now different. This essentializing understanding of culture and heritage often creates divisions between "us" (we who share a given heritage) and "them" (they who do not share this heritage). The results are processes of exclusion or outright conflict when a sense of collective identity and shared heritage is equated with a claim to ownership of a given territory, as we have been witnessing many times during the 19th, 20th and 21st centuries (Kohl and Fawcett 1995; Meskell 1998).

Today, our world has been transformed by processes of globalization and an emerging global heritage revolves around a new agenda of social, political, cultural and ethical issues (Meskell 2015, Harrison 2015, Biehl et al. 2015). One of the factors contributing to this trend is an increasing number of people migrating between world regions, whether as refugees, for work or for family reasons. As a result, cultural homogeneity in many contemporary nation-states is decreasing. Current residents may be permanent or temporary, have citizenship of one or more countries, follow any of a range of religions (or none), use several languages, and practice traditions of every description. In a world in movement and societies

FIGURE 10.1 Cultural heritage in a world in movement. *Portable City-Shenzhen,* installation of suitcase, used clothes, light, map, sound, 148 × 88 × 30 cm, 2008, © Yin Xuizhen. Reproduced with permission of the artist

with a high degree of cultural diversity, a cultural heritage that remains exclusive to distinct cultural groups has lost the integrating function which once gave it legitimacy in the nation-state (Figure 10.1). Cultural heritage no longer has the ability to provide territorially-defined nation-states with distinctive identities and narratives for their citizens to feel a sense of unity. We may sometimes speak of "multi-cultural societies" as if they offered a kind of overarching unity but in many cases contemporary societies are in fact increasingly divided and lack much cohesion and integration (Kalra et al. 2005; Ashworth et al. 2007). Cultural heritage, as we know it, is not able to provide a sense of unity to integrate the diverse collective identities in multi-cultural societies. Indeed, as the social anthropologist Sharon Macdonald (2013: 162) put it, it is at this point unclear "whether it is possible to draw on memory and heritage to form new identity stories that include rather than exclude cultural diversity and 'mixed' culture."

If we wish to retain cultural heritage as a legitimate concern which serves all citizens and residents, there are two principal ways out of this dilemma. One way forward is to emphasize transnational, cosmopolitan, and universal dimensions of heritage. Macdonald (2013: ch. 8) discussed at length a growing "cosmopolitanisation of memory" with the Holocaust and associated memorials and museums throughout Europe as well as in the US and Israel as the most significant example. Yet despite cosmopolitan developments, Macdonald found that the nation nevertheless remained significant in heritage discourses related to commemorating the

Holocaust. Another focus on cultural heritage that is significant to, and shared by, all human beings is evident, for example, in the thinking that lies behind UNESCO's World Heritage list. The World Heritage Convention (UNESCO 1972) recognizes that responsibility for heritage lies with the States Parties to the Convention but it also states that "parts of the cultural or natural heritage are of outstanding interest and therefore need to be preserved as part of the world heritage of mankind as a whole" and that the "deterioration or disappearance of any item of the cultural or natural heritage constitutes a harmful impoverishment of the heritage of all the nations of the world", so that there is a need "for all the peoples of the world, of safeguarding this unique and irreplaceable property, to whatever people it may belong". This so-called World Heritage is selected by experts and States Parties representatives on the grounds of "outstanding universal value", thus intended to transcend any national or ethnic significance (see also Labadi 2013). However, critical observers argued that the application of seemingly global categories such as "outstanding universal value" is actually based on Western notions of heritage and its appropriate management (Smith 2006, Smith & Akagawa 2009, Labadi & Long 2010, Harrison 2013, 2015). These unfulfilled universalist aspirations have been recognized even within UNESCO and those implementing the World Heritage Convention but there are no easy solutions in a context inherently shaped by 20th century Western thinking and owned by the UN's united nation-states.

A second way forward is to identify and promote the use of heritage by "heritage communities" that are not linked to essentializing notions of culture. The idea of heritage communities was first suggested in the 2005 Faro Convention of the Council of Europe which adopted a people-centered perspective and established that heritage must have a value to everyday public life, for example in terms of values, identity, social integration, and economic sustainability. Heritage communities consist of "people who value specific aspects of cultural heritage which they wish, within the framework of public action, to sustain and transmit to future generations" (Council of Europe 2005: Article 2b). These people may be unrelated in terms of territory, cultural background, place of residence or social context but nevertheless form a distributed community. According to the Faro Convention, such heritage communities have "the right to benefit from the cultural heritage and to contribute towards its enrichment" while at the same time sharing "the responsibility to respect the cultural heritage of others as much as their own heritage" (Council of Europe 2005: Article 4). In this sense, a heritage community is not defined exclusively in terms of place, ethnic identity, and sense of belonging but by cultural attachment more generally (Council of Europe 2009). Heritage communities require for their social identity a sense of historical continuity not necessarily linked to a national past (Reicher 2008). Even though the Faro Convention aims to go beyond cultural essentialism, it remains poorly understood in the heritage sector how to address the variety of (sometimes conflicting) needs and desires of different heritage communities (Colomer 2014; see also Waterton 2015 and Lafrenz Samuels 2015: 13–18).

A perspective on heritage that focuses on people rather than things also raises ethical questions in relation to the methods applied in heritage management. Considering the ethical implications of implementing the Faro Convention among minorities and disenfranchized groups, John Schofield called for the inclusion in the heritage sector of social scientists and anthropologists trained in social engagement (2015: 207). By the same token, we suggest that an approach foregrounding heritage communities should lead to the adoption of participatory methodologies, a field largely known in community development (e.g. McIntyre 2008), in participatory budgeting (e.g. Sintomer & Ganuza 2011, Wainwright 2009), education (e.g. Somekh 2005), among many other social sciences (see Reason and Bradbury 2008), including more recently archaeology and cultural heritage (McGhee 2012, Waterton 2015). Participatory action research goes beyond engaging communities or involving stakeholders in democratizing cultural heritage practices. It provides opportunities for co-developing research processes *with* people rather than about or for people. This means that the aim of the inquiry and the research questions develop out of the convergence of two perspectives, that of science and of practice, and that there is a major interest in social change rather than exclusively on scientific research (Bergold and Thomas 2012, Reason and Bradbury 2008). In this sense, action research is not neutral. The application of applied research methodologies is, however, not exempt from ethical scrutiny. Emma Waterton (2015) points out two issues when exploring critically what "community engagement" may mean. First, she notices the necessity to ask who accounts for the "community", as it may include a fuller range of groups that exists within the broader network or assemblage of people, each of them with their own interests but also altogether holding their own relations of power and values (see also Pyburn 2011). Second, we may also focus on the ethical and socio-political arena within which the research is carried out and ask about the project's accountability, questioning the frames of inquiry and the outcomes of social change and practical knowledge (see also Hamilakis 2007).

In the heritage context, early examples of participatory decision-making processes featured in the 1979 Australian International Council on Monuments and Sites (ICOMOS) Burra Charter which placed the local communities at the center of the heritage management process by putting communities of stakeholders in charge of defining the cultural significance of historical places (Sullivan 1997; ICOMOS Australia 2000; Greer, Harrison & McIntyre-Tamowoy 2002). Similar approaches have subsequently been developed in the context of community participation. Here archaeology is practiced for people rather than on people, with participants from the community becoming collaborators rather than research subjects (Hollowell & Nicholas 2009, Pyburn 2009, Neal 2015, Chitty 2017; cf. Holtorf 2007). This chapter discusses these issues in relation to one potential heritage community, the so-called "Third Culture Kids" (TCKs, after Pollock and van Reken 2009). It is based on a pilot study among a selected number of TCKs. This pilot study was framed in a qualitative, participative research strategy (Bergold & Thomas 2012) and aims to be fully implemented in forthcoming research by Laia

Colomer. The research aims at defining the cultural heritage of people with cross-cultural lives and will involve the research partners in the knowledge-production process. Ultimately our chapter contributes to a discussion of a need to think about heritage differently in our time and relates to an existing discussion of New Heritage (Holtorf 2017 and Fairclough 2013).

The cultural heritage of TCKs

TCKs are children who spend a significant part of their formative years outside their parents' native culture(s) and during that time live in several countries other than their passport countries. While abroad they acquire meaningful relations with those other cultures. The term Third Culture Kids was first coined by Ruth Useem in the 1950s and popularized by Pollock and van Reken after publishing *Third Culture Kids. Growing Up Among Worlds* (2009). Today, it is the most accepted term to define this particular population of global citizens.

Traditionally, TCKs represent expatriate groups like members of the Foreign Service, corporate or military "brats" or missionaries. Today, TCKs include increasing numbers of children of families living abroad due to career choices in a globalized labor market (e.g. researchers and academics, skilled workers and individual entrepreneurs, NGO employees, international journalists, international school educators, athletes, etc.) or simply independent and adventuresome families. Unlike most immigrants who for some reason move to another culture so that their children are experiencing a constant dichotomy between the culture of origin and the culture in which they grow up, TCKs grow up in several different cultures moving each time their parents move. For example, one interviewee of the study introduced later, had moved from Belgium to Botswana, Sweden, England, China, and the USA. During this process, TCKs are exposed to many different cultures so that, arguably, as adults they embody globalism and multiculturalism. Kalra et al. (2005: 111–15) pointed out however that we should not overlook the fact that TCKs, unlike many contemporary migrants, are often privileged white children of "expats" that move out of choice rather than necessity. Nevertheless, the emergence and growth of this community of "global nomads" (Schaetti & Ramsey 1999) may very well constitute a prototype of global citizens of future decades: in an increasingly globalized world affected by all kinds of international migrations, a childhood lived in, among, and between different cultural realities may one day be the norm rather than the exception for many people (see also Friedman 2007).

In their ground-breaking study on TCKs, Pollock and van Reken (2009: Part II) discussed a variety of life experiences which TCKs share, and how these experiences provide both benefits and obstacles. Whereas among the benefits are a large cultural and social flexibility and adaptability, a global perspective, and personal skills such as the ability to learn languages quickly and to act as cultural mediators, there is also a downside resulting from the repeated experience of dislocation, grief, and loss. TCKs often feel restless and rootless. They also tend to feel marginal in relation to the dominant culture at their place of residence, being very conscious of their particular psychological, sociological and cultural reality in-between cultures and they may experience "cultural homelessness" (Vivero and Jenkins 1999). As one adult TCK described her situation:

> One can draw key third culture kids characteristics out of my experiences: dislocation, feeling perpetually like an outsider, difficulties with national-cultural identity development, being invisible immigrant once repatriated to my "home" nation, and having my past add up to a succession of losses of places and people.
>
> (Rauwerda 2012: 3)

The single question TCKs dread most is "Where do you come from?" because they do not know exactly what the question is supposed to refer to: their current home, place(s) of upbringing, passport issuing country, family background, or cultural identification(s)? A typical answer by a TCK to the question might be: *"I'm living and working now in New York. but I was born in Nigeria and I was raised in Nigeria, Sweden, Burkina Faso and Vietnam. I went to college in the US".* It becomes clear from this example why TCKs often lack a clear sense of origin, cultural affiliation, geographical attachment, and collective identity. Since TCKs move frequently, they have a different sense of belonging compared to those citizens that are raised in a single culture or immigrants that live under bicultural conditions. Interestingly, their inability to give a straightforward answer to the seemingly straightforward question of their country of origin acts as a cultural marker by which TCKs often recognize each other and thus feel a sense of community.

TCKs are simultaneously belonging "everywhere and nowhere", which gives them the impression that they are lacking full cultural ownership. In this sense, TCKs are raised in a neither/nor world: it is neither fully the cultural world(s) of their parents nor fully the cultural world of the countries in which they were born, nor an amalgamation of the various cultures in which they have been raised (Kalra et al. 2005: 112; Pollock and van Reken 2009). TCKs distinguish themselves from other migrant/expat and diaspora communities in terms of mobility and globality. Their defining feature is that they are serially moving from one country to another, around the world. As a result, their sense of belonging relates neither to *any one* culture nor to *all* cultures experienced. They are rootless and restless, and TCKs invariably recognize these terms as part their personal life experiences (Pollock and van Reken 2009: ch. 9).

This TCK profile is challenging traditional views in social psychology (regarding place attachment, place identity, and sense of belonging; see Lewicka 2011). But it also challenges heritage studies: what is the heritage of citizens whose collective identity is not based on a sense of ethnic or geographical belonging? To date, a consideration of TCKs' collective identity and heritage, i.e. the way in which TCKs recruit reminders of the past in forming their collective identity, is notably absent in the existing academic literature about TCKs, including Pollock and van

Reken's ground-breaking study. In this paper, we are seeking a better understanding of how members of the community of former TCKs, now adults, identify and give meaning to cultural heritage. We are interested in investigating how a community belongs if it lives everywhere and comes from nowhere.

Which heritage is relevant to TCKs?

The cultural identity of TCKs might be a mix of memories, images, and skills from different cultures and places without drawing exclusively on any single culture or region. Alternatively, there might be a distinct and up until now unstudied, specific heritage of nomad citizens.

In order to gain more understanding of this matter, Laia Colomer developed a pilot survey for adult TCKs, aiming to get a sense of the TCK community's relation to cultural heritage. The study had two goals. The first was to investigate the relationship between TCKs and the dominant cultural heritage surrounding them: to what extent, and in what way, is the officially recognized cultural heritage meaningful to former TCKs? The second was to find out whether adult TCKs have their own, distinct cultural heritage, for example by giving meaning to artefacts, traditions, and places that in their respective countries are either not at all or for different reasons recognized as cultural heritage.

The potential interviewees for the pilot survey were selected among TCKs active in social media and contacted through social media or via email. For heuristic purposes particularly active and reflective individuals were selected, some with a professional background in the social studies and humanities. In total, 30 adult TCKs were contacted, with a return rate of 37 percent (11 filled in questionnaires). The following discussion is based on these data. Due to the small size of the sample, we did not assume that the results were fully representative of the totality of TCKs, but they nevertheless were indicative of some trends that are worth discussing now, before further research allows more conclusive results in the future.

The TCKs had lived during their childhoods in some four to five countries, including Canada, China, Botswana, Hong Kong, Brazil, Philippines, Iran, Sweden, Switzerland, Ghana, Cameroon, Lebanon, Ethiopia, Luxemburg, Vietnam, Germany, France, Saudi Arabia, England, US, Belgium, and The Netherlands. They were fluent in three to four languages. In most cases, their parents shared with each other the same passport and are/were not TCKs themselves.

Nomadic heritage

As far as the relation between the interviewees and the cultural heritage in the places they grew up in is concerned (Question 1), all interviewees responded that they recognized that cultural heritage was part of their cultural identity and stated that it was important for their personal and cultural identity. All of them referred to intangible elements of culture (e.g. social behaviors and values, local customs, cultural traditions) that were connected to their personal memories:

> I was deeply influenced by the country but mainly in terms of my social values and behaviours [. . .] I developed a strong sense of community and touchy-feely friendships, for example.
>
> *(Anonymous respondent PS04, referring to Brazil)*

Many also referred to natural conditions (e.g. heat, smell of the air) or particular landscapes (e.g. specific locations, natural features) as something that provided pleasant memories of their upbringing and made them feel cozy, comfortable, or homey:

> Pavements on the streets in Iran, doorbells and some food odours . . .
>
> *(Anonymous respondent PS05)*

> . . . it feels like that climate shaped me: that climate [in Singapore] is what I am most comfortable in . . .
>
> *(Anonymous respondent PS01)*

Recurrent is also the mention of food, particular dishes or cuisine:

> We eat Dutch pancakes and Swiss fondue on a regular basis . . .
>
> *(Anonymous respondent PS02)*

> It is in the food I crave, the jokes I compose, the things that trigger my memories of *home* . . .
>
> *(Anonymous respondent PS08 with emphasis given by interviewee)*

In two cases, the parents tried to maintain their own cultural roots by creating a cultural family identity that followed the family to every country they lived in:

> My parents are fully Lebanese, so even though I spent almost my entire childhood growing up in other countries, the habits and customs of my family and country follow me [. . .] I identify with the customs of the people and the places that make my country of origin special, like the landmarks and historical sites such as the Roman ruins of Baalbek or the palace of Beit et-Dein . . .
>
> *(Anonymous respondent PS05)*

In sum, when it comes to their own heritage and identity, TCKs often but not always mention memories of intangible phenomena related to values and local customs including particular food dishes, tastes, and smells. The two interviewees for whom tangible heritage was significant were those whose families had made a conscious effort to retain their cultural roots.

World heritage

Do TCKs have a special relationship to UNESCO World Heritage sites? Most of the interviewees did not recognize any WH sites in the countries they had lived during their childhood and they did not think either that WH sites were, or could be, especially significant for TCKs:

> [Q2] No, I didn't recognise any of the places; [. . . Q3] . . . they weren't part of my upbringing . . .
>
> *(Anonymous respondent PS03)*

> [Q2] Having visited some of them in Iran, I sometimes I felt like an outsider looking at my favorite place, not really belonging (or wanting to belong?) . . .
>
> *(Anonymous respondent PS05)*

> [Q2] Don't know of any UNESCO's sites in places that I've lived . . .
>
> *(Anonymous respondent PS07)*

> [Q2] No. They have no significance to my heritage and thus don't affect my cultural identity . . .
>
> *(Anonymous respondent PS09)*

None of the interviewees mentioned any UNESCO intangible cultural heritage from the countries in which they had lived.

In sum, no respondents, with the exception of the two families maintaining roots, mentioned a connection to the identity of TCKs nor any recognized local, national, or international cultural heritage. Therefore, it seems that we need to acknowledge that among the TCKs interviewed there is actually a detachment from presently existent expressions of cultural heritage. None of the ordinary forms of defining local, national, or indeed global heritage, both tangible and intangible, appear to be significant to the interviewees.

Towards TCK heritage

Could there be a definable TCK heritage based on tangible or intangible cultural elements that is not normally recognized as cultural heritage, or at least not for this reason, but might be seen by the TCKs as defining and representing their community? Are TCKs a heritage community in the sense of the Faro Convention? Two questions were asked, one open and one with a number of suggested answers that had been derived from the literature and one in-depth interview with a TCK in Stockholm in April 2014. The range of answers to the open question is assorted but again intangible elements are more relevant than tangible ones. One characteristic answer was this:

> Tangible: Passports and Visas, IB exams or O and A level exams, currencies, foods, airports, moving boxes. Intangible: feeling unrooted or homeless/at home everywhere, being adept at understanding what other people mean, even if you don't speak the other person's language . . .
>
> *(Anonymous respondent PS01)*

The answers contain shared abilities learned, elements of a collective identity, and shared memories. At the same time, the answers prove how difficult it is for respondents to move both from the personal situation to the collective, and from the psychological to the anthropological and sociological spheres. Some even sincerely answered, "I do not understand the question". Future research will have to use questions that are easier to understand and better formulated for generating answers to the questions at hand. When asked to rate particular cultural elements that might be significant for TCK collective identity and heritage, the answers were clear and given seemingly effortlessly (see Figure 10.2).

"Family" is very important for TCKs' particular cultural identity. Arguably, the family replaces the stable home which for many TCKs does not physically exist. There is no single place to which family memories are attached, such as permanent residences, summer houses and their surroundings, or landmarks of the city. This is a typical reflection:

> Going back home didn't mean going back home; it meant moving to a new place, and to realise that what was defined as home wasn't home . . .
>
> *(Anonymous respondent PS11)*

For TCKs, "home" is not tangible but intangible; it has always been where the "family" lived at any point in time. In this way, the family itself became this

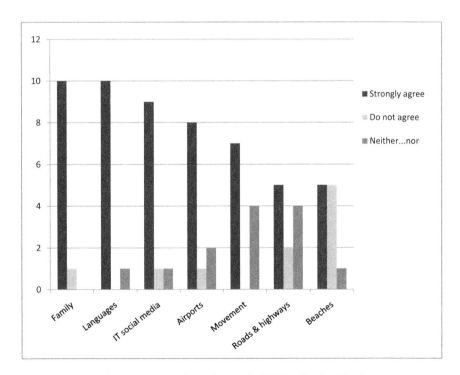

FIGURE 10.2 Cultural elements of significance for TCK collective identity

desired "place", providing personal security and becoming a tangible signifier of everything that "home" is for non-TCKs.

"Languages" are equally significant for TCK identity. During their childhoods, learning languages was a basic communication requirement that allowed them to fit into continuously changing circumstances and blend into all the cultures in which they found themselves. Languages also helped them to develop multi-cultural abilities and aptitudes during their adulthood. Moreover, languages are seen by TCKs not merely as a tool but as a way of developing their personal identity. This is well expressed here:

> Different parts of myself [operate] in different languages because I would, I do, I discuss things differently in different languages [. . .] Germany is a language to argue (. . .). I think about or write down something about my feelings in Italian [. . .]. I used to say that English is a language to communicate [. . .]. So I need to speak all languages to feel complete . . .
>
> *(Anonymous respondent PS11)*

"IT/social media" are the means that allow TCKs to keep in touch with friends, schoolmates, and relatives spread all around the world. Electronic mail, Facebook, Skype, and other communication media have become useful tools for global citizens due to their capacity to bridge large distances, and their significance for TCK identity is not surprising. It would be interesting to analyse in the future how exactly IT/social media are contributing to the TCK community by developing a sense of (heritage) community.

Interesting is an emerging significance for TCK identity of cultural elements such as "airports", "roads & highways" and "movement", the first two being material expressions of the last. Constantly described in TCKs' personal stories, "movement" represents TCK's lives most of all: the consequence of, and metaphor for their de-territorialized, global, displaced, and dislocated lives:

> I think [TCK] is a culture where movement is normal, while for the rest [of people] it is something special . . .
>
> *(Anonymous respondent PS11)*

"Airports" and "roads & highways" are the places where "movement" takes place, where all personal and collective stories and memories begin, end, and start again. However, one respondent (PS08) who had mainly moved in African countries, noticed that besides roads and highways we would need to consider even more types of paths . . . more suitable for non-Western geographies. The hubs and paths of movement may be the most evident physical places significant for TCKs' collective identity and indeed particular sites of memory for TCKs as a heritage community. Whereas Marc Augé (2006) famously argued that airports are non-places, we may consider that for TCKs they are among the most significant places in their lives and can even be described as "homes", familiar places where TCKs feel comfortable, secure, "in-place", and related to their past, present, and future (see also Iyer 2000: 67). Therefore, it may be worth considering "movement's hubs and paths" as places of collective memory (i.e. sites of memory), and therefore as potential heritage places significant to the TCK heritage community. Characteristic is the following description of a TCK's emotions when traveling:

> . . . generally when I move which is also connected to flying, then I feel calm, and it is always the moment where I can think [. . .] it is the calming moment because I don't need to move: something is moving me [. . .] Wait! I cannot say that I do not feel any attachment: to Germany's highways actually!
>
> *(Anonymous respondent PS11)*

Finally, even "beaches" had significance for some TCKs who saw them as gates of departure to another place. One anonymous TCK stated on his blog that beaches are places that exist between other places. But it has to be said that for most of the interviewees they were the least significant cultural element offered.

In relation to the final question, when asked about the potential benefit of a distinct TCK cultural heritage as a tool for establishing their collective identity and improving their quality of life, most respondents saw a potential but they also had doubts:

> I think by identifying the cultural heritage of TCKs we can help people, especially young people, to understand that their cultural identity can be incredibly strong not in spite of their global upbringing but because of their cultural upbringing . . .
>
> *(Anonymous respondent PS02)*

> I do not know. It is a tough subject because not all TCKs will have had the same exact experience, just similar ones. I don't know of it is even possible for all TCKs to identify with a cultural heritage. I think it will help as a start-off point to better establish the collective identity . . .
>
> *(Anonymous respondent PS10)*

Conclusion: towards a cross-cultural heritage

The aim of this pilot study was both to gain a general sense of the relevance of recognized cultural heritage to TCKs, and to find out whether TCKs have their own distinct cultural heritage that lies beyond the dominant heritage. For TCKs who are global citizens and have cross-cultural lives, the national heritage managed in the world's nation-states does not make much sense:

> I feel that the cultural heritage of TCKs is the ability to draw on the global human experience and be comfortable with that, rather than trying to limit heritage to a place or people . . .
>
> *(Anonymous respondent PS04)*

TCKs lack an attachment to national identities and their ideological discourses, and consequently to the cultural metaphors and messages that national heritage expresses. This is perhaps not surprising. Inherently exclusive in character and not necessarily significant to everybody, national cultural heritage is not best placed "to organize diversity within a global community" (Lafrenz Samuels & Lilley 2015: 217). But TCKs seem to feel detached also from UNESCO World Heritage sites, even though these places are supposed to possess "universal value" and are "to be preserved as part of the world heritage of mankind as a whole" (UNESCO 1972). One reason for this may be the fact that the universal values acknowledged by UNESCO are actually rather Western in character, far removed from notions of heritage common in non-western cultures and indigenous communities and therefore anything but truly global (Labadi & Long 2010, Smith 2006, Askew 2010, Harrison 2015). The results of our pilot study suggest that a similar detachment from seemingly universal heritage can also be found among citizens with cross-cultural life experiences. Further research will need to explore the reasons and conditions of this disengagement, but we suspect that part of the answer may have been expressed above by the anonymous respondent PS04 who desired an acknowledgment in heritage of a shared "global human experience" (i.e. a cosmopolitan dimension of what it means to be human).

A particularly interesting result of our survey is that TCKs not only have difficulties fitting into the Authorised Heritage Discourse, but also to imagine their own, alternative forms and expressions of heritage. When confronted with questions on cultural heritage, the TCKs in this study tended to employ common and traditional concepts of culture and heritage, those learned as children and subsequently naturalized. But these concepts do not match the reality of TCKs, which is movable and transitory, whereas for non-TCKs it is usually fixed and stable. John Schofield has been concerned with discrimination that common terminology about heritage and methodologies such as questionnaires (rather than interviews) impose on marginal groups. Members in such groups may not only be suspicious of all references to authority but also disadvantaged through their poor education (real or imagined) that makes written questionnaires a challenge (2015: 206; see also Schofield 2014). But for the generally well-educated TCKs of middle-upper class backgrounds the problem is not one of understanding concepts but the impossibility of moving creatively away from them: heritage terminology still has semantic weight in the Authorised Heritage Discourse and is difficult to escape from in order to be able to formulate other visions of heritage beside monuments, landscapes, and artefacts of "historical interest". The fact that TCKs do not relate very well to conventional forms of cultural heritage does not mean that the task of defining cultural heritage for this community is either unnecessary or impossible. It is only that current notions of heritage cannot accommodate cultural identities in a flow and therefore do not encompass the realities of nomad citizens. In a world increasingly affected by migration, mobility, dislocations, and multicultural values, it is not only valuable but ethically necessary to explore which alternative forms of cultural heritage may be more suitable and appropriate to the TCK heritage community. Movement, airports, roads & highways, home, and family have been preliminarily recognized here as relevant components of TCK collective identity and heritage. The ability of speaking several languages can be seen as part of the acquired competence of TCKs in intercultural communication and the relevance of information and communication technology is arguably nothing else but an adaptation for a well-educated community spread-out globally to the conditions of the network society.

In the future, in order to understand better the significance of heritage outside the heritage sector we will need to design other forms of engagement and be open to give significance to other forms of heritage perceptions. As Schofield noticed (2015: 207), this will need to include other research practices designed to give a voice to people's own perceptions of "the iconic *and* the everyday". The role of experts will be as "facilitators" (Thomas 2008 cited in Schofield 2014; see also Smith at al. 2003, Holtorf 2007). Closely aligned to this, we encourage here the use of qualitative methods to be applied in participative workshops that allow the creation of "spaces of encounter" where notions and issues of heritage can be jointly discussed with heritage communities (after Ganuza et al. 2010). In the case of the globally dispersed TCKs, any such participative workshops will need to expand techniques using Web 2.0 tools and social media networking (e.g. Twitter, Facebook; see also Giaccardi 2012; see also Bouvier 2015).

As we argued earlier, people with cross-cultural life experiences may be the prototype for future citizens. Therefore, it is worth asking now how cross-cultural life experiences are affecting current perceptions of cultural identity and cultural heritage. The present chapter contributes towards this aim by studying first how the community of TCKs relates, or rather fails to relate its collective identity to the dominant heritage recognized and managed in its surrounding culture. Second, the chapter also discusses to what extent TCKs can be considered as a heritage community (in the sense of the Faro Convention) and presents an initial investigation of the significance for TCKs of certain alternative forms of cultural heritage, some of which challenge conventional views of cultural heritage. In doing so, we are advocating an approach to heritage that, partly for ethical reasons, demanding an inclusive approach and considering everybody's perspectives, gives room to other forms of heritage that are meaningful to some people's present experiences and their collective memories (after Smith 2006, Meskell 2010 and Schofield 2015).

Cross-cultural heritage proves to be a key case exemplifying the emergence of a "New Heritage". New Heritage is not about what is left from the past and how to manage it but about people's values, interpretations, uses, and benefits of heritage in society (Holtorf and Fairclough 2013). New Heritage dwells much less on traditionally recognized objects of heritage, and their assumed intrinsic worth, and much more on the meanings and interpretations which people invest in heritage and thus with their lives today. Underlying this is a view of heritage as a particular form of interaction between people and their world and between different people, evoking the past and its remains in specific social contexts. Our emerging understanding of TCKs' cross-cultural heritage is an understanding of one particular community of people and their place in the world. In addition, cross-cultural heritage also exemplifies the possibilities and challenges of community participation in heritage management. In doing so, it challenges the ethics of decision-making about what heritage is and why it matters. Cross-cultural heritage, therefore, requests new ways of imagining and thinking about heritage that are meaningful to global and multicultural citizens in our time.

Acknowledgments

The authors would like to thank Ian Lilley for his comments and Yin Xuizhen for permission to depict her artwork. Laia Colomer would like to thank all the participants that responded to the pilot survey about the significance of cultural heritage to TCKs, whose comments and observations not only provided the basis of this paper but also enriched her views on global nomads and cultural heritage. The research of Laia Colomer on *Cross-cultural heritage: Understanding cultural heritage in a globalised world* has been supported by funding from the European Union's Horizon 2020 Research and Innovation Programme under the Marie Skłodowska-Curie grant agreement No. 658760.

References

Ashworth, G.J., Graham, B. & Tunbridge, J.E. 2007. *Pluralising Pasts: Heritage, Identity and Place in Multicultural Societies*. Pluto Press. London.

Askew, M. 2010. "The magic list of global status: UNESCO, World Heritage and the agendas of states", in S. Labadi & C. Long (eds.) *Heritage and Globalisation*. Routledge, London, pp.19–44.

Augé, M. 2006. *Non-places: Introduction to an Anthropology of Supermodernity*. Verso. London.

Bergold, J. & Thomas, S. 2012. "Participatory research methods: a methodological approach in motion", *Forum: Qualitative Social Research*, 13(1), Article 30. Available online: www.qualitative-research.net/index.php/fqs/article/view/1801

Biehl, P.F., Comer, D.C., Prescott, C. & Soderland, H.A. (eds.) 2015. *Identity and Heritage: Contemporary Challenges in a Globalized World*. Springer. New York and London.

Bouvier, G. 2015. "What is a discourse approach to Twitter, Facebook, YouTube and other social media: connecting with other academic fields?", *Journal of Multicultural Discourses*, 10(2): 149–162. DOI: 10.1080/17447143.2015.1042381.

Chitty, G. (ed.) 2017. *Heritage, Conservation and Communities: Engagement, Participation and Capacity Building*. Routledge. London.

Colomer, L. 2014. "The politics of human remains in managing archaeological Medieval Jewish burial grounds in Europe", *Nordisk Kulturpolitisk Tidsskrift*, 17(2): 168–186. Available online: www.idunn.no/nkt/2014/02/the_politics_of_human_remains_in_managing_archaeological_me

Council of Europe 2005. *Framework Convention on the Value of Cultural Heritage for Society* ["The Faro Convention"], European Treaty Series 199, Strasbourg.

Council of Europe (ed.) 2009. *Heritage and Beyond*. Council of Europe Publishing. Strasbourg. Available online: www.coe.int/en/web/culture-and-heritage/faro-action-plan

Friedman J. 2007. "Cosmopolitan elites, organic intellectuals and the re-configuration of the state", in A. Kouvouama, A. Gueye, A. Piriou & A.C. Wagner (eds.) *Figures croisées d'intellectuels*. Paris: Karthala, pp. 431–454.

Ganuza, E., Olivari, L., Paño, P., Butriago, L. & Lorenzana, C. 2010. *La democracia participativa en acción. Una visión desde las metodologías participativas.* Antígona. Madrid.

Giaccardi, E. (ed.) 2012. *Heritage and Social Media: Understanding Heritage in a Participatory Culture.* Routledge. London and New York.

Greer, S., Harrison, R. & McIntyre-Tamowoy, S. 2002 "Community-based archaeology in Australia", *World Archaeology*, 34(2): 265–287.

Hamilakis, Y. 2007. "From ethics to politics", in Y. Hamilakis and P. Duke (eds.) *Archaeology and Capitalism. From Ethics to Politics.* Left Coast Press. Walnut Creek, pp. 15–40.

Harrison, R. 2013. *Heritage: Critical Approaches.* Routledge. Abingdon and New York.

Harrison, R. 2015. "Heritage and globalization", in E. Waterton & S. Watson (eds.) *The Palgrave Handbook of Contemporary Heritage Research.* Palgrave-Macmillan. London, pp. 297–312.

Hollowell, J. & Nicholas, G. 2009. "Using ethnographic method to articulate community-based conceptions of cultural heritage management", *Public Archaeology*, 8(2/3): 141–160. DOI: dx.doi.org/10.1179/175355309X457196

Holtorf, C. 2007. "What does not move any hearts – why should it be saved? The *Denkmalpflegediskussion* in Germany", *International Journal of Cultural Property*, 14(1): 33–55.

Holtorf, C. & Fairclough, G. 2013. "The New Heritage and re-shapings of the past", in A. González-Ruibal (ed.) *Reclaiming Archaeology Beyond the Tropes of Modernity.* Routledge. London, pp. 197–210.

Holtorf, C. 2017. "What's wrong with cultural diversity in world archaeology?" *Claroscuro* 16: 1–14. Available online: http://ppct.caicyt.gov.ar/index.php/claroscuro/article/view/12433/45454575757929 (accessed 27 July 2018).

ICOMOS Australia 2000. The Australia ICOMOS Charter for Places of Cultural Significance 1999 (with associated Guidelines and Code on the Ethics of Co-existence). Burwood: ICOMOS Secretariat. Available online: https://australia.icomos.org/wp-content/uploads/BURRA_CHARTER.pdf

Iyer, P. 2000. *The Global Soul: Jet Lag, Shopping Malls, and the Search for Home.* Vintage Books. New York.

Kalra, V.S., R. Kaul & Hutnyk J. 2005. *Diaspora & Hybridity.* Sage. London, Thousand Oaks and New Delhi.

Kohl P.L. & Fawcett, C (eds) 1995. *Nationalism, Politics, and the Practice of Archaeology.* Cambridge University Press. Cambridge.

Labadi, S. & Long, D. (eds) 2010. *Heritage and Globalism.* Routledge. London and New York.

Labadi, S. 2013 UNESCO, *Cultural Heritage, and Outstanding Universal Value: Value-based Analyses of the World Heritage and Intangible Cultural Heritage Conventions.* Altamira Press. Walnut Creek.

Lafrenz Samuels, K.L. 2015. "Introduction", in K.L. Lafrenz Samuels & T. Rico (eds.) *Heritage Keywords: Rhetoric and redescription in Cultural Heritage.* University Press of Colorado. Boulder, pp. 3–28.

Lafrenz Samuels, K. & Lilley, I. (2015) "Transnationalism and heritage development", in L. Meskell (ed.) 2015. *Global Heritage – A Reader.* Wiley Blackwell. Chichester, pp. 217–239.

Lewicka, M. 2011. "Place attachment: how far have we come in the last 40 years?", *Journal of Environmental Psychology*, 31(3): 207–230.

Macdonald, S. 2013. *Memorylands: Heritage and Identity in Europe Today*. Routledge. London and New York.

McGhee, F.L. 2012. "Participatory action research and archaeology", in R. Skeates, C. McDavid & J. Carman (eds.) *The Oxford Handbook of Public Archeology*. Oxford University Press. Oxford, pp. 213 – 229.

McIntyre, A. 2008 *Participatory Action Research*. Sage. London.

Meskell, L. (ed) 1998. *Archaeology Under Fire: Nationalism, Politics, and Heritage in the Eastern Mediterranean and Middle East*. Routledge. London.

Meskell, L. 2010. "Human rights and heritage ethics", *Anthropology Quarterly*, 83(4): 839–860.

Meskell, L. (ed) 2015. *Global Heritage: A Reader*. Chichester. Wiley Blackwell.

Neal, C. 2015. "Heritage and participation", in E. Waterton & S. Watson (eds.) *The Palgrave Handbook of Contemporary Heritage Research*. Palgrave/Macmillan. New York, pp. 346–365.

Pollock, D.C. & Reken R.E. 2009. *Third Culture Kids: Growing Up Among Worlds*. (revised edition). Nicholas Brealey Publishing. Boston and London.

Pyburn, K.A. 2009. "Practicing archaeology: as if it really matters", *Public Archaeology*, 8 (2/3): 161–175. DOI: dx.doi.org/10.1179/175355309X457204.

Pyburn, K.A. 2011. "Engaged archaeology: whose community?", in H. Silverman & F. Ruggles (eds) *Cultural Heritage and Human Rights*. Springer. New York, pp. 172–183.

Rauwerda, A. 2012. *The Writer and the Overseas Childhood: The Third Culture Literature of Kingsolver, McEwan and Others*. McFarland & Co. Jefferson, NC.

Reason, P. & Bradbury, H. (ed.) 2008. *The SAGE Handbook of Action Research*. 2nd edn. SAGE. Los Angeles.

Reicher, S. 2008. "Making a past fit for the future: the political and ontological dimensions of historical continuity", in F. Sani (ed.) *Self Continuity: Individual and Collective Perspectives*. Psychology Press. New York and Hove, pp. 145–158.

Schaetti, B.F. & Ramsey, S.J. 1999. "The Global Nomad Experience: Living in Liminality" Employee Relocation Council, September 1999. Available online: www.transition-dynamics.com/liminality.html (accessed June 2012).

Schofield, J. 2014. "Heritage expertise and the everyday: citizens and authority in the Twenty-first century", in J. Schofield (ed.) *Who Needs Experts? Counter-mapping Cultural Heritage*. Ashgate. Farnham, pp. 1–12.

Schofield, J. 2015. "Forget about 'Heritage': place, ethics and the Faro Convention", in Ireland, T. Schofield, J. (eds.) *The Ethics of Cultural Heritage*. Springer. New York, pp. 197–209.

Sintomer, Y. & Ganuza, E. (in collaboration with C. Hergberz and A. Rocke) 2011. *Democracia Participativa y Modernización de los Servicios Públicos. Investigación sobre la experiencia de presupuesto participativo en Europa*. Transnational Institute, Amsterdam. Available online: www.tni.org/en/node/2512

Smith, L. Morgan, A. & van der Meer, A. 2003. "Community-driven research in cultural heritage management: the Waanyi Women's History Project", *International Journal of Heritage Studies*, 9(1): 65–80.

Smith, L. 2006. *Uses of Heritage*. Routledge. London.

Smith, L. & Agakawa, N. (eds.) 2009. *Intangible Heritage*. Routledge. London.

Somekh, B. 2005. *Action Research: A Methodology for Change and Development*. McGraw-Hill Education. Maidenhead.

Sullivan, S. 1997. "A planning model for the management of archaeological sites", in M. de la Torre (ed.) *The Conservation of Archaeological Sites in the Mediterranean Region*. The Getty Conservation Institute, Los Angeles, pp. 15–26.

UNESCO 1972. Convention Concerning the Protection of the World Cultural and Natural Heritage. UNESCO. Paris. Available online: www.whc.unesco.org/en/conventiontext/.

Vivero, V.N. & Jenkins S.R. 1999. "Existential hazards of the multicultural individual: defining and understanding 'cultural homelessness'." *Cultural Diversity and Ethnic Minority Psychology*, 5(1): 6–26.

Wainwright, H. 2009. *Reclaim the State: Experiments in Popular Democracy*. Verso. London and New York.

Waterton, E. 2015. "Heritage and community engagement", in Ireland, T. Schofield, J. (eds) *The Ethics of Cultural Heritage*. Springer. New York, pp. 53–67.

11

THE USES OF HEROES

Justice, Alexander, and the Macedonian naming dispute

Michael Blake

Introduction

On May 18, 2009, a remarkable letter was delivered to President Barack Obama. Signed by 200 scholars of Graeco-Roman antiquity, the letter protested the decision by the United States to use the word "Macedonia" to refer to a small country in the Balkans, only recently independent. Prior to 2004, the United States had referred to this unrecognized state as "the Former Yugoslav Republic of Macedonia" (abbreviated to FYROM)[1]; when it recognized the state as a sovereign entity, the United States had made the decision to refer to it simply as Macedonia. The letter urged the United States government to reverse this decision, and use the term "Macedonia" only in reference to the Greek province of the same name.

Several reasons were given in defense of this policy. The most important is the idea that the modern inhabitants of the self-described Macedonian state are ethnically and linguistically unrelated to the Alexander the Great, the most important figure in Macedonian history.[2] While the territory of the modern Macedonian state was, indeed, conquered by Philip II – Alexander's father – in 358 BCE, conquest does not, insists the letter, create membership; Egypt was similarly conquered by Macedonia, but no-one would rightly regard Egypt as having therefore become Macedonian. The territory now part of the Macedonian state, moreover, has been a part of a dizzying series of empires; the Serbian empire took possession in 1282, the Ottoman Turks in 1392, the Kingdom of Serbs in 1912, and the Kingdom of Yugoslavia in 1918 – before the land became part of the Socialist Federal Republic of Yugoslavia during the Second World War. The result of this was that the population on this territory has been, for centuries, diverse, but is now largely Slavic in ethnicity and linguistic tradition. This fact has not stopped the government of the Macedonian state from claiming Alexander as a national hero; the airport at Skopje, several roads, and the national sports arena all bear the name of Alexander, and several large statues of Alexander have been erected around the national capital.[3] This use of Alexander, says the letter, is utterly unwarranted, given Alexander's lack of connection to the population and territory of the Macedonian state: the land on which that state is built, they argue, was historically distinct from Macedonia proper – the scholars insist that "Paionia" is the proper term for the territory on which the state of Macedonia is situated – and the modern self-described "Macedonians" have no right to usurp the name of Macedonia with reference to themselves:

> We do not understand how the modern inhabitants of ancient Paionia, who speak Slavic – a language introduced into the Balkans about a thousand years after the death of Alexander – can claim him as their national hero. Alexander the Great was thoroughly and indisputably Greek. . . . Why would the people who live [in Paionia] call themselves Macedonians and their land Macedonia? Why would they abduct a completely Greek figure and make him their national hero? The ancient Paionians may or may not have been Greek, but they certainly became Greekish, and they were never Slavs. They were also not Macedonians . . . The theft of Philip and Alexander by a land that was never Macedonia cannot be justified.[4]

The letter goes on to term the uses of Alexander by the Macedonian state as an "abduction," "historical nonsense," a "misappropriation," and "silliness." The letter concludes that the United States has an obligation to communicate to the government in Skopje that "it cannot build a national identity at the expense of historic truth."

This is a remarkable letter; it is rare to see ancient and modern politics engage so directly. The letter is, of course, only one entry in the broader conflict between the government of Greece, which claims that Macedonia is rightly used only to refer to a particular sort of Greek (and a particular province within Greece) – and the government of the Macedonian state.[5] The Macedonian state is pursuing a policy of "antiquisation," seeking to emphasize the historical links between the state's modern territory and its ancient status as part of the greater Macedonian empire. The state is sponsoring archaeological excavation of the territory, seeking to demonstrate the validity of its claims to the Macedonian name; one project involves the mapping of coin excavations, to demonstrate the ancient borders of the Macedonian and Byzantine empires.[6] Greece, in response, has insisted that normalized relations with the government of Skopje require the abandonment of this historical claim to the Macedonian name and the person of Alexander. In 2008, Greece successfully prevented the Macedonian state's accession into NATO, citing the continued use of the term "Macedonia" as justification.[7]

This is a complex situation, and it is beyond my purview to detail what would be required for a successful solution to the problem.[8] I cannot, indeed, give a full accounting of the complex and contested history of ethnic self-identification in the Balkans.[9] I am interested, instead, in the morality of the uses of history and of heroes, and, in particular, to the question of how we might legitimately acquire the right to regard a particular historical hero as *ours*. This is a particularly interesting topic, I think, in an age of widespread migration and demographic change. Who has the right to use an historical figure, and for what purposes? Must there be a linguistic or ethnic link to that figure, for the claim of use to be rightful? Answering this question may move us beyond the morality of history, and tell us something about how to understand the nature of national identity in a modern world of widespread migration. My thesis will be that we have reason to resist the simple, property-based analysis of heroes exemplified by the letter discussed above; we ought, instead, to regard the uses of heroes with reference to the political purposes of heroes in the creation of a national narrative. On this latter conception, there may be multiple states with the right to regard a hero as *their own*; the validity of claims cannot be established simply with reference to descriptive facts, but also with reference to how the hero's story is understood and lived within a particular national community. This latter conception, though, is not morally neutral between different uses of heroes in the creation of nationality. It brings with it demands for principled forms of respect between groups who agree about the heroic nature of historic figures, but disagree about the uses to which that heroism ought to be put. This alternative conception, I will argue, can therefore potentially break the deadlock over who has the right to claim Alexander as hero, by arguing that this question is one that can be resolved only through political engagement of a particular character. Mercifully, though, we have examples of how this sort of political engagement has been accomplished; we might be able to use ideas related to political liberalism to figure out a way forward in the dispute surrounding the rightful uses of heroes.

This chapter will therefore proceed in two parts. In the first, I will try to distinguish two conceptions of how the right to use a hero might be understood – and provide a few reasons to prefer the latter, political, conception. In the second, I will apply this political conception to the Macedonian naming dispute, and give some ideas of what a way forward might look like in this conflict.

The right to a hero: two approaches to the question

One way to ask the question of who has the right to claim Alexander views this question as an essentially *descriptive* one. If there are several claimants to the right, we can examine each of their claims with reference to agreed-upon standards of evaluation; the story that makes the most sense is the one that gets to use Alexander (or, for that matter, the name Macedonia.) This vision of the answer is one that looks to heroes as a sort of *property*; the group with the best chain of title is the one that gains exclusive use to the hero, and the others – whose claim is not so strong – have a moral obligation to cease their use of the figure. A hero, on this account, is a sort of property; if I have the right to that hero, then that means that you don't – and that you have an obligation to respect my exclusive right, as a condition of respecting me. On this analysis, a hero is like a particular parcel of real estate. If there is a dispute in the chain of title, then the right way to solve it is to figure out whose chain is rightful. The disputant with the best chain of title owns the land outright, and this ownership entails the right to refuse others any particular right to enjoy or exploit that land.[10] The property analysis of heroes views them as, essentially, resources; odd resources, perhaps, since the uses of heroes are unlike those of fields and land, but resources nonetheless, to be given to the one whose claim defeats its opponents.

The alternative way of looking at heroes views them not through the lens of property, but through *politics*. What I mean by that is that the disputants must be understood not as parties to a dispute about ownership, but one about how we might deploy history in the present, to use the heroes of the past to create social union and trust in the present. What is worth noticing about this vision of heroes is that no-one needs to acquire, at the end, *exclusive* rights to claim the hero as exclusive property. There might be multiple chains used to support the claim that a given hero is *our own*, and the fact that one given chain is most robust does not in itself entail the conclusion that the competitor accounts are prohibited from continuing to press claims. The idea that there can be multiple chains of descent should be unexceptional to us; we recognize it in a variety of contexts. Think, for example, of the realtor's cliché that George Washington slept here. It is applied, not wrongly, to territorial sites where Washington slept, on which the actual building has since been destroyed; applied, also not wrongly, to the building in which he slept, when that building has been moved to another site; and applied, finally, to the actual beds in which he slept, some of which have been moved to museums after his death.[11] Even if Washington himself had only slept in one bed, in one building, at one site, it would not follow that we could not have multiple agents able to make the statement – Washington slept *here*. The political conception of heroism shares the pluralism of this sort of example, and does not think that any particular story of a hero's people must of necessity preclude the validity of its competitors.

The reason I call this conception *political*, moreover, is that it takes as its focus the ways in which heroism – like history generally – is used in modern political societies, for purposes both good and bad. At its worst, of course, heroism can be used to create vicious forms of social exclusion, using the supposed glory of the dead to justify evil in the present; we need think only of the uses of Horst Wessel by the Nazi party in the 1930s. Not all heroism, though, is malevolent, and some modern democratic theorists have taken the creation of national heroes as part of the process of building a single national democratic community. Will Kymlicka, for instance, argues that nation-building can become ethically defensible when it creates the circumstances for solidarity within a multi-ethnic democratic society – and that the creation of national heroes, by teaching about their deeds and preserving their memories, can be a part of this process.[12] If the modern nation is taken to be a site within which people are expected to have particular duties to one another – to work, in particular, for the success of the national political community, and voluntarily sacrifice to ensure that community's success – then the shared recognition of past heroism can be valuable when it helps ensure the fulfillment of those duties.

The political conception of heroism, in short, does not view heroism as a zero-sum game; your rightful use of Alexander does not necessarily negate my rightful use of him as well. Under some circumstances, of course, the ways in which I use him might be morally prohibited, if they have the effect of making it more difficult for your own polity to use him in the creation of democratic community. I will discuss this idea in the next section. For the moment, though, we ought to focus simply on this idea: that the rightful use of heroes in politics will make reference to the normative foundation of politics itself, and that there can be more than one society with the right to deploy a particular hero for political purposes. What, then, can this conception tell us about the moral preconditions for the rightful use of a hero?

I think there are at least two things to say here. The first is that the facts matter, to a degree; outright falsehoods, insofar as they involve the intentional deception of individuals, are morally bad.[13] They are also, though, comparatively rare. One example might be the supposed forgery of the King Kwanggee-to steles in Korea, which may have been manufactured by Japanese colonial archaeologists, and then used to buttress the claim of a Japanese historical right to the Korean peninsula.[14] This sort of outright deception, though, is not as frequent as the sorts of complaint found in the letter discussed above. The claim made by the scholars is not that the modern Macedonian state is explicitly claiming false facts, but rather using real facts to construct a false narrative – namely, that Alexander "belonged to" the modern Macedonian state. Alexander did, after all, command an empire which contained the physical territory of the modern Macedonian state; that much is not in dispute. The charge is that this nexus is simply not enough to support the particular relationship between Skopje and Alexander. This charge, though, is susceptible – if what I say here is right – to being dispelled simply by noticing that there might be more than one group entitled to say that Alexander is their hero. That the claim from Skopje is less direct than the claim from Athens does not conclude the issue of whether or not Skopje is entitled to claim Alexander. What matters is that a story can be told on which the factual materials in question can sustain a claim of attribution – not whether or not it is the only such story that can be told.[15]

The second thing to note is that the rightfulness of the claim to a particular hero is now going to depend upon how that claim serves the purposes of politics. If the use of the hero is to build responsive political communities, then the needs and interests of those communities must be made a central part of our discussion of heroism. Before we can examine this, though, we need to ask an important question: why think that the political conception is itself the right way to analyze the claim to a particular hero? Why not simply do what the letter does, and reduce the claim to something like a claim over property?

There are, I think, two reasons. The first is the ways in which modern communities, in an age of widespread migration, have good moral reason to resist making claims to heroes dependent upon particular links of ethnicity, language, or descent.

To see this, note the ways in which the drafters of the letter emphasize the ways in which the modern Macedonian state is Slavic by language and ethnicity – and the fact that Alexander himself was neither Slavic-descended nor a speaker of a Slavic language. Stephen G. Miller, one of the signers of the letter and Professor Emeritus at the University of California at Berkeley, notes acidly that Alexander could not even read the writing on the statues of him erected in Skopkje. The linguistic difference, says Miller, is sufficient to make Skopje's claims "historical nonsense." Miller goes on to assert that the inhabitants of ancient Paionia – even had they not been eventually expelled by Slavs – were at most slaves of true Macedonians, and therefore not entitled to use the name Macedonia in reference to themselves.[16]

These claims are worrying, I think, for any number of reasons. One of them is that the idea that the slaves of Macedonians are not entitled to use the word Macedonia is, to put it mildly, dependent upon an odd and not especially appealing notion of national identity. (Imagine if we were to tell the descendants of American slaves they could not now call themselves Americans!) More importantly, though, in an age of widespread migration, to make the right to use a particular hero dependent upon particular facts of descent, language, or ethnicity, is to tell those who do not share those facts that they are not entitled to use that hero in developing their own identities, whether political or personal. That, though, is something we ought to hesitate before asserting. It is, of course, emphatically true that we have reason to worry about ethnic criteria of membership in traditional countries of migration, like the United States. An American political leader who argued that only descendants of the Founding Fathers had a right to invoke George Washington as hero would be making an argument that runs against the American ethos of inclusion for migrants. I do not want to overstate my case, of course; the United States has rarely been as hospitable to immigrants as its rosy self-description. The fact remains that the United States has a normative reason to insist that there needs be no particularistic link to the heroes of American history before someone is rightly able to take these figures as heroic. The most recent migrant to the United States, regardless of ethnic, religious, or linguistic identity, is – or should be – able to regard herself as the inheritor of Lincoln and Washington. So it is in theory, at least, however far we fall in practice.

Similar considerations, though, might inform the politics of states which are less ideologically committed to immigration. There are few states in the world that are not comprised of multiple national, cultural, ethnic, and linguistic communities; neither Greece nor the state of Macedonia are monolithic in these senses. The state of Macedonia contains multiple ethnic forms of identification, and several linguistic communities; indeed, the attraction of a figure like Alexander is precisely the fact that there is so much diversity within the borders of the state, and comparatively little material with which to forge a common political identity. Greece, though, has recently seen migration from Central and Eastern Europe, and has within its borders diaspora communities from Iraq, Pakistan, and India.[17] The states of Macedonia and Greece have the obligation to ensure that whatever forms of national community are created are ones that have the potential to include those who do not share the particularistic markers of descent discussed by Miller. To say that one can only be a true child of Alexander if one shares his ethnicity, or language, or heritage, is to say that this community can never be created. One who is Slavic by ethnicity, for example, is forever precluded from rightly claiming a particular relationship with the historical figure of Alexander. This means, though, that an invocation of Alexander as hero could only be rightful if made within a monocultural society, descended from Alexander and sharing in his own particular identities. Modern societies, though, simply do not have this character; neither Greece nor the state of Macedonia have this sort of uniformity. On this property-based analysis of heroism, then, neither Greece nor the state of Macedonia have the right to invoke the memory of Alexander. A multicultural political community can only rightly invoke a hero if that hero actually serves to create unity, rather than division, in that community; and that can only be done if the hero is understood as something other than the property of a particular ethnic or linguistic population.

This leads, though, to the second reason to think that we ought to choose the political conception of heroism instead of the property-based. It is that we have resources to develop the political conception, which emerge from the literature on political justice and its relationship to diversity. We have, in theory, and sometimes in practice, been able to combine mutual respect and deep disagreement about matters of fundamental value. The key, following on some ideas from John Rawls, is to seek agreement about political values, while refusing to ground political coercion directly on disputed matters of morality. Rawls's political liberalism is, of course, familiar to many of us – but it is important to note that Rawls's view insists that religious adherents, in a multicultural society, have reason to avoid insisting upon unique ownership of historical figures. The most obvious example we might discuss here is Abraham, taken as a foundational figure in at least three religious traditions. Islam, Judaism, and Christianity all make Abraham a part of their own religious identities, all of them in their own particular ways.[18] Adherents of these religions will disagree precisely about what Abraham actually *did* – texts are not constant across the religions – but they disagree more about what was *important* about what Abraham did. All three take Abraham's story as a module within their own religious narratives. They all interpret that story as leading the way towards the rightfulness of their own religious traditions, of course; but they are in agreement that it is Abraham himself that stands as a key figure within their religions as they understand them.

This should not be surprising to us; these faiths are called Abrahamic for a reason. What is important to note, though, is that the use of Abraham by one of these faiths does not push out or exclude the uses of Abraham by the others. The use of political liberalism demands that the adherents of each religious faith restrain themselves from using the coercive force of politics to insist upon religious orthodoxy, or to insist upon the unique rightness of their own interpretation of Abraham's story. Political liberalism depends upon the possibility that this sort of restraint, and plural use of historical figures, is possible. What is remarkable, though, is how in democratic societies this possibility is actually lived as experience. Many societies – including, imperfectly, the United States and the United Kingdom – are able to combine religious pluralism with functioning democratic institutions. Political liberalism, of course, does not preclude each particular religion's thinking that the others are simply *wrong;* religious adherents are called upon to be tolerant towards other religions, not indifferent between them. Very often, though, this tolerance is actually a fact of life within democratic societies; religious diversity does not always lead to religious violence. Instead, at the level of politics, and often at the social level as well, we are able to combine religious disagreement with mutual respect. We may not agree with the worship of those who disagree with us, but we take their worship as having value for them, so much so that we have principled reasons to be tolerant towards that worship. All this is hardly news, but it is important to note that it includes disagreement not only towards doctrine, but towards particular figures such as Abraham.

There are, of course, differences between the case of Alexander and the case of Abraham. In the first instance, I have discussed Abraham in connection with the case of a multicultural democratic society. Alexander, in contrast, is the source of an international dispute; Greece and the state of Macedonia do not share a political community, and what few legal instruments they do share are comparatively weak. Abraham, moreover, stands at the heart of a religious set of traditions; he is used for purposes of faith, not (directly) for purposes of politics. Alexander, in contrast, is a secular figure, used for secular purposes of national pride and political identity. These are, indeed, significant differences. They would require, if we were to spell out a particular way of instantiating the process of living out mutual respect, careful attention to the nuances of how the two situations are different. I cannot hope to do this job here. I want, instead, simply to argue that the job could, and should, be done; that we have reason to think that a political analysis of the uses of Alexander might be possible, and that the invocation of considerations similar to those at the heart of political liberalism might lead us to a just solution in this area. I want, in short, to argue that there are resources in our analysis of political liberalism that might be used to ground a just settlement of these international issues. In the space that remains, I want to give some indications of what such a settlement might look like, by highlighting some considerations that any such settlement will have to come to terms with.

The Macedonian state, Greece, and the politics of stability

The core of political liberalism, I think, is a particular attitude towards the possibility of politics; it is an attitude that insists upon the possibility of democratic governance in the face of deep disagreement about matters of value. The possibility of political liberalism, domestically, is dependent upon the will to seek a stable and just political society, in the face of such disagreement. Political liberalism depends, for its success, upon the will to seek principles that all can regard as acceptable political standards, in the face of such foundational diversity about matters of ethics and metaphysics.

This is, of course, mostly familiar; Rawls's conception of political liberalism, and the international extension of that conception, are well-known to students of political philosophy. What I want to emphasize here, though, is something that is often under-emphasized in our analysis of political liberalism: the fact that political liberalism begins with a particular attitude towards those with whom we are in disagreement. Rawls emphasizes, rightly on my view, that one is compelled to take the mistaken views of others seriously, and to accord them some amount of principled respect – even as one continues to regard them as utterly mistaken. This attitude is buttressed, domestically, through the use of the burdens of judgment. These are considerations designed to make us recognize the epistemic limits on how we can arrive at – and legitimately criticize – the basic metaphysical and moral views of others; we must recognize that all who seek answers to these basic questions are doing so under epistemic limits that preclude any easy condemnation of competing views.[19] Not all those sympathetic to Rawls's project have appreciated his use of the burdens of judgment.[20] I think, though, that there is something important in this idea, that can be spelled out with two related considerations. The first is that there are some cases in which a view might be both mistaken and important in the life of the person living out that view. The ways in which an individual person lives out a religious conception, for example, might compel us to regard that religion with something like an attitude of principled respect – even if we are convinced that the religion itself is utterly false. The second is that there are certain sorts of mistakes that cannot be corrected through intersubjectively valid forms of argumentation. If you believe that two and two make five, it is at least open in principle for me to offer a disproof of the proposition you believe – one that I think you would be utterly irrational to disbelieve. If you are a theist, and I am an atheist, our dispute is not likely to be solved with reference to such non-controversial forms of reason. This has not stopped some stubborn theists (and stubborn atheists) from impugning the reason of their opponents. Most of us, though, are more modest, and regard the errors of our theological opponents as not being errors that can be corrected in such a simple manner. Those who disagree with us may be in error; our ability to demonstrate their error, though, may be vastly more reduced here than in the case of mathematics.

I discuss this idea because I take it that there might be a similar reason for states to regard certain mistaken views of other states through the lens of the burdens of judgment. Rawls, of course, develops similar ideas in his *Law of Peoples*; but I am interested not in his own development of such ideas, but in the attitude that makes these ideas plausible. The core belief I want to explore is that states might have reason to regard the political self-conception of other states as being simply and flatly mistaken – but that the mistake those other states are making as being of such a character as deserving of principled respect. So it might be, I think, with the use of heroes. If the Macedonian state is using the figure of Alexander to build a political identity, it is entirely within the rights of the Greek state to regard that conception as being wrongful – indeed, as faintly silly. This does not, though, negate the idea that Greece might have some principled reason to regard the Macedonian state as having the right to continue to use the figure of Alexander in these mistaken ways. Their claim to Alexander might rest upon considerably more complex and distant claims than the claim made by Greece. This, though, does not preclude the possibility that the mistaken use of Alexander by the Macedonian state has the character of a mistake deserving of principled respect. There are some mistakes, in the area of religion, that we are obligated to respect; I might not agree with your theology, but I am duty-bound to respect the role it plays in your life, and therefore to respect that theology itself. At the very least, I am obligated – in political life – to avoid seeking to displace that theology, or to insist publicly upon its falsity. Some analogue to this, though, seems to hold even for the uses of heroes. If Alexander, as hero, plays a role in the public political culture of the Macedonian state, by unifying and joining the diverse Macedonian people, and creating the circumstances under which a democratic Macedonia emerges and flourishes – then the rest of us, whether or not we like the historical analysis undergirding the Macedonian claim, might be obligated to respect the ways in which Macedonia uses the figure of Alexander.

All this, of course, is fairly abstract. To make it more specific, we can imagine the following general political principle for the use of historical figures in politics: we ought to begin with the presumption that multiple use of historical materials is possible – that the ways in which states use history is such that the same materials might be used by more than one community at any given time. The presumption ought to be that a given hero's use is rightful if it is used to create a more just society – and that this rightful use does not depend upon being the sole community deploying that figure in its political self-understanding. All this, though, is compatible with the possibility of ethical criticism of the ways in which societies actually do use heroes. This criticism, though, would begin with political ethics, and not with history itself. On the political conception I offer here, the use of a hero in a particular way is morally wrongful if it works against the ability of a particular society to do the job of political justice – to be a unified political community, able to engage in the processes of political discourse and justification in a rightful manner. There are, I think, at least two ways in which the use of a hero might be wrongful, on this account – both of which might tell us something about the ultimate resolution of the Macedonian conflict.

The first is what might be called the indirect route: my state's use of a hero might, under some circumstances, crowd out your use of that hero. In what has gone before, I have argued that this is not always what happens; sometimes, you and I are both able to use that hero, and my use does not preclude your own. I do not want to argue, though, that there can be no causal effect of my narrative upon the narratives of others. Under conditions where one party is comparatively more marginal than the other, it might be that the use of a hero by the stronger party might end up deforming that hero in the eyes of the weaker party. The idea of cultural imperialism seems to depend upon ideas like this.[21] The indigenous American population may find it comparatively more difficult to tell stories about their history, when Disney has taken figures from that history and used them in films that will dominate over any competitor narrative produced by natives themselves. Where those narratives are used in the service of political justice, we have political reason to care about those narratives being preserved. We should not think that this phenomenon is always inevitable; the strongest voice does not always dominate. It does mean, though, that those who are strongest might have a special obligation to ensure that they do not crowd out the narratives of the weak.

What does this tell us about Macedonia? Answering this question is not easy, but at the very least we might worry about the validity of the Greek claim that the Macedonian state's claim to Alexander is likely to crowd out the Greek claim to him. The Macedonian state, to put it bluntly, is weaker, more tenuous, and less well-established in global relations than the Greek state; Alexander's Greek ethnicity and language is well-established, and no matter how many statues of him appear in Skopje, the Greeks will likely be able to continue to tell stories of him as a distinctively Greek hero. The marginal party, if any, is the Macedonian state. This state is weaker in terms of the ability to proclaim a narrative to the world; it is also less well-established as a political entity, having only recently emerged from warfare and chaos. It would seem, in short, as if the party that ought to worry about its narrative being crowded out is Macedonia, not Greece. If this is right, though, then Greece cannot rightly claim that Macedonia is stealing its history. If anything, Greece is seeking to take a hero away from a weaker state, which has a crying need for whatever resources might provide national unity under conditions of diversity. Macedonia, right now, stands in need of heroes. Greece, I think, is comparatively immune from Macedonia's use of Alexander, and undermines an already weak society when it seeks to preclude that use.

All of this tells in favor of the Macedonian state's use of Alexander. The second way in which a use of a hero might be politically malign, though, does not. A historical figure might be crowded out, if one narrative use of that figure is more powerful than the other. The figure might, though, also serve the cause of political injustice more directly, by serving to justify territorial expansion and conquest. There is some evidence, though, that the use of the term "Macedonia" by the Macedonian state is doing precisely that. The government at Skopje has encouraged a sort of irredentist mindset, on which the Greek province of Macedonia is rightly part of a Greater Macedonian empire. Bank notes from the state of Macedonia contain pictures of the Greek countryside; Macedonian state political leaders have posed with maps of a supposed Greater Macedonia.[22] All this is, of course, politically malign; the uses of heroism I defend here are only rightful if in service of a legitimate form of political self-government. We can use a hero to defend the claim that we, around here, have obligations and duties to support and preserve each others' rights. We cannot, though, use a hero to insist that the members of other political societies rightly owe allegiance and fealty to us. This is, I think, the flip side of the first way in which heroism might be used wrongly. Above, we saw how a hero can be used by one society to crowd out a competing narrative, and make that latter society less able to do the job of being a just political community. Here, we see how a hero can be used to insist that the latter society has no right to independent existence in the first place. What I defend here is not simply any use of the hero, by any group; it is, instead, the use of the hero in service of political justice. We have an obligation to avoid using the figure of the hero to make political justice more difficult for others. We have an even stronger obligation, I think, to avoid using heroism and history to seek the destruction of someone else's political society.

What, then, can we say in conclusion about the uses of history in the Macedonian state? I cannot offer any easy solutions, or even a map by which some final adjudication might be made. All I can offer is a rejoinder to some bad arguments. If Alexander is to be used rightly, it must be because the political society in which he is invoked is using him for the purposes of justice; his right use is a matter of politics, not of property. Getting rid of bad arguments is a first step – but it is no more than that. Solving the conflict over Alexander requires more skill, and knowledge, than I hope to possess. But we do no-one any favors when we continue to use wrongful arguments in our discussions of this matter; I will therefore be satisfied if I have shown that the contemporary discussion of the naming of Macedonia is a disservice to all the parties involved.

Notes

1 For purposes of this essay, I will refer to the independent Macedonian state not as FYROM, but as "the Macedonian state." I do this for simplicity's sake, while acknowledging that my doing so is only permissible if the arguments against that name's legitimate application will fail. I do not claim that I have been able to offer a dispositive rebuttal against that argument; still less do I claim to have done so before this chapter has even begun.
2 There is no neutral description of Macedonian history, but it is safe to say that all parties regard Alexander as a Macedonian figure, and regard Macedonia in the Ancient period as being significantly akin to Greece in language, ethnicity, and outlook. Stephen Miller offers a summary of these facts in his response to an article in *Archaeology Magazine* detailing the decision by political agents Skopje to claim "ownership" over Alexander's legacy for the modern, largely Slavic state calling itself Macedonia. This letter is available at http://macedonia-evidence.org/letter-1-archaeology.html
3 See "A Macedonian makeover: The capital city gets a controversial facelift," *The Economist,* August 26, 2010.
4 The text of the letter is available at http://macedonia-evidence.org/obama-letter.html
5 Macedonian Greeks' ethnic self-identity is complex, but tends to be understood – by Macedonian Greeks – as being a particular sort of Greek, rather than in competition with Greek identity. The Greek government encouraged this attitude for a long time, encouraging assimilation to the Greek culture. See Jane Cowan, *Macedonia: The Politics of Identity and Difference* (London: Pluto Press, 2000) 96–99.
6 Matthew Brunwasser, "A Letter from Macedonia: Owning Alexander," *Archaeology Magazine* 62(1) January/February 2009.
7 The recent history regarding the relationship between Skopje and Athens is described in Niki Kitsantonis, "Greeks Protest to Defend Right to the Name 'Macedonia," *New York Times,* February 4, 2018.
8 One helpful suggestion is a recent Greek proposal to have the Macedonian state use the term "Upper Macedonia" in official communications. This solution has received mixed reviews in Skopje and in Athens. See "Might the question of what to call Macedonia finally be resolved?" *The Economist,* February 6, 2018.

9 See John Phillips's description: "The Bulgarians asserted that Macedonia was part of great Bulgaria and the Greeks swore that it was a sacred part of Greece. The Serbs insisted it was southern Serbia and the Albanians that much of Macedonia was part of great Albania, the homeland of the ancient Illyrians. The Macedonians' true identity was contested for centuries because of their heterogeneous ethnic mix." John Phillips, *Macedonia: Warlords and Rebels in the Balkans* (New Haven: Yale University Press, 2004), 15.

10 Even real estate, of course, is not quite so simple; this analysis is made more complex by notions such as easements and restrictive covenants.

11 Some of these adventures are discussed in Timothy Foote, "George Washington Slept Here," *Smithsonian Magazine*, December 1999.

12 See generally Will Kymlicka, *Liberalism, Community, and Culture* (Oxford: Oxford University Press, 1989).

13 The position I take here is thus not purely "constructivist" about archaeology, if indeed such a pure constructivism is possible. See generally Chris Scarre and Geoffrey Scarre, *The Ethics of Archaeology: Philosophical Perspectives on Archaeological Practice* (Cambridge: Cambridge University Press, 2006).

14 See Hyung Il Pai, *Constructing "Korean" Origins: A Critical Review of Archaeology, History, and Racial Myth in Korean State-Formation Theories* (Cambridge: Harvard University Press, 2000).

15 It is an open question, of course, as to how little factual relationship we must have to a hero before claiming him or her as our own. I am inclined to think that there must be very little indeed; the experience of Haile Selassie and Jamaica seems to be relevant here. The day of Selassie's one visit to Jamaica, during which he repeatedly refused status as the *Ras tafari* or messiah, is celebrated as *grounation day*; Selassie's own mystification at Jamaica's love for him, and his exceptionally minimal interactions with Jamaica, does not preclude the rightness of lionizing Selassie, nor the legitimacy of grounation day. See generally Ennis Barrington Edmonds, *Rastafari: From Outcasts to Culture Bearers* (Oxford: Oxford University Press, 2000).

16 This point is made forcefully in the Stephen Miller's reply to *Archaeology*. Available at http://macedonia-evidence.org/letter-1-archaeology.html

17 A summary of these facts is found at https://www.migrationpolicy.org/article/greece-history-migration

18 See John Rawls, *Political Liberalism* (New York: Columbia University Press, 1989).

19 See, for example, Leif Wenar, "Political Liberalism: An Internal Critique," 106(1) *Ethics* (October 1995).

20 John Rawls, *The Law of Peoples* (Cambridge: Harvard University Press, 1999).

21 For related ideas, see Iris Marion Young, *Justice and the Politics of Difference* (Princeton: Princeton University Press, 1999).

22 The irredentism of the Macedonian state is also cited by some of those demonstrating in Athens against Skopje's right to the Macedonian name. See Kitsantonis, "Greeks Protest to Defend Right to the Name 'Macedonia'."

12

ARCHAEOLOGICAL HERITAGE AND MIGRATION

Well-being, place, citizenship and the social

Margarita Díaz-Andreu

Introduction

The UNESCO World Heritage Convention of 1972 described heritage as "our legacy from the past, what we live with today, and what we pass on to future generations". This definition about "our" past, that may still be adequate when referring to humanity as a whole, echoed the still ubiquitous belief in the right of nations to "their" past. As we will see later in the article, this belief has been challenged from different angles, as this seemingly innocuous characterisation of heritage is potentially divisive. In the case of Europe, if the legacy the description alludes to is understood as a set of historical events enacted by generations of Europeans whose roots can be traced back into the past, relatively large numbers of the population currently living on this continent would be excluded. The European Commission's *Fifth Annual Report on Migration and Asylum* indicated that 4 percent of the European population in 2013 were third-country nationals (European Commission 2014: 3). To this figure we have to add all those citizens of other European states living in a country different to that of their birth, as well as many non-Europeans whose illegal status excludes them from statistics. The actual percentage of displaced peoples in respect to nationals may triple the figure above. For example, in 2013, 25 percent of the Swedish population were either born or both their parents were born outside Sweden (www.scb.se in Karlsson 2015). Europe is not, of course, an exception. In today's globalised world, in which diverse and fragmented societies are the norm, there is almost no country in the world that does not have an increasing population mix.

There is a growing awareness of the latent problems derived from the impression created by the term "inheritance" included in the 1972 definition of heritage. In European terms, the potential exclusion this entails has been counterbalanced in the last decade by a series of international agreements, such as the Faro Convention on the Value of Cultural Heritage (2005) and the Fribourg Declaration of Cultural

Rights (2007). Both state that everyone has a personal right to heritage. The Faro Convention proposed that all members of society should be involved in the on-going process of defining and managing cultural heritage. These European agreements pose a challenge to heritage institutions on a national, regional and local level. Under the new agreements there is a need to change the way engagement with heritage is sought, not only in the case of new migrants, but also with long-standing communities in Europe, as well as newly formed heritage communities. If we take the example of the UNESCO definition, simply deleting the possessive adjective *our* would give the definition a much more inclusive tone. There would be no *ours* versus *yours*.

This article aims to discuss the interaction between archaeology and contemporary migrations in the context of social cohesion, and the ethical implications that follow from this interaction. Archaeological heritage is one of the means by which today's societies foster the formation and recreation of collective identities. In the following pages an examination will be made of the extent to which archaeological heritage is also able – or potentially able – to fulfil this role for recent immigrants, even when the heritage is not one produced by their genetic ancestors. After a review of the links between archaeological heritage and nationalism, some thought will be given to the potential of archaeology to create a sense of place and to nurture well-being. Some of the initiatives undertaken in different parts of Europe aimed at integrating migrants into archaeological activities and promoting their sense of belonging will be identified. Attention will then focus on Catalonia and on the practices undertaken to actively create citizenship with a social inclusion agenda.

Archaeological heritage and the nation

Identity, the identification of individuals with broader groups on the basis of differences that are socially sanctioned as significant, has many aspects and archaeology could be suitably associated with many – perhaps even all – of them. This is because every identity has an origin and ways of symbolising and imagining it. There are many examples demonstrating that archaeological heritage has been used and abused to signify, create and recreate religious (Meskell 1998), ethnic (Silberman 2010), regional (Zobler 2011), national and even international (Díaz-Andreu 2007) aspects of identity. As these and many other cases show, the use of the past to signify identity is never neutral and it may be ethically correct or, to the contrary, partially or fully inappropriate, i.e. morally wrong. On a positive note, archaeological heritage has the potential to create community, making it more coherent and thus increasing the well-being of its members (Baumeister and Leary 1995). However, as mentioned, archaeology can also be abused and foster exclusion. Today there is real danger in countries governed by coalition governments with right-wing leanings that the field of culture, traditionally considered as of lesser importance than health or finances, will be left to the extreme right-wing partners. They are usually more than happy to promote the xenophobic politics of exclusion of what are considered non-national ethnic communities (Gustafsson and Karlsson 2011, Jensen 2011, Kvaale 2011).

It is important to appreciate why archaeology can be an effective means for signifying identity and how it has been doing so for the last two centuries in the case of nationalism. It is necessary to ascertain not only whether there is scope for change, but indeed a moral obligation to transform the way we understand it. The reason behind archaeology's potential to denote identity is very much linked to the attraction wielded by antiquities. The understanding of the past that has predominated in the last two centuries, first in the Western world and then globally, is very much linked to a key transition in world history marked by the end of the Ancient Regime and the emergence of nationalism as the basis of international politics at the end of the eighteenth century. In the world of nations, the demonstration of the existence of a national past means the right to claim a future of political independence, or indeed to maintain a country's independent status.

Archaeology became a professional discipline funded by the state thanks to nationalism (Díaz-Andreu 2007). Nationalism is a political ideology which maintains that nations have the right to self-government. A nation needs a past to demonstrate its own existence and the particular nature that makes it eligible to be considered an independent political entity. Because history – and therefore also archaeology – provides the basis for the political right to a nation's independence, archaeology became increasingly professionalised during the nineteenth and twentieth centuries. Archaeology museums created narratives about the past, explaining in chronological order the origin and development of the nation. Ancient monuments had to be preserved and inspectorates were created to care for them. Meanwhile the need to train museum curators and inspectors encouraged the founding of university chairs.

When archaeology was first professionalised, archaeologists were explicitly proud to work for their nations, focusing either on the antiquities in their own countries or in places around the world, the latter mainly in areas that, more often than not, were located in the regions under the imperial influence of their own countries. Therefore, their work was part of the national agenda (for the connection between imperialism and nationalism see Díaz-Andreu 2007, 2018). The narrative of origins thus created was translated into archaeology museums, schoolbooks, novels, cinema and many other media. Today, in contrast to this earlier period, archaeologists living in long-established nations are usually unaware of their political role, as archaeology has been subsumed as just another practice of banal nationalism. This is to say that the internalisation of national identity makes individuals stop perceiving their actions as political because, according to Billig's proposal (1995), archaeology is potentially a part of the routine of national forms and symbols that allows the transformation of nationalism into national identity. The products of the archaeological profession – national conferences, the language used in publications and the territory covered in journals and books – are daily reminders of national identity, despite the (frequent) lack of awareness among archaeological heritage practitioners and indeed among users.

In contrast to ethnic purity and cultural and national homogeneity, today the world is going through dramatic changes. Despite the maintenance of nationalist feelings everywhere in the world, and indeed the recent revival of very marked nationalist feelings in many places, the coherence that independent nations (perhaps) once had is currently challenged by supra-national institutions such as the European Union, as well as by international companies that try to circumvent national regulations, and by mass-migrations, transnationalism and diaspora. The cultural homogeneity that nations once claimed to have, has disappeared due to mass migration encouraged by a mercantilist need for cheap labour. The human basis of the nation is multicultural, i.e. individuals whose connections to cultures are not clear-cut but rather partial and plural; individuals for whom cultural traditions are interacting systems instead of fixed, independent practices (Morris, Chiu and Liu 2015). In the face of these changes it is vital that we reflect on the role archaeology has in today's world. Can we maintain archaeology, with its national baggage, in the globalised world? What are the ethical implications of doing this? Should we assume that descent from cultural groups in the past bestows on groups and individuals the ownership and care of cultural heritage? These are important questions to answer if we are to ponder the adequacy of archaeology in a world in which an increasing percentage of the population living in a country has an immigrant background.

A way forward: archaeology and place

On a recent visit to the US to attend a conference, a group of delegates, including myself, were kindly taken to visit one of the archaeological sites in the area. The archaeology of the area was explained by an enthusiastic PhD student. I asked him about his family background and his answer was the one I expected: his forebears had come to America from a myriad of European countries and he himself was not from that part of the US. I suddenly wondered why he should be interested in the archaeology he was explaining to us and about which he was tirelessly working to produce a doctoral thesis. If the past is about knowing about your ancestors – an assumption that is often made in Europe and many other parts of the world – here I had an example of someone who was fully engaged with the archaeology of the area, but whose ancestors were from elsewhere. He was not indeed an exception, as around 98.5 percent of the United States' population has an immigrant background, a percentage that excludes the 1.5 percent of Native Americans (Comer 2013: 74). Given my involvement in Catalonia in projects in which social inclusion and migration are a component (see below), and having been thinking about issues concerning immigrant communities' attachment to archaeological heritage, I suddenly realised that the immigrants' position regarding the heritage in Catalonia and in Europe as a whole was not that different to that of white Americans' feelings towards pre-Columbian archaeology; in neither case could a claim of ancestry be made. I asked one of the other speakers at the conference, another white American, and he answered as follows:

> For me it is about place. It is about where you are and where you make your
> home. So, even if I am not directly connected to an archaeological site or a
> specific cultural tradition, it is still where I am living, it is part of where I am
> and then a part of who I am because it is my home . . . I am very interested
> in Native American history and I find it relevant because it is a part of my
> landscape, my place, and this becomes a part of who I am.
>
> *(Chip Colwell, personal communication, 11 January 2015)*

Chip Colwell's answer does not mean that he is not fully aware of the colonial
and post-colonial implications of archaeology in the US, about which he has
written much (for example, Colwell-Chanthaphonh 2009). When I had asked
the PhD student the same question the previous day, his answer had been
very similar.

Back in Barcelona I decided to ask some of the students in a Catalan language
class I was attending about their attachment to heritage. They were all immigrants,
but of very different ages, statuses and situations. Their answers varied, but some
repeated some of the ideas expressed above. A student from El Salvador, twenty-
two years old with only basic studies, commented that:

> I would imagine that old buildings with a history are very important for
> the city and country. . . . If they were knocked down the country would
> lose a lot . . . would lose wisdom . . . I don't know whether my opinion
> counts, but I would not agree if a building with its antiquity and its history
> is knocked down.

Similarly, a well-educated, middle-class Italian man who had already been living
in Barcelona for the last six years mentioned that he had visited several museums,
mainly of art, but also the museum at the Born Cultural Centre. He went there
because he wanted to learn more about the history of the city and liked seeing re-
enactors dressed up. He stated that knowing about history was necessary because it
made people understand many things that could not be perceived otherwise. He
also especially liked Roman archaeology because of the connection with Italy.
He was adamant that the Roman walls in Barcelona should not be destroyed
"because a piece of history should not be removed".

My survey is plainly anecdotal and skewed towards people who, even though
in some cases have no higher education, aspire to expand their knowledge (as
shown by their interest in learning the vernacular language of the place where
they live). However, it seems interesting to note that the opinions of these two
interviewees make a clear connection between their perception of archaeology
and historical monuments and their well-being. Although place is not mentioned
in the case of the migrants to Barcelona questioned, I would argue that if they care
it is because they live in Barcelona and have identified to some degree with the
city. Their connection with the monuments is not based on the idea of ethnicity,
but of experiencing the place, feeling part of it.

The use of place for the making and organisation of collective identities has been a focus in the field of human geography. Ashworth, Graham and Tunbridge argue that an individual's need to belong to spatially defined social groups is as important today as it was two centuries ago when it was used to characterise nation-states. The difference lies in the complexity of identities in the globalised world (Ashworth, Graham and Tunbridge 2007: 1–2). The authors distinguish four key concepts intrinsic to the debate on heritage, identity and place: culture, assimilation, multiculturalism and pluralism. Culture is seen as practices and a system of signification by which people make sense of the world, a way of life.

In a recent study for English Heritage (whose name has now significantly changed to Historic England), three types of connection between historic environment and sense of place were identified: place distinctiveness or what makes a place distinctive; place continuity, i.e. the way a place supports people's sense of continuity; place dependency, i.e. how a place empowers individuals to reach their goals; and a sense of place. In addition to these, community relations within a place are also important (Graham, Mason and Newman 2009: 3). Unfortunately, migration was not considered in this study.

Archaeology and social cohesion in a multicultural society: what has been done so far

How to encourage a sense of belonging among the foreign and national immigrant population? And what are the ethical implications of doing so? There is a recognition of diversity in Europe, but this does not mean that the immigrant population has a sense of belonging. An archaeology museum that provides a message about the nation's ethnic roots emphasising (or even only implying) a direct genetic connection between the people living in the past with the current population, does not empower immigrants and therefore does not encourage social cohesion. The concern in Europe for immigrants and integration is clearly exemplified in a recently published guide for policy-makers and practitioners with the title of *Building migrants' belonging through positive interactions* (Orton 2012). Andrew Orton, who is a social scientist, does not mention ethics in his document, but makes statements that are ethically-informed. As he puts it:

> Giving migrants a voice, recognising their true value and building their sense of belonging to receiving societies, in short empowering migrants, is the only appropriate policy choice in a democratic society. It is this choice that will enable us to ensure fair and just societies for all, and allow migrants to both be integrated and feel integrated.
>
> *(Orton 2012: 9).*

The document he produced for the Council of Europe contains a series of recommendations based on the premise that "enabling diverse positive interactions builds belonging and cohesion" (Orton 2012: 9). By this it means that everyday processes which allow people to foster networks of supportive relationships should be encouraged by policy-makers and practitioners. Interaction is seen as key to avoiding communities living parallel lives with little contact. How can archaeological heritage promote contact?

It is not an understatement to say that in Europe archaeology and the heritage sector have largely remained unengaged with contemporary globalisation and in particular with global-scale migration and the challenges this poses on many levels, including narratives, public outreach and recruitment. The European country that seems to be at the forefront of this is Britain. In the UK, there is increasing involvement of non-professional archaeologists in archaeological practice and, among these, there seems to be a recent emphasis on including individuals of immigrant background. An example of this is given in one of the recent numbers of the magazine British Archaeology. The feature was about Mr Delwar Hussein Hussein, who had become enthusiastically involved in the excavations taking place in the extension to his local mosque, the Bait-ul-Aziz Mosque and Community Centre in Southwark, London (Pitts 2014). Pride in his contribution to the investigation of the past of his local mosque transpired from the article, as well as his sense of belonging to that place and, by extension, I would add, to the whole country.

In Sweden, too, relevant work has been conducted. Anita Synnestvedt's work in Bergsjön, a suburban area of Gothenburg, Sweden, inhabited today by a high proportion of immigrants, illustrates how interest in these issues has been present for at least a decade. The "Multicultural meetings by an ancient remain" project took place in 2006. It was centred on the excavation of the chamber tomb of Siriusgatan (1800–1500 BC). Synnestvedt aimed to connect interpretation with how the site had been used throughout time up to the present day and to explore how the monument was perceived by the local community, a neighbourhood with an ample variety of cultural backgrounds. She managed to engage a wide range of participants: about 150 pupils aged from seven to twelve and staff from the nearby primary school, most of them of immigrant background, the monument's caretaker, previous residents of the area, people from other parts of the city, associations, heritage managers and politicians. Roll-up banner stands were used to explain the main periods where the findings were dated: prehistory, 1920s and 1950s. A final banner with the title "Outlook in the world" helped explain the similarity of the excavated structure to others found around the world. After a week of excavating in which children and adults participated, a party involving the whole community was organised. The project was an excellent example of how the local community, regardless of their ethnic background, can become interested in knowing about their landscape's past. Sadly, no long-term evaluation of the project impact was undertaken due to lack of funds (Synnestvedt 2009 and personal communication 8 February 2015).

As a consequence of European projects, community archaeology has reached countries that do not normally follow the trends of the English-speaking world. Thus, the Archaeology Unit in Saint-Denis, a city 9 km to the north of Paris, started an outreach programme. Given that a quarter of its citizens are of nationalities other than French, it is not surprising that among those participating in the activities there are also migrants (Rodrigues in Synnestvedt 2014: 16). Among many other activities there have also been rescue excavations with demonstrations by craftsmen, sometimes given by residents from other parts of the world such as Ivory Coast. Finally, the excavations at the îlot Cygne were used as a training worksite for students and residents with open-day excavations, visits for school-children, teaching activities, European Heritage Days and local events (Rodrigues 2012). Rodrigues's work can be presented in a whole new light after the 2015 police raid in Saint-Denis, when the suspected mastermind of the November 2015 Paris attacks and some of his collaborators, all suspected members of the Islamic State, were identified in the area.

In addition to excavations, other projects linking archaeology and recent migrants to Europe are being undertaken in museums. In the wider field of muse-ums there has been an effort to 'museumify' migrants, to make them the object of enquiry either by building specific museums, discussing migration in particu-lar instances in the permanent exhibition or organising exhibitions on migration (Basso Peressut and Pozzi 2012). Some museums have done this from the perspec-tive of the "New Museology", which highlights their explicit responsibility to address social and political problems, encourage social change and empower indi-viduals, regardless of their social or ethnic background (Gerbich and Kamel 2012: 199). Most of these exhibitions are related to art and when archaeological objects are used, they are selected because of their aesthetic qualities.

In Norway there have been at least two surveys exclusively focusing on immigrants, both undertaken in 2010–2011, the first at the Oslo Museum and the Norwegian Folk Museum and the second at the University's Museum of Cultural History (Prescott 2013: 62–63 and this volume). Although the results were skewed, for only young people between the ages 15 and 30 years old, being mainly those attending a university or university college, they confirmed the "lack of interest and involvement among the major non-European immigrant groups". They showed that cultural activities were not "a priority compared to work, homework, Quran schools, resting, etc." and that young people "experi-ence little encouragement from parents to use museums and culture institutions that are not ethnically specific" (Prescott 2013: 63). However, one is left won-dering what results a similar survey of working-class, non-migrant Norwegians would have provided. Interestingly, in the qualitative interviews undertaken, students of a migrant background expressed their desire for historical and cultural exhibitions to include issues linked to their experiences of hybridisa-tion, and not necessarily issues related to their countries and cultures of origin (Prescott 2013: 63).

Among the publications of the European Museums in an age of migrations project (MeLa) (see www.mela-project.eu/contents/the-mela-books-series), archaeology is only mentioned in passing and the implications of museums as multifaceted places of identity and place are not explored in the case of those displaying the material culture of the past. Archaeology, however, was the focus of the project Placing Voices, Voicing Places in the inner city of Dublin, Ireland.

As a result of this a series of recommendations to the Irish government were made concerning the need to review current government policies on integration and cultural diversity, Heritage Council strategic plans and goals and the Landscape Characterisation Assessment process. It was also advised that museums should have standard programmes and policy tools that include intercultural dialogue and cultural planning to encourage an effective, culturally-sensitised policy on diversity (Cooke et al. 2008: 6).

Archaeology and social cohesion: Catalonia as a case study

In the last third of the nineteenth century Catalonia was a labour-exporting area with a migratory flux mainly towards Latin America. Industrialisation changed that situation. From an initial period in which Catalan peasants left their villages to work in the new factories, in the 1910s and 1920s migration was fed by people from neighbouring regions of Spain. After the Civil War, migration from all areas of Spain to Catalonia intensified with the population increasing by a hundred thousand every year between 1950 and 1975 (Pujadas 2007, Zapata-Barrero 2006: 191–196). In 1975, 44 percent of the population of Barcelona had been born outside Catalonia (PBI 2008: 3). The last decade of the twentieth century and the first of the twenty-first century brought a new type of migrant with an international background. From 2.8 percent of foreigners in 2000, according to the latest official count (2014), this percentage increased to 16 percent in 2010 and it is now 14.5 percent (Institut d'Estadística de Catalunya (IDESCAT), www.idescat.cat). A wide variety of languages is now spoken in Catalonia (Lingua Món ny).

Migration policies in Catalonia

Catalonia has had a continuous policy on migration since 1992. In that year an Inter-Departmental Commission for Monitoring and Coordinating Actions on Immigration Affairs was set up by the Generalitat de Catalunya, the Government of Catalonia. It produced the Inter-Departmental Immigration Programme (1993–2000) with the general aim of promoting the integration of migrants and the specific objective of coordinating all the departments dealing with migration. This plan was followed by a second from 2001 to 2004, a third, the Plan for Citizenship and Immigration (2005–2008), and a National Agreement on Cooperation (2009). One of the main emphases of these plans has been the promotion of the Catalan language as a medium for improving social cohesion. The effects of these policies and the interest of the municipalities have been felt in museums, with exhibitions on migration and multicultural festivities (KuanUm 2011, van Geert 2014: 207–210). In the context of the first International Forum of Cultures (2004), the Museum of the History of Immigration in Catalonia was established in Sant Adrià de Besòs (van Geert 2014: 206).

In addition to the Government of Catalonia, the Provincial Government of Barcelona and some town councils have drawn up policies on migration.

Examples of the latter are the town councils of Terrassa and Manlleu in 2003, whose initiatives partly derive from the serious ethnic tensions existing in their communities. In Barcelona, the Intercultural Plan has also been developed (PBI 2008, van Geert 2014: 212).

Museums, archaeology and migration

As in the whole of Europe, in Catalonia the archaeological community has been reluctant to engage with the social context of its focus of study. There are, however, exceptions, mainly related to projects organised in museums. One of the earliest examples, if not the first, began in 2005 at the Barcelona Museum of History (MUHBA, Museu d'Història de Barcelona). Located in Barcelona's old quarter (Ciutat Vella), the Patrimonia'm project encouraged several schools located in its neighbourhood to participate in a joint project. This project's aim was to "improve social cohesion, communicating the city's heritage, promoting the values of citizenship and establishing connections between historical monuments and local communities" (Garcés, Liz and Terrado 2009: 124). Several schools joined the project and the many websites with different activities linked to it speak of its success (MUHBA ny). Having been initially designed for the inner city, its coverage has now been enlarged and historical sites such as the medieval monastery of Pedralbes, to the northeast of the city, and the nineteenth-century aqueduct of the Ciutat Meridiana neighbourhood (MUHBA ny) are now part of the heritage included in the activities. The project is increasing awareness of and pride in Barcelona's heritage among schoolchildren, with the idea that they will also transmit this to their families (Liz 2009).

Other projects include those undertaken by the firm KuanUm. Since 2005 these have been related to the town councils of Cornellà, Sant Boi and Viladecans, three municipalities to the southeast of the city of Barcelona which had immigrant populations of 15.56 percent, 10.4 percent and 9 percent respectively in 2013 (the latest available data), having risen from 1.6 percent, 5.9 percent, 1.4 percent and 1.4 percent in the year 2000 (figures from IDESCAT). KuanUm has been organising tours and workshops without distinguishing ethnic background. Regarding the visits to archaeological sites, they are mainly undertaken in Sant Boi (Figure 12.1). They are adapted to the level of children's language understanding and age. Archaeology is used to establish relationships with the places of origin, as a way of encouraging feelings of familiarity with the place where the migrants are now living, and therefore their feeling of well-being. KuanUm members find that the material culture makes it easier to highlight affinities in the case of migrants from Eastern Europe, North Africa and the Near East, although it is always possible to talk about processes instead of objects and structures (Huélamo and Solías 2016).

Another case of a museum trying to develop projects in which migrants are consciously included is that of L'Hospitalet. In this town, which is now attached to the city of Barcelona, the migrant population rose from 5.9 percent in 2000 to 54.73 percent in 2013 (IDESCAT). The Museo de L'Hospitalet organises visits for

FIGURE 12.1 Participants at a school located in the old town centre of Barcelona at the "Eating like Romans: panis et Moretum" sensory workshop, 29 March 2007. (Photograph: KuanUm)

migrant newcomers with the aim of telling them about the traditional architecture and history of the area. Their experience is that most attendees are adult women and that men do not engage in this type of activity. The museum has also recently teamed up with the local schools to encourage children to explain the museum exhibition to their peers (J.M. Solías, personal communication, Feb 2015).

Other projects in museums have not so much dealt with bringing local residents into contact with the area's heritage and the museum's collections, but with opening up the museum to social events, some of them related to one or several ethnic groups living in the area. One example of this was the Museum of Sant Boi, whose permanent collection is heavily based on an archaeological display (www.museusantboi.cat/), which organised a North African Tamazight evening with food, music and traditional dances in 2008 (van Geert 2014: 208).

The Rua Xic Project (2014)

Most of the large museums in Catalonia, however, have been slow to react to the social challenges posed by immigration. There are exceptions and a recent activity in which another archaeologist, Apen Ruiz, and I have been involved represents one of them (www.gapp.cat/ruaxic/). However, the initiative did not come from the museum, but from a group of young MA graduates with a History of Art background. In June 2014 they decided to form a group under the name of "Enfilant museus", which loosely translates as "setting museums on track". Enfilant realised that the Museum of Archaeology of Catalonia (Museu d'Arqueologia de Catalunya, (MAC)) seemed to be turning its back on the Poble-Sec, the neighbourhood in which it is located. Having obtained the museum's agreement regarding the creation of a project with local residents, they contacted Marabal, a cultural association based in Poble-Sec. Set up in 2008, it organises theatre workshops and courses, theatre and dance performances, active reflective shows and community arts projects (www.marabal.org). One of the activities that Marabal has organised since 2011 is the Rua Xic, a street parade on which the local people work for months designing and preparing the costumes, accoutrements, music, etc. It was decided that the 2014 Rua Xic would be related to the MAC, and add to the parade a theatre piece to be played at the museum.

After the first project design phase between January and March 2014, a campaign was begun to attract residents. For the 2014 Rua Xic, Marabal managed to put together a diverse group of people aged from eight to sixty-five years old. The ethnic composition of the group reflected up to a point that of the neighbourhood as, although it had a large number of Spaniards, both from Catalonia and other parts of Spain, it also had members from Latin America, Eastern and Northern Europe and North Africa. However, no Asians joined the group, despite the fact that they could be as much as 10 percent of the ethnic make-up of the area (IDESCAT). The very first group workshop took place on 3 April and it was followed by five more weekly sessions with group interaction activities based on the theme of multiculturalism. The first visit to the museum was on 10 June and in it group members played a role game and followed clues to discover pieces in the collection that had been chosen for their links to themes previously discussed at the April and May sessions. Two more workshops were held after that visit and a lip dub was organised in early July.

The workshops resumed after the summer break when the group was divided into two different parts, one for the play and the other in charge of preparing costumes and accoutrements. The play was written and directed by Marabal member Òscar Galindo and minimally supervised by the archaeologists in the team. It was rehearsed for two and a half months. Archaeological advice was also sought by the second group. The day selected for the Rua Xic was Saturday 22 November 2014. The festival started in Santa Madrona Square, where a professional group hired for the occasion danced on stilts. There was also music and face painting for children and tickets for the play were distributed in four tents erected to symbolise the four ancient cultures – Iberian, Phoenician, Greek and Roman – that would be key to the play. The actors arrived in the square shortly before the parade started heading towards the museum. They were all dancing to the rhythm of accompanying music and the dance continued at the front of the museum, where the play began with the death of the main dancer, Adama. Bearing her on their shoulders, the actors entered the museum.

The play was performed in the Roman exhibit room, a hexagonal space where statues and mosaics are on display. A balcony on a third level overlooks this area and it was there that the audience of about one hundred and fifty was located (Figure 12.2). An interview made that very morning among the public in Santa Madrona Square had highlighted the fact that a high proportion of local people had never been in the museum. The play discussed a series of ethnic tensions and hostilities among the four ancient cultures and their resolution. At the end of the play the people clearly felt empowered. A good feeling had been created and everybody involved in the play felt extremely positively about the experience. In the interviews immediately after, the museum keeper Joan Muñoz insisted on the openness of the museum to the local neighbourhood, although he acknowledged the other museum staff's fears about having the play performed among the Roman statues (Ruiz Martínez 2014).

The Rua Xic was a success as an inter-cultural project. As project members explained in a reflective workshop a week later, the activity had been important for many of them at personal level. In fact, many are still in touch through WhatsApp and regularly meet, and many have participated in the following Rua Xics since then. The main aim of the project was social and artistic and in those two fields the

FIGURE 12.2 Rua Xic being played at the Roman room, Museum of Archaeology of Catalonia, on 22 November 2014. The actors in the photograph come from Morocco, Roumania, Colombia, England, Argentina and Catalonia. (Photo: Qian Gao)

results were better than expected. With this activity the museum also saw its rooms being visited, in many cases for the first time, by local residents, many of them with migrant backgrounds (Díaz-Andreu and Ruiz 2017).

Conclusions

The world is changing with globalisation. Mono-ethnic nation-states, if they ever existed, have definitely been superseded by multi-ethnic, multicultural nation-states. Archaeology has been slow to react to this new situation. The history of archaeology shows that archaeological narratives of origins have clearly been linked to the reinforcement of a mono-cultural, homogeneous national past. For the last twenty years the literature produced about this has provided endless examples of how it has led to exclusion of some sectors of the total population. Unfortunately, all the reasons why this has happened – mainly through assuming a link between culture and people – are still common in today's archaeological and cultural heritage management discourse (Hodder 2010: 869, Högberg 2015: 48–49). Instead of abandoning the support for archaeological heritage, this article has argued the need to adapt it to the global world, not because it is convenient, but because the new narratives of place and well-being are a better fit with the way communities live. Moreover, it can be argued that abandoning archaeology and searching for origins would lead to profound social damage. This is because the demand for archaeology is linked to identity, to the human need to belong, to have a personal attachment to groups and communities (Baumeister and Leary 1995). Despite the challenges of globalisation, the perdurance of the nation-state as the basis for national and international politics gives archaeology an important role in reinforcing this sense of belonging in the wider community in which one lives, regardless of a person's place of birth and the particular cultural practices they follow in their daily lives. It is archaeologists' moral responsibility to make archaeology a medium for social fulfilment in today´s globalised society.

Archaeology has an ethical role to play and there is a need for an active involvement of archaeological heritage practitioners in the fostering of well-being in society. Archaeologists have a duty to be one of the agents for the promotion of interculturality. The link between archaeological heritage and identity and a sense of belonging reinforces the need to maintain support for the former, although it should be conditional on it fulfilling its role as a cohesive rather than a divisive factor. This makes it urgent to reconsider the ways in which archaeological heritage has the potential to create community in today's global and multicultural world, both where we live – Catalonia in my case – and in Europe and the world as a whole.

Acknowledgements

The ideas in this article have taken a long time to develop. They originated with talks given in Oslo, Cambridge and Leicester during the 2012–2013 academic year. My stay in the last of these was related to my position as Visiting

Professor at that university. I am grateful to Chip Colwell, my fellow students in the Catalan class, the members of GAPP, the Grup d'Arqueologia Pública i Patrimoni, and fellow members of the Heritage and Values project (JPI-JPEH) – Qian Gao, Ana Pastor, Apen Ruiz and Amilcar Vargas – for their comments and suggestions. I am especially grateful to all the participants in the Rua Xic. It was a great experience.

References

Ashworth, G., B. Graham, and J. Tunbridge. 2007. *Pluralising Pasts: Heritage, Identity and Place in Multicultural Societies*. London: Pluto Press.

Basso Peressut, L. and C. Pozzi (eds.) 2012. *Museums in an Age of Migrations. Questions, Challenges, Perspectives*. MeLa book series 1. Milan: Politecnico di Milano.

Baumeister, R. F. and M. R. Leary. 1995. The need to belong: Desire for interpersonal attachments as a fundamental human motivation. *Psychological Bulletin* 117:497–529.

Billig, M. 1995. *Banal Nationalism*. London: Sage.

Colwell-Chanthaphonh, C. 2009. Reconciling American Archaeology and Native America. *Daedalus* 138:94–104.

Comer, D. C. 2013. Archaeology, minorities, identity, and citizenship in the United States. In P. F. Biehl and C. Prescott (eds.), *Heritage in the Context of Globalization. Europe and the Americas*: 69–76, New York: Springer (SpringerBriefs in Archaeology, Vol. 8).

Cooke, P., A. Feldman, C. O'Donnell, T. O'Keeffe, and S. Tuck. 2008. *Placing Voices, Voicing Places. Archaeology in Inner-City Dublin: Spatiality, Materiality and Identity-Formation Among Dublin's Working Class and Immigrant Communities*. Online.

Díaz-Andreu, M. 2007. *A World History of Nineteenth-Century Archaeology. Nationalism, Colonialism and the Past. Oxford Studies in the History of Archaeology*. Oxford: Oxford University Press.

Díaz-Andreu, M. 2018. Archaeology and Imperialism: From Nineteenth-Century New Imperialism to Twentieth-Century Decolonization. In B. Effros and G. Lai (eds.), *Unmasking Ideology in Imperial and Colonial Archaeology: Vocabulary, Symbols, and Legacy* 28–64, Los Angeles: UCLA, Cotsen Institute Press. (Ideas, Debates, and Perspectives 8).

Díaz-Andreu, M. and A. Ruiz 2017. Interacting with heritage: social inclusion and archaeology in Barcelona. *Journal of Community Archaeology & Heritage* 4: 53–68.

European Commission. 2014. 5th Annual Report on Immigration and Asylum (2013). www.europarl.europa.eu/meetdocs/2014_2019/documents/com/com_com%282014%290288_/com_com%282014%290288_en.pdf.

Garcés, M., J. Liz, and C. Terrado. 2009. Patrimonia'm. Un treball cooperatiu del Museu d'Història de Barcelona i les escoles de ciutat vella. In P. González Marcén (ed.). *Patrimoni, identitat i ciutadania: un nou paper per a l'arqueologia i la historia*: 123–136, Bellaterra: Universitat Autònoma de Barcelona.

Gerbich, C. and S. Kamel. 2012. Welcome on the Diwan! Experiences with the visitor panel of the Museum für Islamische Kunst at the Pergamonmuseum in Berlin (Germany). In N. Schücker (ed.). *Integrating Archaeology. Science – Wish – Reality*: 199–204, Frankfurt am Mein: Römisch-Germanische Kommission.

Graham, H., R. Mason and A. Newman. 2009. *Literature Review: Historic Environment, Sense of Place, and Social Capital*. London: English Heritage.

Gustafsson, A. and H. Karlsson. 2011. A spectre is haunting Swedish archaeology – the spectre of politics: Archaeology, cultural heritage and the present political situation in Sweden. *Current Swedish Archaeology* 19:11–36.

Hodder, I. 2010. Cultural heritage rights: From ownership and descent to justice and well-being. *Anthropological Quarterly* 83:861–882.

Högberg, A. 2015. The heritage sector in a multicultural society: A discussion from a Swedish perspective. In P. F. Biehl, D. Comer, C. Prescott, and H. A. Soderland (eds.), *Identity and Heritage. Contemporary Challenges in a Globalized World*: 47–54, New York: Springer.

Huélamo, J. M. and J. M. Solias 2016. *Kuanum. Reflexions al voltant del llegat dels sentits*. In M. Díaz-Andreu, A. Pastor and A. Ruiz (eds.), *Arqueología y comunidad: el valor social del patrimonio arqueológico en el siglo XXI*: 147–168. Madrid: JAS Arqueología.

Jensen, M. B. 2011. Comment on "A spectre is haunting Swedish archaeology" from a Danish point of view. *Current Swedish Archaeology* 19:37–43.

Karlsson, H. ed. 2015. *The contemporary past as an inclusive cultural heritage. A case study of the so called Air Torpedo of Bäckebo, Sweden*: Paper presented at the Heritage Values and the Public workshop held at the University of Barcelona 19–20 February.

KuanUm. 2011. Can Mas, un barrio con corazón. *KuanUm blog* accessed February 2015: kuanum.blogspot.com.es/2011_03_01_archive.html.

Kvaale, K. 2011. Something begotten in the state of Denmark? Immigrants, territorialized culture, and the Danes as an indigenous people. *Anthropological Theory* 11:223–255.

Lingua Món. ny. Las lenguas de la inmigración en Cataluña. Accessed February 2015: www10.gencat.cat/casa_llengues/AppJava/es/diversitat/diversitat/llengues_immigracio.jsp.

Liz, J. 2009. Patrimonia'm. Un proyecto de proximidad y trabajo cooperativo entre el Museo de Historia de Barcelona y las escuelas e institutos de Ciutat Vella. *Blog de Edumuseos*.

Meskell, L. 1998. Oh my goddess! Archaeology, sexuality and ecofeminism. *Archaeological Dialogues* 5:126–142.

Morris, M. W., C.-y. Chiu, and Z. Liu. 2015. Polycultural psychology. *Annual Review of Psychology* 66:631–659.

MUHBA. ny. Patrimonia'm – a heritage project for schools. Accessed February 2015: museuhistoria.bcn.cat/en/taxonomy/term/433.

Orton, A. 2012. *Building migrants' belonging through positive interactions. A Guide for policy-makers and practitioners. Council of Europe policy document*. Brussels: Council of Europe.

PBI. 2008. *Pla Barcelona Interculturalitat*. Barcelona: Ajuntament de Barcelona. Online.

Pitts, M. 2014. My archaeology. *British Archaeology* 136:14.

Prescott, C. 2013. Heritage and the new immigrant minorities: A catalyst of relevance for contemporary archaeology? In P. F. Biehl and C. Prescott (eds.), *Heritage in the Context of Globalization. Europe and the Americas*: 59–68, New York: Springer (SpringerBriefs in Archaeology, Vol. 8).

Pujadas, I. 2007. Les migracions dels anys seixanta a Catalunya. *Butlletí de la Fundació Lluís Carulla [Special issue: Les onades immigratòries en la Catalunya contemporània]* 7:36–41.

Rodrigues, N. 2012. Saint-Denis, archaeology, territory and citizenship (Archeologie, territoire et citoyennete). Assessment and prospects. In N. Schücker (ed.). *Integrating Archaeology. Science – Wish – Reality*: 17–21, Frankfurt am Mein: Römisch-Germanische Kommission.

Ruiz Martínez, A. 2014. Rua Xic in Poble Sec, Barcelona. heritagevalues.net/rua-xic-in-poble-sec-barcelona/.

Silberman, N. A. 2010. Rewriting Jewish history. Recent excavations have transformed our understanding of the lives of European Jews during the Middle Ages. *Archaeology* July/August:18, 58–61, 65–66.

Synnestvedt, A. 2009. Archaeology as a meeting point for multicultural regeneration. In *AHI (Association of heritage interpretation, Conference report from the Vital Spark Interpretation Conference in Aveimore 2007*. Online.

Synnestvedt, A. 2014. *Archaeology, Art and City Planning. Gothenburg Workshop for Inspiration and Sharing Experiences. 27–28 March 2014. NEARCH workshops in Gothenburg 1 New scenarios for a community-involved archaeology*. Gothenburg: University of Gothenburg.

van Geert, F. 2014. The recognition of migrations in the construction of Catalan national identity? Representations of the history of migrations and cultural diversity in Catalan museums (1980–2012). In L. Gourievidi (ed.). *Museums and Migration: History, Memory and Politics*, London: Routledge.

Zapata-Barrero, R. 2006. Immigration, autonomie politique et gestion de l'identité: Le cas de la Catalogne. *Outre-Terre* 4:189–209.

Zobler, K. A. 2011. Syrian national museums: Regional politics and the imagined community. In H. Silverman (ed.). *Contested Cultural Heritage Religion, Nationalism, Erasure, and Exclusion in a Global World*: 171–192, New York: Springer.

13

'EVERYBODY'S DIFFERENT – AND YET WE'RE ALL THE SAME'

A transcultural project in a multicultural class

Cynthia Dunning Thierstein

> Évoluer dans une classe où les élèves ont des langues maternelles et des histoires différentes ne peut être que bénéfique pour les autres enfants: ils apprennent à s'adapter à un monde ouvert et pluriel, qui sera de toute façon le leur.
>
> *Marie Rose Moro*

Introduction

Biel/Bienne (Canton of Berne, Switzerland) has a long tradition of immigration. It started in the middle of the 19th century with the arrival of French-speaking watch-makers from the nearby Jura mountains. They were soon followed by construction workers from rural areas near and far.[1] This was the very beginning of the bilingualism which is a hallmark of the town today.

During the economic boom which lasted from 1945 to 1975, labour was needed to keep up with the workload produced by an economy in full swing. This labour came mainly from Italy in the form of seasonal workers. In 1965, a quarter of the active population were foreign residents, not including political refugees from Eastern Europe and the workers' children. This foreign work force was composed of 80 percent Italians and 10 percent Spaniards. In 1968 several movements tried to counter immigration with populist initiatives[2] that were fought against in Biel/Bienne (although with not much success), giving the city a reputation of being favourable towards immigrants. In the 1980s, migrants started to come from other parts of the world. Their profiles were now more diverse, including refugees, asylum-seekers as well as students and highly qualified people. In Biel/Bienne, which has neither a university nor tertiary centre, and is far from the diplomatic sphere, this wave of migrants was mostly made up of political refugees from South America, Vietnam or Eastern Europe, increasing the percentage of foreigners to 18 percent of the city's population. In 1992 there were people from over 100 countries living in the city and by 2010 the percentage of foreign residents – originating from 143 countries and speaking more than 70 different languages – was around 29 percent and is still constantly growing.[3] The most recent immigration comes from North Africa and the Near East.

A total of 33.1 percent of the city's population speaks languages other than the official languages of the town which are German and French. The majority have a migrant background. Statistics show that 53.5 percent of the foreign residents are economically active, although most are lower ranked employees and 22 percent have no higher education than the mandatory schooling.[4]

This situation certainly is problematic, in particular for the local population, part of which is afraid of the changes in society the migrants may provoke. There is a clear demand for rapid integration, which starts at school.

Migrants and education

The relationship that migrants have with the local cultural heritage is a difficult one, either provoking social isolation or on the contrary, masking the origins and identity of the immigrant communities. Therefore it is a challenge at least to understand the cultural traditions of each community, and accept their existence without necessarily having to assimilate them. This is a difficult task in particular for teachers, who are generally the first adult reference people that migrant children are in contact with.

The pedagogical response to high immigration rates in the 1960s and 1970s was to see heterogeneity as a disturbance, to focus on assimilation, and to limit itself to intensive language courses and lessons on local cultural knowledge. Heterogeneity was still seen as a problem in the 1980s, since the schools had to cope with problems caused by migrant children. The answer was then to support and promote the children not only in the school but with extracurricular activities. The 1990s saw a revolution in the education of migrant children with the acceptance of intercultural pedagogy, considering homogeneity as a fiction and defining heterogeneity as a challenge that can be overcome with the development of the main school language (French or German in the case of Biel/Bienne) as second language and a greater parental participation. This developed in the 21st century into a pedagogy based on diversity, which considers heterogeneity to be normal and deals with problems through an appropriate handling of language, cultural, social and performance-related differences.[5] During this phase, many extracurricular activities and parallel structures were abandoned. In reality, the evolution has not been so clear; all cantons, cities or schools find themselves at different stages of adaptation and the pedagogy of diversity still seems to be more of a wish than reality.

In 2009, one third of all classes in the canton of Berne, mostly in the cities, were multicultural or multilingual.[6] This development is also a clear consequence of the fact that many children are now no longer direct migrants but children of migrants, born in the country. Teachers have to learn to cope with this new reality.

In Biel/Bienne, the structures of the city, responsible for education, focus on encouraging integration from the earliest age possible, working with pre-school children and their parents as well as the teaching of a second language in kindergarten. The encouragement continues with continuous institutional support throughout the school curriculum. All-day school is particularly important to this concept of education through immersion, since this puts migrant children into continuous contact with their native schoolmates, although special classes for the integration of recently arrived migrants exist in higher levels.[7] Migrant children also have the opportunity to learn their original languages and understand their culture in classes organised by embassies or private associations on an extracurricular basis. But the development of transcultural educational concepts still belongs to the field of research, while many projects have been initiated by teachers themselves in different classes, or sometimes whole schools in the case of special activities (such as a school feast). Certain projects are led in association with the Pedagogical University in Berne, which offers a curriculum on school and migration.[8]

Recent literature on migrant youth defines the different spheres of influence that accompany migrant children through their educational careers, and which must be considered in the pedagogical processes throughout the time they are in school.[9] Although the experiences lived by migrant children are often similar to those of the native children in similar social circumstances, some particularities do exist, especially in the first sphere of influence which is the *immigration process*. It includes the reasons for immigration as well as the way the family or group have been welcomed in their new surroundings. The second sphere of influence is the *family environment* which plays a role in the socio-economic context in which the child will grow up. *Schools and other educational structures* play an important structural and emotional part, since they often influence the formative development of the child. These last two elements are in close relationship to a fourth sphere of influence which is the *social capital* including three fields: the family, the community and the institutions. All these elements allow children to develop *psychosocial resources* such as resilience and motivation, which they can use to advance their educational careers (Figure 13.1).

But another important sphere of influence is certainly cultural heritage and it reflects upon all the elements mentioned above. The first ethical dimension can be traced to the heritage the migrants bring from abroad, which reflects particularly on the immigration process and family environment. On one hand, migrant communities are encouraged to remain connected with their own heritage by communicating their difference with the local "indigenous" community. On the other hand, they are asked to integrate new heritage values when entering another country and specially when confronted with different organisational structures such as school.

One essential part of this new shared community life is defined in the classroom. And this life may be even more diverse than the life outside the classroom, particularly for migrant children who grow up in partly closed communities.

Educational inputs

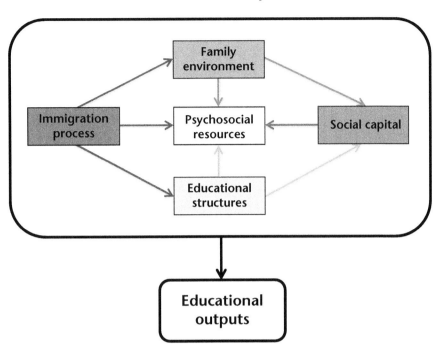

FIGURE 13.1 Influence of educational inputs on the formative process. After Bader, B. and R. Fibbi, 2013, p. 12

A second question arises concerning the way to communicate ideals of shared living in harmony within the same community. Integration in this context means defining a cohesion factor and the development of values that are the same for all. Therefore it is important to find a subject or theme having similar values in the external communities to reinforce the internal one composed in the classroom. This cohesion will serve as a base for further understanding amongst the children in and out of the classroom, forming therefore a new community conscious of its similarities in their differences. Communities change – the classroom will also – but certain values will remain and be transported to other groups forming new communities, spreading the word in a form of active engagement.[10]

Ethics concern everybody working in heritage and archaeology. If you want to engage in heritage activities, you have to find a meaningful way to do it.[11] In his article on the Faro Convention,[12] Schofield defines the social importance of "places" that get their heritage value from the stories and experiences that are attached to them. This applies to places considered as particular by groups of individuals as well as those that are special for personal reasons. Heritage matters,[13] not only as a place, but also through the subjects approached by heritage and particularly by archaeology. Therefore the social importance matters equally for gestures and activities attached either to rituals or to everyday life, such as the making of bread for instance. The *universality* and *inevitability* (to use the words Schofield does) of these actions give them a strong social relevance as much as any valued place would. Valorisation is based on understanding and teaching how to understand differences and similarities throughout time and space.[14] Who, besides the actors themselves, can testify to the social relevance of activities and gestures that are part of a very long historical process, if not archaeologists, historians or anthropologists?

Certain authors[15] propose that archaeologists participate in societal change through working with teachers in and out of the classroom. Archaeology is used as a tool for the building up of a social coherence between children of different origins forming a community in the classroom. The social values developed in the classroom should give reference points that are common throughout space and time outside this privileged setting. Integrating heritage into the educational programme may help to define a common ground showing shared values placed in the past and which still have influence in everyday life today. Thus it is possible to stabilise and develop further understanding of differences. The result is learning to work together and earn respect from one another. Archaeology in education can show young people how to understand and appreciate diversity in the past as well as in the present and therefore learn to live in a society composed of different communities, migrant or not.[16] This project inscribes itself in this context.

The project: 'Everybody's different – and yet we're all the same'

It is within this perspective that the idea to develop a project using historical aspects and topic-centred theatre arose, with the intention of bringing together children of a multicultural and multilingual school class in order to reflect on their differences as well as on their similarities while discovering objects of cross-cultural significance in time and space and thus allowing them a better understanding of each other and their local social environment today.

The educational aims are manifold: development of social competence, self-recognition, creativity and the understanding of our links with social history. The project is particularly close to the school curriculum, integrating the teaching of history with other branches like citizenship, hands-on and creative activities as well as the use of body language in a theatrical context.

Methodology

Holistic learning lies at the heart of our project, and we concentrate on the children's experiences in combination with historical and ethnological elements, stories and rituals.

For this experiment, we chose the theme of "bread", a universal food-stuff which has been known since prehistory and is found almost all over the world.[17] It also has great social, religious and political significance, and therefore allowed us to consider many approaches and develop many activities related to history, ethnology and other social sciences. The cultural aspect reflected by our subject, which was bread throughout time and around the world, was meant to confront a common past legacy, reaching down to the Neolithic agricultural revolution, with modern heritage showing a very rich range of bread-making techniques from all over the world. This permitted children from diverse origins to discover common ground in the past and the present, and allowed them to learn to work together.

Several key concepts followed us throughout the project:

- *Diversity* of kinds and forms of bread throughout the world, reflecting the diversity of the origins of the children.
- *Similarity* of the main ingredients of bread (flour, water and salt) reflects continuity in its fabrication and a comparable way of preparing bread throughout time and around the world.
- Bread is a staple food and its continuous presence, in many forms, has given it an important role in human existence, becoming an emblem of repletion, of labour, of life. For that reason, bread is present in all sectors of human activities. "*Panem et circenses*"[18] reminds us of the importance of bread as a political instrument of appeasement. The famous statement, wrongly attributed to Marie-Antoinette, "*S'ils n'ont pas de pain, qu'ils mangent de la brioche*"[19] shows us that the lack of staples such as bread or rice may lead to a revolution. Bread is present in many rituals as an emblem of fertility and has a deep spiritual significance in Judaeo-Christian traditions.

Different teaching methods were used simultaneously

The first and most important approach was based on *theme-centred theatre*.[20] This method allows children to approach different themes in a playful way, recreating movements in relationship with a particular situation or inventing scenes relative to the studied topic. They discover objects and situations through physical access, allowing them to understand and tackle issues in a global way. Each pupil can emphasise individual capacities, with skills being fostered by movements and of theatrical improvisations. The educational possibilities in the field of theme-centred theatre are numerous and can be adapted to the particular situations of each school-child.

Archaeologists and heritage specialists rarely know how to see, feel and comprehend the children, while their teachers live with them and know their background. Therefore, with the help of the teacher, we applied active pedagogy and cognitive learning by encouraging communication between the children and the group, which permitted the participants to express their motivations and feelings. This was done with the help of practical exercises requiring everybody's participation. Personal work was used to develop autonomy and self-confidence.

Implementation

During a whole school year, from September 2013 to July 2014, we followed a school class with children from diverse cultural backgrounds, repeating actions of long ago, reviving rituals and participating with all five senses, trying to understand a common past history despite the differences of origins. The twenty 10- to 11-year-old children were originally from Afghanistan, Brazil, Congo, Germany, Iraq, Kosovo, Macedonia, Pakistan, Portugal, Serbia, Slovakia, Sri Lanka, Switzerland and Turkey. Some were born in their mother-country, other were born in Switzerland. Furthermore a certain number of pupils had learning disabilities which slowed down the class activities considerably. The main protagonists were a professional actress, who is also a teacher, and an archaeologist. The class-teacher was also always present, helping when necessary.

Five modules were put into practice in the five days throughout the school year. Each module had its own aims which all led to the main objective of developing a better understanding of each other and today's local social environment through the understanding of historic and ethnological elements.

Each module was built in a similar way, with an introduction, two to three distinctive activities and a retrospective view of the day.

The first module's aim was to get to know each other and discover the breads of the world. The children greeted each other in their mother tongue or the language of their country of origin using traditional gestures if they were known. They also used the name of a type of bread existing in this country and brought the recipe to school. Thus the parents were also brought into the project, sometimes giving input on older traditions. The children tried to personify themselves with their breads and presented themselves and their origins in a theatrical way. During the second part of the morning, it was important for each pupil to understand that they all form part of one whole. With a game of "Memory",[21] they discovered all kinds of breads existing around the world and could find out which ones they knew about (Figure 13.2). An accent was put on local Swiss breads, allowing the children to integrate their knowledge of local products as well. The results were presented as a map of the world where the countries of origin of all the children were represented with small self-made flags linked to the recipes and pictures of their traditional breads (Figure 13.3).

The second module was devoted to the historical aspects of bread. With pictures corresponding to bread-making in the Neolithic period, by the ancient Egyptians, during the Roman Empire and in the Middle ages, the children, divided in four groups, tried to classify the different ingredients, stages and ways of production through time. This led to thorough discussions on the evolution of agricultural techniques, on differences in the components of bread-making, as well as what the value of bread had in these historical periods. These considerations were brought to life through small stage plays whose texts and forms were prepared by the pupils and presented in class. The second part of the module consisted of a typological exercise. Ten types of bread, defined by their contents and ways of baking, were put on the blackboard. The children received written descriptions of these

FIGURE 13.2 Children attributing the names of breads to the corresponding illustrations. (Photo: Mathias Tschantré)

bread types and had to find the matching picture. They also had to classify the "Memory" cards corresponding to the bread types. Thus the children learned that the main ingredients of bread have already exited for more than 7,000 years and that the making of bread is linked not only to alimentation but also to agricultural practices and the evolution of techniques, and this in all periods of time all over the world. Typology is a very important instrument in archaeological research, and it was used here not only to show its significance, but also to make the link between the diversity of forms and the similarity of ingredients.

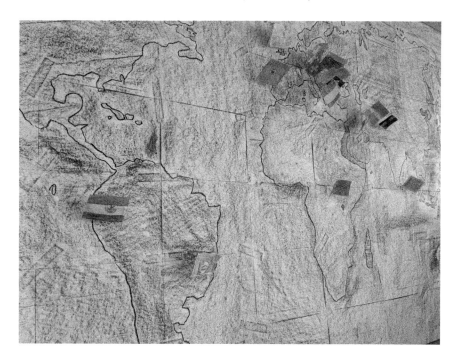

FIGURE 13.3 Map showing the places where the children came from. (Photo: Mathias Tschantré)

The making of bread was the main theme of the third module. It was accompanied by the production of flat bread (which resembles prehistoric bread) with the help of a Turkish cook, who allowed all children to prepare and bake a "pita" which they could eat during the break. But first, the pupils had to find out the main constituents of bread. It was a good opportunity to discover where the different types of flour ingredients come from (maize from America – taro from Africa – wheat from the Near East) thus using the world map once more. Touching, smelling and tasting all these components was an important experience, which found its way into the small theatre plays and the "Bread dance" which was to be part of the final module. Each child then gave a small presentation of their particular recipes, explaining what is so special about it. The ingredients for the recipes were then separated into groups (red for flour / blue for water / yellow for salt / green for yeast / etc.). This showed that all the types of bread had at least three common elements: flour – of whatever grain, water, and salt.

The making of flat bread was a touching experience, since many of the children already knew its particularities from home, and often showed off trying to make the best one! Others were bored and made little effort, especially since it was something boys don't generally do! Nevertheless, this experiment showed us how deeply imbedded certain traditional customs and practices still are amongst these children who mostly grew up in Switzerland.

With the fourth module, we wanted to discover the customs and rituals around bread and let the children create their own ritual around the "artistic bread" they had invented themselves. The first part consisted of a story-telling round, with pictures showing bread in a symbolic context: Christmas or Easter breads, bread made

FIGURE 13.4 Artistic bread: this one represents an imaginative form of the Slovak emblem. (Photo: Mathias Tschantré)

for a marriage, the birth of a child or for someone's death, etc. The accent was also placed on the fact that in some countries, without bread, other foods take over this role, such as in northern Africa where dates or other food goods play a more important role. All the breads presented are festive and their importance is clear from the use of many more ingredients than the bare staples of flour, water and salt.

Then a story was especially chosen in order to speak about solidarity.[22] The astonishing fact was that this particular story was taken up as a main theme during the plays the children invented for the fifth module. The second part of the lesson was occupied by making an "artistic loaf of bread" (Figure 13.4) and giving it a particular meaning, which was then explained to the whole class. The last part of this module was based on the invention of small plays on the different themes that had been spoken about since the beginning of the project as well as the creation of a "Bread dance" combining movements related to the making of bread, its ingredients, traditional movements and how one should feel if one were a piece of bread! This module brought forth the children's emotions and creativity, which was then fully expressed during the last module.

The fifth and final module was the preparation and realisation of a party where all the parents, teachers and other participants were invited to celebrate the end of the project. It consisted of a culinary part, with the preparation of bread, soup and "damper bread"[23] for all to try and cook. The most exciting part of the party was

FIGURE 13.5 Rehearsing the "bread rap". (Photo: Cynthia Dunning Thierstein)

the show. It was composed of the "Bread dance" as it had been built up during the fourth module, as well as six plays taking on subjects such as the invention of the first bread amongst the gods of the universe, the story of a robbed baker who found his flour again, or the legend of the poor old lady and her rich neighbour whose bread always became hard as a rock. The show closed on a "bread rap" (Figure 13.5) which the teacher and pupils organised – music, words and dance – to our great surprise and to the pleasure of all. It was a real expression of collaboration between all parties; children, teachers and parents: a manifestation of understanding of each other and of today's local social environment. It was the last day of school, and this class, who could now speak of having come together, would be leaving for other schools, hopefully with each child newly motivated to develop their own future educational careers.

The project was completed with teaching materials in French and German for teachers who would like to repeat the project with their classes. It is, however, important that the project be carried out in collaboration with specialists – archaeologists as well as actors – since only they can bring the knowledge and authenticity necessary for a successful outcome.

Lessons learned and conclusions

The whole project was based on collaboration between the children and their teachers, shared activities and dialogue. It allowed all the participants to reflect upon the past and the present. Through their own personal experiences in the classroom, the participants learned to recognise diversity in their heritage, generated by different practices and ways of living they bring from home.

In this case, the subject of bread throughout time and space brought the children to identify and accept their differences, even if they were still too young to formulate them precisely. But also it allowed them to define similarities, helping them develop cohesion and build a one-time community in the classroom.[24] Social archaeology . . . seen in a practical way.

The difficulties some children had with their immigration background were experienced through their educational problems, the absence of concentration or extreme liveliness. The project channelled some of these difficulties, allowing the children to express themselves freely through theatrical activities and physical work.

So, we applied theme-centred theatre to familiarise the children with actions and movements used in different historic periods, leading them to understand both the past and the present. Re-enacting these past actions also validates those of today, which are, in the end, not so different at all. The living experience through theatrical and hands-on activities in relation to bread-making allowed the children to take possession of the material and identify themselves with it. Also, having to work together facilitated mutual acceptance and respect for all.

Working on a common subject, but being allowed to demonstrate one's differences was therefore extremely rewarding.

It was important to involve the families throughout the project since this is the main way to develop a social exchange and to accompany the learning process with the various inputs from around the world. The children had to ask their parents what bread belonged to their culture, and how it could be made. The rolling pins brought to prepare the flat bread, for example, corresponded to those used in each child's country. Parents also contributed at home, telling stories and explaining traditions in relation to bread. These were sometimes shared during the activities. The family was also present at the party, where each family group mixed either with members of the same cultural background or with others – neighbours, teachers and friends.

The importance of the school structure in this project does not need to be underlined. The school was the venue for the activities, and the classroom was also a "melting pot", where ideas came together and could be expressed. The best results of this cooperation were certainly the "bread rap" and the theatrical performance during the party.

I believe that the project would not have been half as successful without the highlight of the party: this was the expression of the social capital, as we defined it at the beginning of this chapter, bringing together family, different communities and school as a place of exchange, enrichment and finally solidarity.

Needless to say, this kind of project can be done in all school classes with children of different backgrounds, not only with differences of origins, but also with social disparities or even with classes where children of different ages and levels come together.

If the integration of migrant children was our initial objective, this was very quickly replaced by transcultural experience offering new languages for us as well as for the children involved. Heritage, and archaeology as one of its main vectors, works with the material past to understand the world of today and prepare for the future. It not only considers objects and data, but materialises through dialogue and common experiences.[25] Bearing this in mind, then the experience described above can be considered as a model project of novel heritage methodology in particular in relation to ethical integration practices with migrant children.

Acknowledgements

I would like to express my thanks to the programme "tête-à-tête" of the Direction of public education of the canton of Berne, the city council of Biel/Bienne, Zonta-Club Biel/Bienne, and Villa Kebab for their financial and personal support, without which this project would have never happened. Special thanks go to Mathias Tschantré who let us go through this project with his class and Isabelle Freymond, who knows how to combine theatre and pedagogy in ways that are always engaging.

Notes

1 The history of migration in Biel/Bienne is taken from different chapters in the most recent publication on the history of the city: *Bieler Geschichte. 1815 bis heute*, p. 667–672, p. 717, p. 884; p. 892–895, p. 944–948.

2 The so-called Schwarzenbach-Initiatives against over-population and foreign infiltration.

3 The foreign residents counted for 30.19 percent in June 2013 (Bieler Tagblatt, 13.8.2013). The average annual percentage of immigration is 2.5 percent.

4 www.biel.ch/files/pdf4/pra_sm_fact_sheet_01.04.2014_d_f.pdf, consulted 09.12.2014. This corresponds to the Swiss national means with 55 percent active working foreigners, of which 25 percent do not have a higher education than mandatory schooling (Espa 2014: Enquête suisse sur la population active, ESPA (2014). Neuchâtel: Office fédéral de la statistique : www.bfs.admin.ch/bfs/portal/fr/index/themen/03/02/blank/data/03.html#; consulted 09.12.2014).

5 Waldis, B. 2009. Bericht "*Migration und Schule*", p. 8, Tabelle 1.

6 Waldis, B. 2009. Bericht "*Migration und Schule*", p. 6.

7 This will be enhanced further with the enactment of the Cantonal law on the integration of the migrant population in the canton of Berne (Lint) on January 1st 2015.

8 I thank Peter Walther, responsible for the department of Schools and Sport of the city of Biel/Bienne for his explanations concerning integration of the migrants in the municipality.

9 Bader, B. et R. Fibbi. 2012 (2013). *Les enfants des migrants: un véritable potentiel*, p. 11–13.

10 Waterton, E. 2015. *Heritage and Community Engagement*, p. 54.

11 Schofield, J. 2015. *Forget About Heritage: Place, Ethics and the Faro Convention*, p. 197.

12 Ibid., p. 198.

13 Ibid., p. 208.

14 Moro, M. R. 2012. *Enfants de l'immigration, une chance pour l'école*, p. 86.

15 These archaeologists are Jepson (2004) and Stone (2000), cited in McDavid, C. and Brock, T. P. 2015. *The Differing Forms of Public Archaeology: Where We Have Been, Where We Are Now, and Thoughts for the Future*, p. 167.

16 Little, B. 2012. *Public Benefits of Public Archaeology*, p. 396.

17 The bibliography for this project was mainly based on the works of Max Wehren, who spent most of his lifetime collecting information on the making of bread throughout all periods of time.

18 Juvenal, *Satire X*, 77–81.

19 This citation probably has its origin in Jean-Jacques Rousseau's *Confessions*, book 6: "Enfin je me rappelai le pis-aller d'une grande princesse à qui l'on disait que les paysans n'avaient pas de pain, et qui répondit: Qu'ils mangent de la brioche." http://fr.wikipedia.org/wiki/Qu'ils_mangent_de_la_brioche_!

20 More on theme-centred theatre in : http://tzt.ch/c/74/das-tzt-wurde-von-heinrich-werthm%C3%BCller-im-rahmen-seiner-lehrt%C3%A4tigkeit-an-der-johann-wolfgang-goethe-universit%C3%A4t-frankfurt-am-main-entwickelt-der-anstoss-zur-entwicklung-des-tzt-war-die-%C3%BCberlegung

21 The sets of "Memory" cards were specially made for this project.

22 It is the story of a poor lady who had no flour to bake some bread for her children and asked the neighbour for some help. The rich neighbour refused and a spell fell upon her, transforming all bread she made or bought into stone until it was her time to ask the poor neighbour for help, which she, of course, accepted. Thus the spell disappeared and they could share the bread together.

23 "Damper bread" is an Australian specialty consisting of dough curled around a stick and cooked over an open fire.

24 Harrison, R. 2015. *Beyond "Natural" and "Cultural" Heritage: Toward an Ontological Politics of Heritage in the Age of Anthropocene*, p. 27–28.

25 Ibid. p. 35 citing Holtorf, C. and G. Fairclough. 2013. The new heritage and re-shapings of the past. In A. Gonzáles Ruibal (ed.) *Reclaiming Archaeology. Beyond the Tropes of Modernity*, Routledge, p. 197–210.

References

History of Biel/Bienne and migration

Biel/Bienne. Statistisches Fact Sheet *Données statistiques*. Stand *Etat* 01.04.2014. Hrsg. Wirtschaft /Stadtmarketing. *Ed. Economie / Marketing de la ville.* www.biel.ch/files/pdf4/pra_sm_fact_sheet_01.04.2014_d_f.pdf, consulted 09.12.2014

Enquête suisse sur la population active, ESPA (2014). Neuchâtel: Office fédéral de la statistique. www.bfs.admin.ch/bfs/portal/fr/index/themen/03/02/blank/data/03.html#; consulted 09.12.2014.

Gaffino, D. and R. Lindegger (Hrsg.). 2013. Bieler Geschichte. Band 2. 1815 bis heute. Mit Beiträge von T. Kaestli in Zusammenarbeit mit H. Rickenbacher und D. Gaffino. Hier + Jetzt, Verlag für Kultur und Geschichte, Baden.

Migrants and education

Bader, B. and R. Fibbi. 2012 (2013). *Les enfants des migrants: un véritable potentiel.* SFM (Swiss Forum for Migration and Population Studies) Neuchâtel; SG and CDIP, Berne (Rapport final CONVEGNO 2012) (only pdf). http://edudoc.ch/record/110244/files/convegno2012_bericht_f.pdf; consulted 9.12.2014.

Moro, M. R. 2012. *Enfants de l'immigration, une chance pour l'école.* Entretiens avec Joanna et Denis Peiron. Bayard.

Waldis, B. 2009. *Bericht Migration und Schule,* Planungsauftrag des Rektorats zu den Lehrangeboten an der PHBern. Pädagogische Hochschule PHBern, Bern.

Migrants and archaeology

Jameson, J. H. Jr. 2006. Towards an inclusive public heritage. In: *Interpreting the Past. Vol. IV. Who owns the Past? Heritage Rights and Responsibilities in a Multicultural World.* Flemish Heritage Institute (VIOE) and Ename Center for Public Archaeology and Heritage Presentation, p. 211–219.

Lowenthal, D. 1985. *The Past is a Foreign Country.* Cambridge University Press

Ethics

Harrison, R. 2015. Beyond "Natural" and "Cultural" Heritage: Toward an Ontological Politics of Heritage in the Age of Anthropocene. *Heritage & Society,* 8 (1), 24–42.

Little, B. 2012. Public benefits of public archaeology. In R. Skeates, C. McDavid, and J. Carman (eds.), *The Oxford Handbook of Public Archaeology.* New York: Oxford University Press, p. 395–413.

McDavid, C. and Brock, T. P. 2015. The Differing Forms of Public Archaeology: Where We Have Been, Where We Are Now, and Thoughts for the Future. In C. Gnecco and D. Lippert (eds.), *Ethics and Archaeological Praxis, Ethical Archaeologies: The Politics of Social Justice 1.* Springer, p. 159–184.

Schofield, J. 2015. Forget About Heritage: Place, Ethics and the Faro Convention. In Tracy Ireland and John Schofield (eds.), *Ethical Archaeologies: The Politics of Social Justice 4.* Springer, p. 197–209.

Waterton, E. 2015. Heritage and community engagement. In Tracy Ireland and John Schofield (eds.), *Ethical Archaeologies: The Politics of Social Justice 4.* Springer, p. 53–67.

Theme-centred theatre

http://tzt.ch/c/74/das-tzt-wurde-von-heinrich-werthm%C3%BCller-im-rahmen-seiner-lehrt%C3%A4tigkeit-an-der-johann-wolfgang-goethe-universit%C3%A4t-frankfurt-am-main-entwickelt-der-anstoss-zur-entwicklung-des-tzt-war-die-%C3%BCberlegung; consulted 9.12.2014.
ICH DU WIR: Lektionensets zu : Sozialkompetenz, Gender, Konsum, Konflikt, Kommunikation, Sexualität. Tzt-Verlag, Meilen.

Teaching materials on bread in French and German

Dokumentationsstelle der Schweizerischen Brotinformation (SBI) (www.schweizerbrot.ch/de/broschueren/downloads.html) *Service de documentation de l'Information suisse sur le pain ISP (www.painsuisse.ch/fr/brochures/telechargements.html)*, consulted 9.12.2014.
Juvenal (Decimus Iunius Iuvenalis), Saturae. *Satura X*: www.thelatinlibrary.com/juvenal/10.shtml
Rousseau, J.-J. (1889). *Les Confessions*, illustrations de M. Leloir. Tome I, livre 6. Editions Launette, Paris: http://fr.wikisource.org/wiki/Les_Confessions_(Rousseau)/Livre_VI
Währen, M. 2000. Gesammelte Aufsätze zur Brot- und Gebäckkunde und - geschichte. Deutsches Brotmuseum, Ulm.

14

THE PLACE OF THE MIGRANT

Heritage and ethics in the transnational space of a Sydney park

Denis Byrne

Introduction

The various mobilities that comprise migration – including flows of people, objects, and ideas – exist in relation to what have been called 'immobilities or moorings' (Sheller, 2011: 1). These latter include networks of family that typically moor first generation migrants to their point of origin, even while they are working to anchor themselves in the destination landscape. The phenomenon of chain migration means that significant proportions of the population of particular villages and rural areas in origin countries often end up living in the same city or even in the same suburb of their destination country. The Salvadoran village of El Palón, for example, has partly reproduced itself in West Adams, Los Angeles, while the Mirpur rural area of Bangladesh has done the same in Tower Hamlets, London (Saunders, 2012). Circulatory flows of people, objects, money and knowledge link the home place and the new place, a phenomenon which is conducive to flexible, mobile notions of belonging (Sheller, 2003: 276–277) that elude the category of stable, permanent belonging that has been central to the modern nation-state's project of national identity building.

While deterritorialisation of social life is taken to be a hallmark of globalisation (Harvey, 1989; Scholte, 2000) this is not incompatible with the continued centrality of place in social life, it simply means that individual lives are no longer tethered to singular territories. Nor is it incompatible with a commitment to the activity of placemaking. Scholars increasingly appreciate that placemaking is central to the process of migration (e.g., Hou, 2013; Rios and Vazquez, 2012). In this chapter I focus on migrant placemaking in Sydney, Australia, looking not at built space but at the natural environment of a national park and the ways recently arrived immigrants have made a place for themselves there by virtue of repetitive acts of embodied presence.

Sydney is unusual in having large areas of native bushland surviving deep within the cityscape. These include the environment of the Georges River National Park,[1] an area of bushland extending along both sides of a river located approximately twenty kilometres southwest of the central business district. Steep bush-covered slopes run down to alluvial flats along the river, some of these flats having been extended by reclamation (infilling) of mangrove wetlands in the mid-twentieth century to form lawned picnic grounds. In 1992 when the present national park was declared, the picnic grounds were retained in recognition of their importance to people in the neighbouring suburbs. At the top of the slopes the bushland extends for a short distance out into the flat surrounding country before it gives way quite abruptly to a suburban landscape of detached houses.

Pre-colonial Aboriginal occupation along the river has left traces in the form of rock paintings, shell middens and scatters of stone artefacts (Goodall and Cadzow, 2009). The British arrived in Sydney in 1788 and from the early nineteenth century the suburbs along the northern side of the Georges River (closest to the city centre) were being settled by successive waves of low-income Anglo-Celtic[2] working class families. From the 1970s these suburbs received new waves of migrants, including refugees fleeing post-conflict Vietnam (Thomas, 1999) and Arabic-speakers fleeing civil war in Lebanon and violence elsewhere in the Middle East (Dunn, 2004). These people are sometimes referred to as 'recent migrants' to distinguish them from earlier waves of mostly Anglo-Celtic migrants arriving in Australia. In the present day, these southwest suburbs have the highest concentration of recent migrants in Sydney, a city of 4.4 million people of whom 40 percent in 2011 were born overseas.[3] Of the 360,000 people living in the southwest Sydney census area in 2011, 51 percent were born overseas and 79 percent had at least one parent born overseas.[4]

In the early 2000s the Office of Environment and Heritage NSW (OEH)[5] became interested in the question of how migrants of a non-Anglo-Celtic background relate to the environment of national parks located near their places of residence: to what extent, for example, do they visit the parks and feel comfortable in them? (Thomas, 2001; Thomas, 2002). The subject of this chapter is a program of research carried out by OEH and the University of Technology Sydney, which looked in detail at the way Arab and Vietnamese immigrants living in southwest Sydney perceived and experienced the Georges River National Park (Byrne et al., 2006, 2013; Goodall and Cadzow, 2009, 2010). In the course of this work it quickly became apparent that these people did not merely passively adapt themselves to the established cultural landscape of the park but worked to make it amenable to their own social needs in a manner that merged their conceptions of what a park should be with their growing understanding of the limitations and possibilities of the environment they had migrated to.

The ethics of placemaking in national parks

Place is an outcome of social 'work'. According to Arjun Appadurai (1996: 181), people rarely take locality for granted but rather 'seem to assume that locality is ephemeral unless hard and regular work is undertaken to produce and maintain its materiality'. This work may involve ritual enactment or it may consist of more mundane activities in which people, mostly unconsciously, become identified with localities via the action of memory, emotion, imagination and sociality. The work of making places out of spaces is now seen as a fundamental priority of human existence (Casey, 1993). Certainly it is central to the experience of migration. The overwhelming majority of migrants arriving in Australia settle in urban rather than rural environments but, given the way bushland exists close to or even inside the urban and suburban settings in Sydney, migrants may easily find themselves in the midst of a 'natural' environment they neither understand nor possess adaptive strategies for. Depending on where they come from, they experience subtle or dramatic differences in climate, seasonality, vegetation and fauna. Those arriving from humid-tropical southern Vietnam in the 1970s and 1980s often described their surprise and discomfort with what they perceived to be its dryness (Thomas, 2001). This resonates with research in the USA which found that many migrants arriving in Los Angeles from humid countries such as Vietnam perceive California's dry Mediterranean environment to be a 'wasteland' (Trzyna, 2007: 39).

Since the innovative work of Jane Jacobs (1961) and William H. Whyte (1980), urban planners, community groups, local governments, geographers and others have made an effort to promote greater understanding of the way the inhabitants of particular streets, neighbourhoods, villages and other localities have worked to make these spaces habitable by imprinting them with the patterns of their own local lives. Even if this entails only minor physical changes to these spaces, the concept of placemaking recognises the agency of ordinary inhabitants in formatting and reformatting their environment: urbanites socialise capitalism's concrete jungle, villagers reinterpret and rework the traditional built environment they are born into. Placemaking is not, however, something humans simply do to the environment; it entails responsiveness to its cues and possibilities which implies a symmetry in human–nonhuman relations (Feld and Basso, 1996; Ingold, 2000; Massey, 2005; Stewart, 1996; Tilley, 1994). Placemaking thus necessarily has ethical entailments.

Human placemaking in national parks occurs in a setting that includes numerous nonhuman actors, including plants, birds, mammals and reptiles as well as rocks, soil, and flowing water. They have an existence, which, while not unaffected by our existence and actions, is independent of it. Unlike human artefacts, their capacity to act on us is not the outcome of 'causal sequences' that we have initiated (Gell, 1998: 16). It might be argued that one of the reasons we enter national parks is to experience being in an undomesticated space and to make ourselves available to the kind of interaction with nonhumans that we are not in control of. Human visitors to national parks approach plants, animals or other natural phenomena in the park environment and these latter also approach people: a bird flies into our field of vision, a wildfire races up the gully towards us, a possum attracts our attention when it moves. Nature *comes at* park visitors also in the sense that plants, animals and ecologies transmit effects to embodied visitors: visitors smell certain plants, sense them visually and are affected by their 'charisma' (Head and Atchison, 2009: 239).

Visitors may react with fear at the sight of a snake. This particular symmetry in human-nonhuman relations does not imply equity in human-nonhuman power relations since, as we are only too aware, at a macro level our capacity to impact plant and animal species vastly outweighs their capacity to impact us. It is indeed partly in response to this imbalance that national parks and other protected areas have been established as refugia for nonhuman species.

This raises the ethical question of whether recent migrants and citizens in general should engage in placemaking activities in national parks. One answer would be that as cultural beings humans are incapable of not making places out of spaces and that even national parks are cultural constructions. But, more importantly, the issue is surely the extent to which placemaking alters or degrades the environment. I turn now to consider picnics as an instance of placemaking.

Picnics in the park

Although it was never intended or designed for such a purpose, the Georges River National Park has provided a great many recent migrants in southwest Sydney with their first experience of Australian nature and also with a relatively non-threatening environment in which to become accustomed to it. A key factor in this is the existence of the picnic grounds along the river that were mentioned earlier. In parts of the park these form a band of flat ground, covered with lawn, occupying the space between the river and the steep bush-covered slopes a few hundred metres away. In our interviews with Vietnamese and Arab (mainly Lebanese) visitors to the park we found that most enjoyed seeing the bush from a distance, at the edge of the picnic lawns, but had little or no desire to actually enter it. People spoke of enjoying having the bush as a backdrop to their picnics on the lawns. In this context, the lawns might be said to constitute a liminal, in-between, or mediating space between the river and the bush. Here they can enjoy being close to the bush without being inside it.

The picnics that migrants 'stage' in the Georges River National Park are an important form of placemaking wherein these people, young and old, make the transition from a state of being visitors in somebody else's space to a state of having their own place there. However, in our interactions with the national park rangers and park managers the park we soon discovered that some of them were uncomfortable with this notion of placemaking. From their point of view, the park was a culture-neutral natural landscape which visitors of all cultural backgrounds were free to enjoy but not to change in any way. From this viewpoint, the park could not be subject to placemaking by migrants or anyone else because it was a 'place' already. Even though they understood that the picnics had no lasting impact on the park landscape they were uncomfortable with the idea of the park being 'culturally constructed' differently by different groups. To them, a national park was by definition a *natural* landscape. They managed to hold on to this conception even though they knew the picnic grounds had been created in the 1950s and 1960s on terrain formerly occupied by mangrove wetlands. Our argument that the whole notion of a national park was a product of a specific Western cultural tradition of nature appreciation (Meskell, 2012) failed to move them.

The fact remained, however, that for the Arab and Vietnamese migrant groups in our study, the park as a whole and certain areas of it in particular were becoming sites of attachment and belonging via processes of placemaking. Picnicking played a key role in this. Picnics staged in the park tended to involve groups larger than the nuclear family (Byrne et al., 2013). For Arab–Australians interviewed, an average picnic would be attended by 10–50 people who were mostly members of an extended family: 'cousins and their cousins', as one young interviewee put it. Much larger picnics were also organised to mark special occasions, such as the birth of a child, or to bring large fraternities of people together. An example of the latter are the annual picnics held in the Georges River National Park by the families of emigrants from the village of Toula in northern Lebanon (see Figure 14.1). Most picnics are held on weekends and public holidays, many people participating in one almost every week of the year. While our interviewees described the picnics primarily as social events, it became clear that for most of them the picnics represented the primary vector that brought them into the national park and into contact with Australia's natural environment.

Large group picnics have been a feature of migrant existence in a number of countries. The British Italian community, for example, has held picnics at Shenley near London (Fortier, 2000: 108). In Los Angeles, large annual picnics were held by those who had migrated from other states, particularly during the Depression

FIGURE 14.1 Lebanese–Australians picnicking in Georges River National Park.
(Photo: Denis Byrne)

years of the 1930s. These 'state picnics' included the famous Iowa Picnic at Bixby Park, Long Beach, which in 1940 attracted 100,000 people.[6] These picnics were not about ethnicity, they were about homesickness, shared identity and a shared experience of being outsiders in a new city.

At the Georges River National Park picnics a sensory environment, or sensorium, was created that enveloped the participants. Its elements included the smell and taste of food from 'home', the sound of music from 'home', the sounds of familiar language and the vision of people of familiar facial features. At picnics by Arab–Australians it included the aroma of the hookah (*sisha* in Arabic). Writing in the context of British–Indian migrant experience in London, Divya Tolia-Kelly (2004: 285) describes this kind of sense memory as a 'placing mechanism'. Scents and sounds can 'operate as a gateway into other environments' (Tollia-Kelly, 2004: 286), namely in this context, the home environments of the Middle East. But it is not a case of people being 'transported' to these other places; rather of a hybrid or transnational place coalescing in the space people currently inhabit. There is a symmetrical sense in which people resident in the homelands of the Middle East have co-presence at the Georges River picnics by virtue of the technologies of transnational phone calls, messaging and photo- and video-sharing. Via technologies like Google Maps they may easily discover the location, layout and topography of this park that has become a key habitat for their relatives and friends in Sydney and which, by extension, has become a habitat for them. As Julie Chu (2010: 38) in her landmark work on transnational placemaking reminds us, you don't have to actually leave the homeland to be emplaced elsewhere.

To the casual observer, migrant picnickers on the Georges River might seem to have created a microenvironment for themselves that, rather than linking them to the environment of the park, insulates them from it. Yet clearly they are exposed to the sensorium of the surrounding environment: the scent given off by native vegetation baking in the sun, the sound of bird calls, the vision of the cloud patterns over the river and the bushland beyond. This and the sensorium of their picnicking infiltrate each other and out of this intermingling a new place is made. Migrants rework the destination (Silvey and Lawson, 1999: 124) but they are also reworked by it.

In the course of the picnics, associations are created between a locale and the social experiences people have there. Eisenhauer and his colleagues have documented this in a well-known study of recreational use of public lands in Utah, stressing that 'activity at a locale is necessary for a space to be regarded as a place' (Eisenhauer et al., 2000: 423). I assume most park managers in Australia would similarly recognise that the activities engaged in by park visitors are constitutive of the bonds they form with a park environment. However, since the natural environment of a park is alive, active and 'vibrant' (Bennett, 2010), human activity in the park always has the aspect of culture-nature *interactivity* in terms of which the other-than-human elements of the park are affected and the park 'environment' is altered. A simple example of this would be the feeding of birds by picnickers, an event which via repetition over time influences bird behaviour. Clearly it is not simply a case of migrants adapting to park environments but of migrants and parks being reconstituted by their co-presence.

Some of our interviewees spoke with great affection of places in the park where they had picnicked habitually. I accompanied a group of second-generation Arab–Australian young men on a visit to a location they had often picnicked with their families when they were small children and where, when they had grown up and acquired their first bicycles, they returned to without their families. 'We grew up here', one of them said of the place. This old picnic spot was part of the familiar landscape of their growing up, at once unremarkable to them but also intimately known and fondly remembered (Byrne et al., 2013: 13). This was a close-knit group of young people, a number of whom were now at university, whose social bond had been formed partly during those long-ago afternoons down by the river. They had this place in common. On the occasion of our visit they pointed out to each other how much certain trees had grown since the days when they were children, implicitly if not consciously registering the fact that they and the place had grown up together. Within the temporal scale of their individual and collective lives and perhaps those of their children – for those who went on to have children – this old picnic spot was a heritage place. The ethical question of how migrants acquire a place-based heritage in their destination locale is interesting in that it implicitly challenges the conventional notion of heritage as something inherited rather than something made.

Emphemerality, looseness and the situation of the immigrant

A particular aspect of the places 'made' via picnicking is that picnics entail few if any physical alternations to the landscape. The picnic infrastructure of portable barbeques, folding chairs, blankets and straw mats, sun umbrellas and MP3 music players is packed up and taken home. The picnic leaves a footprint only in the form of flattened grass or scraps of food quickly removed by insects, birds and other animals. In its physical aspect, the picnic is ephemeral. The 'place' in one sense dissolves after each picnic only to reform again at the next staging. These places do however have a continuous existence in the minds of 'repeat- picnickers' who come to think of them as *their* places. This is a non-exclusive claim, one that recognises that other people use the same space at other times. There is competition for these spaces, though, and on summer weekends an advance party of the picnic fraternity may go to the park early in the morning to stake their claim to the familiar spot. While, as mentioned earlier, Appadurai (1996: 181) has stressed the need to maintain the materiality of locality, locality (or placeness) can often be sustained even where materiality is ephemeral.

Anthropologist Setha Low and her co-workers (Low et al., 2005) have studied the way Latino and other migrant groups became a presence in parks in New York. In their research at Jacob Riis Park, New York, for the US National Park Service, they observed that Latino groups picnicked in the 'back beach' area of the park where they 'enjoy music and dancing – especially Latino rhythms and salsa – and would enjoy summer afternoon concerts that remind them of home (and bring a bit of home to their new beach)' (Low et al., 2005: 125). Low and her colleagues make the point that, for all their emphemerality, these places are of key importance to migrant groups at a time when they are tentatively establishing a presence in national parks. Low et al. maintain that park staff should not merely welcome people of all ethnicities but be sensitive to the kind of placemaking behaviour their research documented. While robust in some ways, there is nevertheless a particular fragility about places that come into being in this way. Their invisibility (to outsiders) means they are unlikely to appear on management plan maps and thus may be vulnerable to revegetation or park development works.

If picnics sites have this aspect of emphemerality, it may also be said that national parks are attractive to recent migrants partly because they constitute what Catharine Ward Thompson (2002: 69) calls 'loose space' – spaces that are not 'fixed' or 'constrained' in the way that built urban space tends to be. National parks are relatively unstructured and unsupervised spaces that are far more open and unconstrained than most of the built public spaces of cities. From the point of view of the migrant park visitor, the river and the native bushland (and its associated biodiversity) are also 'loose' in that, while they can be encompassed by private or state property rights, their life essence is non-proprietary: it cannot be owned by any one culture group.

In an indirect way, this brings us to the ethical domain of the heritage-belonging nexus in the context of a multicultural society such as Australia's. Indigenous Australians numbered 548, 370 at the time of the 2011 census, constituting 2.5 percent of the total population. The other 97.5 percent of the continent's population arrived after 1788, thus conferring a special resonance to the idea of Australia as a migrant nation. While the current non-indigenous population derives from over 200 countries, the great majority who are from countries other than Ireland and the United Kingdom arrived in the aftermath of World War II. It was then that the White Australia policy was adjusted to permit and even encourage immigration by non-British Europeans. From the 1970s race ceased to be used as a criterion in migration policy, opening the way for an influx of migrants from Asia and elsewhere in the non-Western world. The cultural diversity of post-World War II Australia did not equate with a democratisation of belonging, however. In the 1950s and 1960s government programs actively encouraged immigrants to assimilate to what was perceived to be the core Anglo-Australian culture. At the level of emplaced heritage, this core culture was manifest in the old colonial government buildings, Christian churches, private mansions and pastoral estates which, prior to the 1970s, had been recorded by National Trust organisations modelled on the British National Trust. Even after the adoption of multiculturalism as a policy in 1973 and the official embrace of cultural diversity as a positive concept, non-Anglo migrant cultures were conceived as standing beside and enriching a pre-existing core culture rather than reconfiguring it (Hage, 1998). They were conceived 'as in-comers to a prior ancestral space, impacting a spatialized body from without' (Anderson and Taylor, 2005: 3).

The 'ancestral space' that migrants enter and with which they are expected to integrate is essentially that of a white settler nation that has appropriated selected elements of indigenous heritage. The nation-state is territorialised such that the land/environment it encompasses is conflated with the social, economic and political dimensions of the nation to form a unitary entity. The discourse of cultural heritage is enlisted to help flesh out and stabilise this entity. As Ghassan Hage (1998, 2003) maintains, the construction of the unitary, territorialised nation is not dispensed with under multiculturalism; rather it accommodates the migrant other, accepting and even welcoming the cultural diversity migrants bring. They are welcome to make this place their own but not to remake it. The uneasiness of national park rangers and managers, most of whom have a background in conservation biology, with the idea of migrant placemaking appears to stem from their desire to keep human placemaking out of those few spaces on the planet that serve as a refuge from damaging or lethal human impact on other species. This is problematic in that, consciously or otherwise, it plays into the proposition that national parks, and specifically the Georges River National Park, have not already been impacted and shaped by humans. In fact, this park has been shaped by Aboriginal people prior to their dispossession of the landscape in the nineteenth century (Goodall and Cadzow, 2009), by white suburban settlers in the post-World War II era (Goodall, 2010) and subsequently by the national park landscape management regime. It posits humans as outside the field of nature, conceived here as wilderness. As Bannon (2011) has so cogently argued, what is needed in order to preserve 'nature' is a conception of 'wildness' that, rather than precluding human presence, fosters a non-destructive mutuality between human and non-human species. The picnics that Lebanese and Vietnamese migrants hold in the park neatly exemplify such mutuality: they are a form of placemaking that is open to the flesh of the world (birds, bees, human bodies, rivers, trees) and is not destructive of it.

National parks as transnational space

In Australia and perhaps other countries with a high and culturally diverse migrant intake, immigration is widely perceived as a linear, one-way movement of people. This is reflected in the way the category of 'migration heritage' is framed by heritage institutions and practitioners according to themes of arrival, settlement and adaptation, a framing that 'contains' the migrant story within the host country's borders. What this view fails to notice is that each migrant group is likely to see itself as belonging simultaneously to its destination country and its origin country. Homeland belonging is experienced by some migrants as intense and pervasive and by others as situational and less intense. It assumes a material dimension via a circulatory flow of objects between origin and destination locales and by the engagement of migrants in practices of transnational building construction. During the nineteenth and twentieth centuries, for example, Chinese immigrants in Australia sent remittance money back to their home villages in southern Guangdong to fund the construction of new houses, temples, ancestral halls, schools, shops, roads and bridges (e.g., Hsu, 2000; Williams, 2003).

Commenting on transnationally facilitated building activity that has taken place in emigrant villages in Lebanon, Hage (2002: 12) has asked, 'what is more part of Australia's multicultural heritage than the many villages and towns from which Australia's migrant population has originated?' And yet these villages and towns are excluded from the purview of Australian heritage practice. The transnational connectivity of migration heritage sites is not explicitly referenced in heritage practice but nor is its elision likely to be consciously enacted; rather, via a process of methodological nationalism (Wimmer and Glick Schiller, 2002), it seems to be taken for granted by practitioners 'that the boundaries of the nation-state delimit and define the unit of analysis' (Levitt and Glick Schiller, 2004: 1007). The 'bordered' approach to migration heritage stands in contrast to the situation in the humanities and social sciences more generally where since the 1990s there has been a burgeoning interest in the concept of transnationalism. The term is generally used to refer to kinds of cross-border social connectivity that, while it has long characterised migration and sojourning, from the late twentieth century has been amplified by relatively cheap air travel and advances in electronic media (Appadurai, 1996; Ong, 1999). In this aspect of globalisation, certain villages in countries like Lebanon and China are now more intimately connected to suburbs in Sydney than they are to other population centres in Lebanon and China. Transnationalism is a concept with significant implications for the way national parks are socially constituted in Australia: the parks draw migrants to them but park space is also drawn into transnational space.

The dynamics of transnationalism are perhaps most easily seen in the setting of urban migrant enclaves. When, for example, a group of Lebanese men gather in south-west Sydney to listen to the news from Lebanon on the radio they are situated in a Lebanese diasporic 'ethnoscape' (Appadurai, 1996). They can see Beirut quite clearly in their minds, which is to say they can spatialise what they are listening to, often in great detail. But this is also an embodied experience: the way they sit around the table, the way they sip their tea, the gestures of their hands in response to what they are hearing, all signal that their bodies and minds are in a space that is neither Beirut nor Sydney but, rather, a Beirut–Sydney continuum. This is the 'diasporic state of mind' that Ien Ang (2011, 86) writes of.

Moving to the situation of national parks, Vietnamese migrants interviewed for our study spoke of how the Georges River would often evoke for them the rivers of Vietnam on which or near which many of them had grown up. More than just a remembering of the homeland, this evocation took the form of an embodied experience: they felt as though they were *in* their homeland or, in our terms, in a transnational space that transcended the borders of Vietnam and Australia. For some people, the simple act of holding a fishing rod triggered 'embodied memories' (Connerton, 1989) that took them back to those times they had stood beside a river with a rod in the old country (Goodall et al., 2009). As researchers, we began to appreciate that when we saw a Vietnamese person walking beside the Georges River, while they were ostensibly wholly within the bounds of the national park they were nevertheless situated in a transnational space (see also Low et al., 2005: 33). We could not accurately describe what the national park meant to these visitors without also describing what Vietnam meant to them. The presence of Vietnamese–Australians in the park implied that Vietnam, in transnational form, was also present there.

There is also a significant religious dimension to the transnational spatiality that engulfs the park. Vietnamese Buddhists are known to go to national parks in the Sydney area to meditate (Thomas, 2002: 102) and Thai Buddhist 'forest monasteries' have been established in bushland on the outskirts of the city (Byrne et al., 2006). The association of forests with meditation is deeply established within the Theravada tradition as it exists in Sri Lanka, Burma, Thailand, Cambodia and Laos. It appears now to have been extended to embrace the Australian bush. Turning to Islam, it is common to see Muslim Arab migrants standing or kneeling on the riverside lawns of the park to pray at the times designated by their religion. One of our Muslim interviewees remarked that since all of nature is God's creation, to be standing or kneeling on the ground in the park is about as close to God as one could be. Islam maintains there is no such thing as a profane world: in the words of the Prophet, 'the whole of this earth is a mosque' (Wersal, 1995: 545). Muslims praying in the Georges River National Park face towards the *Kaaba* in Mecca. The invisible line orienting and connecting them to Mecca, as well as the act of praying itself, might be thought of as bringing Islam into the park or as placing the park within the cosmology of Islam. Meditating or praying are not, however, acts which colonise park space for particular religions, rather these acts occur partly because individual actors experience the park environment as conducive to spiritual experience (Byrne et al., 2006). Or, in the case of Muslims, it may simply be that they happen to be in the park at prayer time and the 'looseness' of park space allows them to pray there whereas in another public space, such as a shopping mall, football stadium or public library, it would not. There seems no question that religious ritual and spiritual experience can play a role in placemaking but, as in the case of picnicking, the places it helps 'make' in national parks are ephemeral and non-proprietary. In this regard they are suited to the ideal of national parks as culturally open spaces.

Transnationalism and connectivity conservation

Transnationalism unsettles the idea of the nation as a spatially bounded entity. It might also be said to challenge the conventional way of thinking of national parks as firmly bounded and stable units of space. The national park concept had its origins partly in Western romantic conceptions of 'wilderness' (Schama, 1995) but was also very much bound up with the emergence of the national state. To elaborate on what has already been stated above, national parks helped provide the 'imagined community' (Anderson, 2006) of the nation with a tangible, iconic topography (Thomas, 2001: 23–25; Crusin, 2004: 22–29). They helped the nation's citizenry to grasp the physical-geographic totality of the nation, described by Thongchai (1994) as the national 'geobody', and to develop a sense of belonging to it.

The International Union for Conservation of Nature (IUCN) and other international conservation bodies have given the national park concept an aspect of internationalism but this has not diminished the close engagement of the concept in national identity formation.

I have found it productive to think about transnationalism in relation to the concept of connectivity as it pertains in the fields of nature conservation and protected area management. The concept of wildlife corridors and the broader theory and practice of connectivity conservation (Bennett, 2003; Sandwith and Lockwood, 2006) appear to have originated in an appreciation that the boundaries of protected areas are more likely to have been drawn in relation to the geometrics of the cadastral grid and to political considerations than to the real spatiality of species distribution and mobility – the reality, for instance, of a breeding population of kangaroos whose short- and long-term movements cross into and out of the borders of a national park at will. This view and the management approaches flowing from it reconceptualise national park boundaries as necessarily permeable and conditional rather than solid and fixed. In order to serve their protective function it is realised they must be integrated with other fragments and corridors of conserved habitat, including private land under voluntary conservation agreements and timber-production forests. This cross-boundary approach is seen to better approximate the actual life patterns of plants and animals. humans included

In a parallel development, the theory and practice of nature conservation has acquired a new consciousness of indigenous and local people's dependency on the resources of protected areas and of their cultural connectivity to landscapes, both of which are frequently cut across by protected area boundaries (Byrne and Ween, 2015; Peluso, 1995; Zerner, 2003). 'Countermapping' approaches have been devised to assist indigenous and local people to contest the kind of state boundary-marking that has often seen protected areas created without local informed consent (Byrne, 2008; Peluso, 1995; Ross et al., 2010) and, in Australia, Indigenous Protected Areas have been created and joint-management agreements over national parks negotiated. There is also a growing appreciation of the social and emotional connectivity that exists in places like Australia between national parks created over former pastoral lands and those non-indigenous people who formerly owned and farmed that terrain (Brown, 2012).

While there continues to be an appreciation that what protected areas are protected *from* are human processes inimical to the wellbeing of humans and other species, there is an increasing awareness that human social connectivity with, and valuation of, these spaces is critical to their long-term existence and functioning. The concept of transnationality provides a perspective in which social connectivity can be considered in the wider, cross-border frame that modern-era migration and sojourning has given rise to. For example, ideas about national parks now readily flow backwards and forwards between Australia and Vietnam along diasporic lines. The Georges River National Park is now 'known' in southern Vietnam courtesy of transnationally transmitted photographs and phone videos, increasingly frequent homeland visitation, and other vectors. Moving in the other direction, traditions and contemporary practices of nature appreciation and nature visitation in Asia and the Middle East now inform patterns of park visitation by many thousands of first- and second-generation migrants in Australia. For park management, multiculturalism and transnationalism are not so much challenges as assets – assets that we are still learning to capitalise on. As hyper-development in Asia degrades that region's environment (e.g., Wen and Li, 2007), Australia has come to be valued by many in Asia as a tourism and migration destination on account of its 'environmental assets'. There is a transnational sense here in which Australia is becoming one of Asia's protected areas, or a protected area of an Asia-Pacific transnational field. Whatever qualms some Australians might have at this prospect, it carries the implication of a vastly expanded potential support base for the county's protected areas.

Conclusion: picnics and the ethics of belonging

Down beside the Georges River, as the sun dips below the trees, the Lebanese–Australian picnickers begin clearing away the remains of the food; blankets are folded, straw mats are rolled up. The paraphernalia of picnicking is carried away and packed into the boots of cars. Goodbyes are said. It is as if the picnic place itself is being packed up and taken away. And yet while the 'place' is partly composed of stories, memories and emotions, which indeed reside with individuals and depart with them in their cars, other elements of the place seem to adhere physically to the locale. Given that the same groups of picnickers tend to return to the same spot on subsequent occasions, that particular locale acquires for them an associational load. The place becomes 'sticky' with affect, to use Sarah Ahmed's (2010: 35) term; it acquires the potentiality of transmitting particular affects to particular bodies. The actions and experiences that have occurred at the picnic site have been continuous with its materiality – with, for instance, with the grass and the smell of the grass, the soil and its sometimes dampness, sometimes dryness, the brittle gum leaves scattered on the grass and the water of the river that the Lebanese boys love to ride jet skis on. These are supposed to be stable elements of the territorial nation and yet they readily lend themselves to being participants in a new hybrid place with material connections to Lebanon and Mecca and the suburban houses a few kilometres from the park where the picnic kebabs and salads are prepared.

However, in the larger frame of the Australian social–political order, belonging-to-place tends to be measured in tangible rather than ephemeral terms. The problem with picnics as 'made' places of an enduring nature is that the places in question are invisible to those who do not belong to the migrant groups who create them. Had my colleagues and I not attended some of the picnics beside the river we would not have known that that these areas of lawn were storied places for particular migrant families. While the old wooden boatsheds which stand beside the river just beyond the boundary of the park are likely to be protected for their heritage value by the local government, these picnic spots will not be. This is not problematic insofar as there is little likelihood of the picnic grounds being destroyed, given their presence in a national park. And if every place of significance to every person or group was to be given a heritage classification they would not only fill the entire landscape but would overlap and superimpose themselves on each other. The obsession with preservation that informs much contemporary heritage discourse has been a target of recent critique (Holtorf, 2011; Poulios, 2010).

But heritage preservation is not the ethical issue here. What is at stake is whether a person's belonging to a place should be measured in terms of tangible heritage traces. The tendency to equate built heritage with belonging creates a hierarchy of those deemed to be more 'in place' over those less so. In the Australian context, this inevitably privileges the belonging of the pre-World War II waves of Anglo-Celtic migrants over the belonging of post-war migrants from other parts of the world. The former have not only had more time and resources to build, they have been part of a colonial process that has authorised and encouraged them to occupy space and to build in it. Of course, the dominant group in Australia does not perceive this to be the case. As Peggy McIntosh claimed, in her seminal essay of 1988 (McIntosh, 1989), most white people are oblivious to the privileges whiteness confers on them.

There is a real need for heritage practitioners and commentators in Australia to attend more to the ephemeral dimension of the place-based heritage record created by post-World War II immigrants in Australia. We need to know more about how newcomers develop a sense of belonging by being and acting in place. Almost inevitably this placemaking occurs in spaces where others before them have built or culturally configured, examples being the Indian restaurants that occupy nineteenth century Anglo houses in Harris Park, western Sydney, and Lebanese picnic places situated in the Georges River National Park. There is, theoretically, no end to the multiplicity of places that can be made in the same space. Equally, for all the nation-state's insistence on the territorial loyalty of its citizens, belonging is fluid and multiple in its subjectivity. The ability of society at large to see and acknowledge would seem a prerequisite or at least a support for the 'cosmopolitan makeover' that Australian multiculturalism is in need of (Collins, 2013: 173).

Acknowledgements

I acknowledge the research contribution of my colleagues, Allison Cadzow and Heather Goodall, to the project this chapter is based on. The project, 'Parkland, Culture and Communities' was co-funded by the Australian Research Council under its Linkage programme and the Office of Environment and Heritage NSW. I gratefully acknowledge all the Arab and Vietnamese Australians who agreed to participate in the study.

Notes

1 The park homepage: www.environment.nsw.gov.au/nationalparks/parkHome.aspx?id=N0080
2 'Anglo-Celtic' refers to Australian settlers from Britain and Ireland.

3 Australian Bureau of Statistics (ABS), Greater Sydney Statistical Division, 2011 census. www.censusdata.abs.gov.au/census_services/getproduct/census/2011/quickstat/1GSYD. Consulted February 2013.
4 ABS Sydney South West Statistical Division, 2011 census. www.censusdata.abs.gov.au/census_services/getproduct/census/2011/quickstat/127. Consulted February 2013.
5 NSW is an abbreviation of New South Wales, one of Australia's six states.
6 See www.latimes.com/news/local/la-me-then11-2008may11,0,188403.story

References

Ahmed, S. (2010). Happy objects. In M. Gregg and G. J. Seigworth (eds.), *The Affect Reader*, pp. 29–51. Durham, NC: Duke University Press.

Anderson, B. (2006). *Imagined Communities*, revised edition. London: Verso.

Anderson, K. and A. Taylor (2005). 'Exclusionary politics and the question of national belonging: Australian ethnicities in "multiscalar" focus'. *Ethnicities* 5(4):460–485.

Ang, I. (2011). 'Unsettling the national: heritage and Diaspora'. In H. Anheier and Y. R. Isar (eds.), *Heritage, Memory and Identity*, pp. 82–94. London: Sage.

Appadurai, A. (1996). *Modernity at Large: Cultural Dimensions of Globalisation*. Minneapolis, MN: University of Minnesota Press.

Bannon, B. E. (2011). 'Flesh and nature: understanding Merleau-Ponty's relational ontology', *Research in Phenomenology* 41:327–357.

Bennett, A. F. (2003). *Linkages in the Landscape: The Role of Corridors and Connectivity in Wildlife Conservation*, 2nd edition. Gland, Switzerland and Cambridge, UK: IUCN.

Bennett, J. (2010). *Vibrant Matter: A Political Ecology of Things*. Durham NC: Duke University Press.

Brown, S. (2012). 'Applying a cultural landscape approach in park management: an Australian scheme'. *PARKS: The International Journal of Protected Areas and Conservation* 18:101–110.

Byrne, D., Goodall, H., Wearing, S. and A. Cadzow (2006). 'Enchanted parklands'. *Australian Geographer* 37(1):103–115.

Byrne, D. (2008). 'Counter-mapping in the archaeological landscape'. In B. David and J. Thomas (eds.), *Handbook of Landscape Archaeology*, pp. 609–616. Walnut Creek CAL: Left Coast Press.

Byrne, D., Goodall, H. and A. Cadzow (2013). *Place-making in National Parks*. Sydney: Office of Environment and Heritage NSW and University of Technology Sydney. www.environment.nsw.gov.au/nswcultureheritage/PlaceMakingGeorgesRiver.htm

Byrne, D. and G. B. Ween (2015). 'Bridging the culture-nature divide in heritage practice'. In L. Meskell (ed.), *Global Heritage: A Reader*. London: Blackwell.

Casey, E. S. (1993). *Getting Back into Place: Toward a Renewed Understanding of the Place-World*. Bloomington IN: Indiana University Press.

Chu, Julie Y. (2010). *Cosmologies of Credit: Transnational Mobility and the Politics of Destination in China*. Durham and London: Duke University Press.

Collins, J. (2013). 'Rethinking Australian immigration and immigrant settlement policy'. *Journal of Intercultural Studies* 34(2):160–177.

Connerton, P. (1989). *How Societies Remember*. Cambridge: Cambridge University Press.

Crusin, R. (2004). *Culture, Technology, and the Creation of America's National Parks*. Cambridge: Cambridge University Press.

Dunn, K. (2004). 'Islam in Sydney: contesting the discourse of absence'. *Australian Geographer* 35(3):333–353.

Eisenhauer, B. W., Krannich, R. S. and D. J. Blahna. (2000). 'Attachments to special places on public lands: an analysis of activities, reason for attachments, and community connections'. *Society and Natural Resources* 13:421–441.

Feld, S. and K. H. Basso (eds.). (1996). *Senses of Place*. Santa Fe: School of American Research.

Fortier, A. (2000). *Migrant Belongings: Memory, Space, Identity*. Oxford: Berg.

Gell, Alfred. (1998). *Art and Agency: An Anthropological Theory*. Oxford: Clarendon Press.

Goodall, H., Cadzow, A., Byrne, D. and S. Wearing. (2009). 'Fishing the Georges River: cultural diversity and urban environments'. In A. Wise and S. Velayutham (eds.), *Everyday Multiculturalism*, pp. 177–196. Houndsmills, Hampshire, UK: Palgrave Macmillan.

Goodall, H. and A. Cadzow (2009). *Rivers and Resilience: Aboriginal people on Sydney's Georges River*. Sydney: University of New South Wales Press.

Goodall, H. and A. Cadzow (2010). 'The People's National Park: working class environmental campaigns on Sydney's urban, industrial Georges River, 1950 to 1967'. *Labour History* 99:17–35.

Hage, G. (1998). *White Nation: Fantasies of White Supremacy in a Multicultural Society*. Sydney: Pluto Press.

Hage, G. (2002). 'Citizenship and honourability: belonging to Australia today'. In G. Hage (ed.), *Arab–Australians: Citizenship and Belonging Today*, pp. 1–15. Melbourne: Melbourne University Press.

Hage, G. (2003). *Against Paranoid Nationalism: Searching for Hope in a Shrinking Society*. Sydney: Pluto Press.

Harvey, D. (1989). *The Condition of Postmodernity*. Oxford: Blackwell.

Head, L. and J. Atchison (2009). 'Cultural ecology: emerging human-plant geographies'. *Progress in Human Geography* 33(2):236–24.

Holtorf, C. (2011). 'On the future significance of heritage', *Norwegian Archaeological Review* 44(1):64–66.

Hou, J. (2013). *Transcultural Cities: Border Crossings and Placemaking*. London and New York: Routledge.

Hsu, M. Y. (2000). *Dreaming of Gold, Dreaming of Home: Transnationalism and Migration Between the United States and South China 1882–1943*. Stanford: Stanford University Press.

Ingold, T. (2000). *The Perception of the Environment*. London: Routledge.

Jacobs, J. (1961). *The Death and Life of Great American Cities*. Harmondsworth, UK: Penguin.

Levitt, P. and N. Glick Schiller. (2004). 'Conceptualizing simultaneity: a transnational social field perspective on society', *International Migration Review* 38(3):1002–1039.

Low, S. M., Taplin, D. and S. Scheld. (2005). *Rethinking Urban Parks*. Austin, TX: University of Texas Press.

Massey, D. (2005). *For Space*. London: Sage.

McIntosh, P. (1989) 'White privilege: unpacking the invisible knapsack. *Freedom Magazine*, July/August: 10–12.

Meskell, L. (2012). *The Nature of Heritage: The New South Africa*. Oxford: Blackwell.

Ong, A. (1999). *Flexible Citizenship: The Cultural Logic of Transnationalism*. Durham, NC: Duke University Press.

Peluso, N. L. (1995). 'Whose woods are these? Counter-mapping forest territories in Kalimantan, Indonesia', *Antipode* 27(4):383–406.

Poulios, I. (2010). 'Moving beyond a values-based approach to heritage conservation', *Conservation and Management of Archaeological Sites* 12(2):170–185.

Rios, M. and L. Vazquez. (2012). *Diálogos: Placemaking in Latino Communities*. London and New York: Routledge.

Ross, A., Sherman, K. P., Snodgrass, J. G., Delcore H. D. and R. Sherman (eds.). (2010). *Indigenous Peoples and the Collaborative Stewardship of Nature*. Walnut Creek, CAL: Left Coast Press.

Sandwith, T. and M. Lockwood. (2006). 'Linking the landscape'. In M. Lockwood, G. L. Warboys and A. Kothari (eds.), *Managing Protected Areas*, pp. 574–602. London: Earthscan.

Saunders, D. (2012). *Arrival City: How the Largest Migration in History is Reshaping Our World.* New York: Vintage.

Schama, S. (1995). *Landscape and Memory.* London: Fontana.

Scholte, J. A. (2000). *Globalization: A Critical Introduction.* St Martins: New York.

Sheller, M. (2003). 'Creolization in discourses of global culture'. In S. Ahmed, C. Castaneda, A-M. Fortier and M. Sheller (eds.), *Uprootings / Regroundings: Questions of Home and Migration*, pp. 273–294. Oxford and New York: Berg.

Sheller, M. (2011). 'Mobility', *Sociopedia.isa.* www.sagepub.net/isa/resources/pdf/Mobility.pdf

Silvey, R. and V. Lawson. (1999). 'Placing the migrant,' *Annals of the Association of American Geographers* 89(1):121–132.

Stewart, K. (1996). *A Pace on the Side of the Road.* Princeton: Princeton University Press.

Thomas, M. (1999). *Dreams in the Shadows: Vietnamese-Australian Lives in Transition.* Sydney: Allen and Unwin.

Thomas, M. (2001). *A Multicultural Landscape: National Parks & the Macedonian Experience.* Sydney: NSW National Parks and Wildlife Service and Pluto Press. www.environment. nsw.gov.au/nswcultureheritage/MacedonianExperience.htm

Thomas, M. (2002). *Moving Landscapes: National Parks & the Vietnamese Experience.* Sydney: NSW National Parks and Wildlife Service. www.environment.nsw.gov.au/nswcultureheritage/MovingLandscape.htm

Thongchai, W. (1994). *Siam Mapped: A History of the Geobody of Siam.* Honolulu: University of Hawai'i Press.

Tilley, C. (1994). *A Phenomenology of Landscape.* Oxford: Berg.

Tollia-Kelly, D. P. (2004). 'Landscape, race and memory: biographical mapping of the routes of British Asian landscape values', *Landscape Research* 29(3):277–292.

Trzyna, T. C. 2007. *Global Urbanization and Protected Areas.* Sacramento: California Institute for Public Affairs. www.InterEnvironment.org/cipa/urbanization.htm

Ward Thompson, C. (2002). 'Urban open space in the 21st century', *Landscape and Urban Planning* 60:59–72.

Wen, D. and M. Li (2007). 'China: hyper-development and environmental crisis', *Socialist Register* 130–146.

Wersal, L. (1995). 'Islam and environmental ethics: tradition responds to contemporary challenges', *Zygon* 30(3):451–459.

Whyte, W. H. (1980). *The Social Life of Small Urban Spaces.* Washington D.C.: The Conservation Foundation.

Williams, M. (2003). 'In the Tang Mountains we have a big house', *East Asian History* 25/26:85–112.

Wimmer, A. and N. Glick Schiller. (2002). 'Methological nationalism and beyond: nation-state building, migration and the social sciences', *Global Networks* 2(4):301–334.

Zerner, C. (ed.). 2003. *Culture and the Question of Rights.* Durham, NC: Duke University Press.

15

SHARING HISTORY

Migration, integration and a post-heritage future

Johan Hegardt

Introduction

> On Thursday 25 February 2016, a leading Swedish morning paper writes in
> an editorial with the heading "Slut för tystnadens strategi" (The end of the
> strategy of silence) that there has been a dramatic change in Swedish politics.
> All of a sudden, the editorial concludes, the Social Democratic government
> has addressed the issue of integration. Most parties have followed suit.
>
> *(Dagens Nyheter 2016)*

For many years, and without much debate, the leading political parties in Sweden
have quietly agreed not to address integration. The reason is the politics of the
right-wing party Sverige Demokraterna (Sweden Democrats), a party that has seen
a rapid growth in recent years. Different opinion polls in 2015 revealed that almost
20 percent of those entitled to vote would vote for the party. This was a shock
for the established parties, but they could not deal with it because the Sweden
Democrats had built their identity on the question of immigration. Their argument
wass that immigration is always a socio-cultural and socio-economic problem, and
if Sweden is to accept immigration, immigrants must be integrated or even assimilated in Swedish society, its customs and heritage. A multicultural society is a
society of conflict, enormous government spending and socio-economic alienation, the party argued.

Dealing with integration would mean accepting that the Sweden Democrats
were addressing an important issue. The leading parties did not want this debate
because the Sweden Democrats actually increased in popularity after such debates.
Therefore, it was quietly agreed not to talk about integration and hope for the best,
which probably was that the voters in the end would become tired of a party never
achieving any of its political aims.

Having been monopolized by the Sweden Democrats, immigration issues thus became a non-issue among the established parties and disappeared out of focus. The word *immigrant* was also dismissed from the political narrative. First it was replaced by the term *new Swedes* and later by the term *newly arrived*. The bizarre strategy behind this oblivion and twisting of words was that if immigrants did not exist there was no issue to be discussed and the Sweden Democrats would be logically neutralized. The voters didn't agree. They knew that immigrants did exist and they turned to the Sweden Democrats in larger numbers.

Things have changed dramatically since then, and it is the consequences of this dramatic change that the chapter addresses. Sweden received more refugees per capita than any other European country, including Germany, in 2015. Society and the welfare system are under severe threat, or this is at least what the established parties underline. The Schengen agreement is suspended and everyone traveling into Sweden must be able to confirm his or her identity.

The demand coming from a majority of the leading parties is that the flow of people fleeing from the Syrian war, North Africa or Afghanistan must be stopped. But thousands have already arrived and it is impossible to look the other way. Something must be done, and all of a sudden the established parties are addressing the issue of migration, immigrants and integration, and – like a miracle – the Sweden Democrats in 2016, for the first time in many years, are losing voters.

This introductory example from one of the world's leading welfare societies is not at all uncommon in our present world. Most nations in Europe are dealing with a similar situation; others are doing what they can to reject all immigrants. At the same time we witness a rising pressure on democratic institutions and on the press in some European societies.

Explicitly or implicitly, heritage is at the center of the whole issue. The general argument is that our heritage – as in values, welfare systems, religious beliefs, economic systems, social stability and even race – is under threat, not only because of migration but also from a world turning into a spinning globe of cosmopolitanism, globalization and social inequality. The demand coming from everywhere is that we need bulwarks, we need to return to a bygone nation-state stability, we need order, but we also need identity, we need to know who we are, which group we belong to, what skin color we have, our gender or sexual preferences! What we are witnessing – not only in Europe – is the relationship between heritage, identity and politics, which of course is what heritage has always been about.

In this chapter I use Sweden as a point of departure for a broader discussion on the issue of heritage, identity and politics. I begin with a history of Swedish heritage management and after that turn to the social-political background of Swedish museum staff and heritage functionaries. I want to point to a shift in Swedish heritage politics from heritage as homogeneity to multiculturalism and identity politics, which is very much the present state of the art, but, as we have seen, a political position that is now discussed because of the real or imagined pressure from migration and the need for a more explicit relationship to integration.

In the following parts of the chapter, I want to present some thoughts related to a post-heritage world where instead of heritage we discuss history as something shared or held in common. I end the chapter by presenting a more practical use of a *shared history* where I work together with a museum and an art gallery. I also want to discuss integration. Here I use a definition from science where integration means the merging of two or more parts into a *completely* new whole, which is essential for this chapter, because if not, we are dealing with assimilation and that, I believe, is a word most of us do not want to use.

Swedish heritage management

Swedish heritage management is the history of its legislation since the first act was passed in 1666, and the institutions and functionaries that have been and are responsible. Behind an explicit civic structure an often hidden idea of ethnic continuity and identity can be found in the legislation – the idea of a pure Swedish race and a united nation (see also Hegardt 2011a & b; Hegardt & Källén 2011). Laws are always related to power and majority, morals and norms and to identity and being (Derrida 2005).

Swedish heritage management can be classified into three historical contexts: heritage as myth, heritage as genealogy and heritage as science and nation-narration. It is also possible to distinguish a fourth – heritage in a cosmopolitan world. Here I only discuss the last two, because it is between heritage as science and nation-narration and heritage in a cosmopolitan world that we find the issues at stake today. I have discussed the previous two in an article from 2014, but heritage as myth can be summarized as a heritage that signifies a mythological and heroic past, present in the landscape as symbols. Through such myths the present past becomes useful in the political, religious and social context of the time. Such a perspective on heritage was common in Sweden during the sixteenth and seventeenth centuries. During the eighteenth century in Sweden a utilitarian approach, reason and specialized historical research opened a new approach to heritage and history – genealogy and chronology. The chronology of the nation and the genealogy of the King and the nobility became important. At this stage the present past is thus historicized.

Since the mid seventeenth century Swedish society has been under the control of and organized by its civil servants. During the early nineteenth century new sciences such as archaeology, ideas of progress launched by German Enlightenment philosophers such as Kant and Hegel, positivism and natural science and the idea that the nation is an ethnic and linguistic entity, proposed for example by Fichte and Herder, emerged. Such perspectives, combined with a civil structure of functionaries, contributed to chronological studies of Swedish heritage. However, the most important boost to Swedish heritage consciousness came through the Dane Christian Jürgensen Thomsen's (1788–1865) publication of his Three Age System, featuring the Stone Age, the Bronze Age and the Iron Age (Thomsen 1836). In the late nineteenth century, heritage management became more centralized and related to bureaucratic institutions and museums in Stockholm. The heritage legislation from the late seventeenth century was rewritten and would be rewritten again several times during the twentieth century to adjust to a changing society and centralized bureaucracy (Hegardt 2014: 7176).

When the National Museum was finished in 1866 the Museum of National Antiquities was placed on the ground floor. The antiquity collection followed Thomsen's ideas and the galleries illustrated, like pictures in a book and in a proper chronological order, the progression of the nation. Narration was crucial when explaining how the nation had come into being. It was important to show a united people and one race. The Museum of National Antiquities, today renamed the Swedish History Museum, was bursting at the seams in the 1920s, overfilled with objects. The bits and pieces of the nation coming into being, once glued together, were now slowly falling apart. At the same time, Swedish society underwent political and economic crises. Nina Witoszek (2002) has described these crises as a proof of temporariness, eliminating the idea of a secure and infinite historical process. To meet these crises, a welfare society – *folkhemmet* or "the people's home" – was introduced. Europe was viewed with skepticism as neofeudal, patriarchal and unequal. Conflicts and tensions were to be avoided by the "imperative of harmony" and society was to be built on rationalism, compromises and consensus. According to Witoszek, Sweden from that time defined itself as the nation of goodness. Heritage management and museums followed suit in this new social construct. It was Per Albin Hanson (1885–1946), the leader of the Social Democratic Party, who in the 1920s introduced the welfare society and *folkhemmet* and in the mid 1920s Sigurd Curman (1879–1966) took over the Museum of National Antiquities, launching a new museum and heritage politics based on *folkhemmet*. It was time to glue the bits and pieces of heritage back together again, this time on the principles of *folkhemmet*, consensus, compromise, rationalism and the society of goodness. It was also decided that a new museum must be built, erected at the end of the 1930s (Hegardt 2014: 7177).

The Museum of National Antiquities worked with an advanced chronological perspective illustrating the united Swedes and how their special race came into being. In the 1920s and the 1930s these perspectives were emphasized and moved into heritage management under the authority of the Heritage Board. National consensus based on rationalistic epistemology became important and heritage legislation and organization were founded on civic organization rather than on an explicit ethnic or linguistic principle. Nevertheless, the capacity of civic society to organize heritage is related to the ethnic and linguistic idea of a united Swedish race. It is important to underline that Swedishness has been inscribed and narrated as heritage with the aim of guaranteeing stability and the homogenous nation, first disturbed when faced with cosmopolitan diversity and global economies in later decades of the twentieth century. Color consciousness (Appiah & Gutmann 1996) in Sweden is based on the idea of a stable historical race of blond and blue-eyed people with a common heritage. Implicit racism is the outcome of such perspectives, becoming a practical reality in the late twentieth century due to increasing immigration. Through heritage and the *good* society, Swedes have viewed themselves as superior without having to face the people classified as inferior from a standpoint of a racialized discourse. When these *inferior* people suddenly turned up as immigrants, the country had to face itself, its history and its idea of heritage. Public-service authorities have rightly been accused of having profound problems with structural racism (Hegardt & Källén 2011; de los Reyes & Kamali 2005; Pred 2000).

The relationship between heritage and Swedishness, historical continuity and authority of heritage management and society as a stable united nation of one people and one race, is a crucial problem. Heritage as a national and ethnical signifier has been shown to be dangerous and thus obsolete (Hegardt 2011c). The critical point made is that heritage management can no longer build its existence on the idea of national continuity.

It is obvious that continuity and Swedishness do not work in a society marching into a global world with cosmopolitan responsibilities. The uncertainty that has followed has opened the way for right-wing parties, but also for other political groups, local organizations, museums and authorities and the public to appropriate heritage in line with the old idea of historical continuity, a united nation and Swedishness and building their arguments on traditional heritage narratives, for example by replacing the word *race* with the word *culture* and striving to enclose Sweden, regions or local areas through its heritage.

In 2005, I conducted a study together with the Department of Sociology of Education and Culture at Uppsala University to find out who studies cultural historical subjects and heritage management related subjects at the different universities in Sweden (see also Hegardt 2005; Hegardt & Källén 2011). It turned out that the majority of students came from ethnic Swedish middle-class families. Finding a job and becoming a functionary in the heritage management system was the primary wish of these students. This means that these individuals will reproduce and guard the narratives of Swedish heritage, because it is through these narratives that they gain their position and income, and also their cultural capital, which is extremely important, and they achieve this inside a system organized by the State and civil society. The narratives thus become State-governed and managed by functionaries employed by the different authorities.

Sweden must find a new definition of what it means to be Swedish, and this goes for many other nations in Europe and around the world. From my point of view the word *cosmopolitan* (Appiah 2007) describes the situation best. If one looks closer into what is called Swedish heritage one finds that only a fragment can be defined as Swedish in accordance with the national definition of the word. People from all parts of the world have brought material objects to this country from all parts of the world. Historical buildings and other structures have been built by workers and paid for by wealthy people who have come from all over the world. Intangible heritage is a consequence of people meeting with people from many parts of the world. Every museum in Sweden is filled with objects that strengthen this perspective. What is needed is a definition of being Swedish that expands the borders of the nation-state, perhaps in line with Bhabha's (2004) idea of hybridity. Nonetheless, true and authentic Swedishness and heritage only exist inside a very narrow and imagined community (Anderson 1991), and as Appiah has stated it: "Cosmopolitanism isn't hard work; repudiating it is" (Appiah 2007: xviii).

The disappearance of the immigrant

From this argument based on Hegardt (2014) it becomes clear that Swedish society has a long history of civil servant organization and the functionaries' responsibilities to ensure that Swedish heritage reflects not only Swedishness but also the Swedish welfare society. The idea of the *good* society complicates the issue even more. Being Swedish implies a responsibility to the idea of the *good*. This in turn further implies that not integrating is similar to not accepting that one of the world's leading welfare societies is not only a society among other societies, but also a *good* society. But what we find here is also a clear example of the double bind. As we have seen, the idea of Swedish heritage and Swedishness is strictly speaking a racialized issue closely related to the idea of *folkhemmet* and the welfare society and consequently the *good* society. When immigrants try to become integrated Swedes they will always be unmasked because of their skin color, their names, accent or lack of understanding Swedish traditions and rituals. To be able to deal with this problem, Swedish politicians have for many years argued in favor of the multi-cultural society. But the multicultural society created new problems, for example racialized identity politics among different immigrant groups, creating their own cosmopolitan communities, religious identities, social and ethnic rules, for example within families, and so on.

The consequence of not addressing the issue of migration and integration of immigrants before 2016 was also that they ended up in large numbers on the outskirts of mainstream Swedish society. Unemployment, social problems, criminality and even radicalization became a reality. But neglecting the immigrants and letting them disappear from the discussion has also had a major impact on migration and immigration heritage and its history, because if the issue of migration and immigration is not addressed than there is no reason to discuss migration, immigration heritage and its multilayered and multitemporal history.

Yet the new politics addressing migration, immigrants and integration has no interest in discussing a new whole, an understanding of integration that I mentioned in the introduction. Instead the discussion is about workplaces and education, and even though no one uses the word assimilation, except the Sweden Democrats, this is what it's all about. By finding work, immigrants will automatically turn into more ordinary Swedes and the social problems and even the problems of radicalization will disappear, is the common political opinion. This also means that any heritage related to migration and immigrants will be pointless. Instead it is Swedish heritage that comes into focus again as the model for integration, and this has to do with the idea of the welfare society not only being a welfare society but also the *good* or even the best society in the world. If immigrants learn to understand

Swedish heritage and find jobs they will again disappear, although this time not outside mainstream Swedish society but by becoming a part of it. Holding on to migration and immigration heritage would do nothing good in such a process. Therefore, the Swedish Cultural Minister started a campaign in 2014 to open the Swedish heritage landscape for everyone. A democratic heritage is the slogan: "The Swedish government is working together with different agents in order to present a heritage policy with space for different stories and many voices. The common heritage is in constant development and is constantly being formed by people together."[1]

I sympathize with the Minister's agenda, which in many ways mirrors the latest discussion in international heritage management, but what is missing here is a deeper understanding of the history of Swedish heritage management, a history that I have described above, a solution to the problem of the double-bind, a responsibility to address the history and heritage of migration, but most of all an understanding of the practical and theoretical implications of real integration, which in my opinion should create a new whole.

What is also interesting here is that not only addressing the issue of integration but also the new strategy of a democratic heritage is very much a direct response to the Sweden Democrats' ambition to monopolize the heritage issue for their own political propaganda and turning it against immigrants. It is clear that the politics expressed in the Minister's memorandum are not meant for those who vote for the Sweden Democrats, approximately 20 percent of the voters, nor for a conservative middle class, but for everyone else, whoever they might be. What this implies is that the "space for different stories and many voices" and "being formed by people together" is radically narrowed down to the group of everybody else. Precisely because of this, and because heritage cannot be shared, heritage becomes a problem rather than a possibility and it becomes a field for conflicting political perspectives instead of an open space for everyone. This is not something isolated to Sweden, but an international problem. We therefore need to move beyond the heritage issue and explore a future without heritage as we know it and define it today, and into a post-heritage understanding of history as something that can be shared within the context of historical consciousness.

Heritage without history?

It is interesting to note that heritage is mostly understood and discussed as an a-historical phenomenon to be used in the present and therefore also risking misuse in the present. Laurajane Smith ends her thought-provoking book like this:

> It is through understanding the use that places and processes of heritage are put to in the present, the way the present constructs it, the role that heritage plays and the consequences it has, that a useful sense of what heritage is and does can be achieved.

(Smith 2006: 308)

But arguably the preconception behind this conclusion must be questioned. Today we are witnessing a never-ending stream of academic publications agreeing that heritage is a consequence of the present (see also Harrison 2013). I do sympathize with the idea of doing things right, but must ask whether it is really true that it is the present that is the producer of heritage and it is equally true that we produce the past in the present, as Harrison for example writes: "It is only with an active engagement with the past we produce in the present that we can generate the individual and collective memories that will bind us together in the future" (Harrison 2013: 231).

Discussing the work of Alois Riegl (1858–1905) and its reception in the Soviet Union, Irina Sandomirskaia, Professor of Cultural Studies at Södertörn University, recently argued (2015) that Riegl was one of the first scholars who actually dismissed history from the study and conservation of art and monuments. For Sandomirskaia, he is thus an early forerunner of today's idea that heritage is an a-historical phenomenon and that heritage studies are an a-historical practice.

Heritage studies might gain from not being a part of history as a discipline, for example not having to engage in a debate about what actually happened a few hundred years ago. But this does not have to imply that whatever we might call heritage is not also something historical.

Marcia Sá Cavalcante Schuback, Professor of Philosophy at Södertörn University, has introduced me to the Italian word *beni vacanti*, which means *ownerless property*. What is *heritage* if not a property without an owner? If it had an owner we would not be able to deal with it the way we do because it would in that case be a question of heritage proper, i.e. something that is and will be inherited over the generations and therefore legally belong to someone. According to the Oxford Dictionary of English *heritage* is a "property that is or may be inherited; an inheritance – they had stolen his grandfather's heritage". The *heritage* that engages thousands of academics, politicians and NGOs, but also ordinary people, local organizations, indigenous groups and minorities around the world is something else and of course cannot be inherited in the proper definition of the word. Inheritance is the legal or informal gesture of passing on something once owned from one hand to another, from one generation to the next, from the dead to the living. Most things that we today call *heritage* have not been passed on to us from a former owner, but exist in the present as *beni vacanti* because of a cut in the process of inheritance, a cut that creates a void between people in the present and people in the past, between us and them. Therefore, *heritage* must be understood as something historical rather than something a-historical, but with a temporality based on cuts and voids, a temporality that *beni vacanti* is a consequence of.

Because *heritage* is ownerless property it can be appropriated by anyone in the present that has power enough to do so, mostly state authorities, state-related trustees, NGOs and of course academics. It can be politicized or turned into an economic or sustainable resource. Because we view it as something a-historical it can be used for almost any reason. We educate people with the skills to handle this ownerless property, functionaries and others who become the guardians of this otherwise ownerless property and who, if needed, can create a narrative that defends their position as guardians of this *property*, as discussed above.

It is therefore not as the present or as heritage that *heritage* is important – if it is important – but as something historical. Why has history been explicitly dismissed from heritage, and could an inclusion of history in our understanding of heritage make it possible to address heritage in a post-heritage context?

There are different answers to these two questions, of course, but one answer to the first part of the question might be that history is understood as problematic. Historians focus on the past and its historical processes and events, irrelevant to those who want to make use of *heritage* in the present. A second perspective is that history has had a tendency to be used in the creation of nation-states and nationalistic perspectives. History is understood as the coming into being process of nations, and only those who have a clear and long historical relationship to this process are accepted inside the borders of the nation as history, which makes history a marker of a national identity, as discussed earlier in this chapter.

The use of the word *heritage* implies that we are talking about something inherited, but at the same time we cannot talk about it as inheritance. The paradox thus reads that heritage is something that once existed and has been left to us as heritage, but can we accept the responsibility or the limitation that comes with it as history? There is a belief that we can deal with *heritage* in almost any way, but not as something historical.

But is this a reasonable way to proceed? I don't think so and for many reasons. One is because skipping history is counterproductive to what we actually want to achieve, which might be, for example, a responsible and sustainable relationship to *beni vacanti*. We might also ask why history must be a chauvinistic or musty pursuit of historical facts within an academic discourse? Yet my impression is that the heritage field, whether we are dealing with politicians, academics or indigenous groups, needs this image of history, maybe not always overt, but immanent in the historical development of heritage studies. The discipline of heritage studies is a much younger field than history, and for me at least it is fairly clear that the identity of heritage studies needs the discipline of history as a counter position or a negation, but the consequence is that heritage studies are throwing out the baby with the bathwater, because when skipping history it also dismisses the historical aspect of *beni vacanti*, the ownerless property, with its multilayered temporalities, voids and cuts.

The whole issue of *heritage* is speeding into a dead end, or even worse. It has become the locus of identity and therefore a conflict trigger, fragmenting the world into razor-sharp identity politics. It is explicitly or implicitly connected with memories that no one remembers, it justifies itself as heritage, a heritage that no one has inherited, it dismisses history and by doing so opens up to anyone with enough power to appropriate this memory without remembering, this heritage without inheritance, in whatever way is suitable for gaining power. To repeat myself, we need to address a world beyond heritage, a post-heritage world that interprets and understands history as something that can be shared within the context of historical consciousness, which is within a proper understanding of integration as something that shapes a new whole in the future, a new whole beyond heritage. We need, I hesitate to state, to move away from the concept of *heritage* and find a new understanding of history in a cosmopolitan world of movements, regardless of whether this movement is a consequence of migration, business, research or love.

I am not maintaining that this is an easy undertaking, but I have started to explore the issue together with Färgfabriken in Stockholm and Örebro County Museum in the city of Örebro. It is important to underline that we are dealing with two different projects or rather discussions, one at Färgfabriken and one at the Örebro County Museum, and that these two projects are in the making, work in progress, so to speak. Here I briefly present the theoretic framework that these two projects or discussions rely on.

Färgfabriken

Färgfabriken is an art gallery and a display room that has, since its start in 1995, served as a platform for contemporary cultural expressions with an emphasis on art, architecture and urban planning. It is a trust owned by the Lindén group and is thus a private institution. Färgfabriken's projects involve situations not only in Sweden but throughout the world. The institution has developed methods with the purpose of exploring and trying to understand the complexity of our constantly changing world. The word *färgfabriken* means literally "the paint factory" and the premises were once used for producing paint. But in this case it can also mean the color factory, the factory that produces color or puts color on a changing world, because the word *färg* both means "paint" and "color" in Swedish.

In 2015 I introduced the concept of *shared history* at a workshop at Färgfabriken. Since then a small group of curators at Färgfabriken and I have been discussing the concept. By *shared history* I mean the integration of two or more historical experiences into a new whole. I base my understanding on three theoretical concepts: hybridity (Bhabha 2004), the sublime historical experience (Ankersmit 2005) and the practical past (White 2014).

I quoted Appiah above and his statement that "cosmopolitanism isn't hard work; repudiating it is", and I think that Appiah is perfectly right. Bhabha's idea is that hybridity is the state of the art. As in the case of cosmopolitanism we work hard to make sure that we repudiate hybridity. Ankersmit's idea of the sublime is that we begin with or have, or at least there exists, a sublime historical experience, something precognitive, which means something that exists or comes *before* our understanding of historical knowledge. In short, we experience the historical *before* we turn it into something cognitively knowable and therefore it might also be possible to work against this sublime experience, for example by placing the past in different boxes, ordering history by chronology or the preconception that we produce the past in the present. White's idea is that the past is something that we make use of in our everyday activities in the present. We need the past to orientate in the present. It's yesterday that makes today possible, which I think is a fair understanding of White's intention.

Every one of us has a sublime relationship to history, and we understand, whether we like it or not, that *culture* is much more hybridity than essential and that we depend on the past – yesterday – in our everyday activities. Together they shape our historical consciousness. At the same time, democratic as well as non-democratic institutions, authorities and governments need the opposite, or at least a more general and manageable understanding of history, culture and the past. We also see how heritage becomes a tool in both non-democratic and democratic countries. Sweden, Denmark and Hungary use heritage in different ways and so do Russia and China, but with the common understanding of its usefulness in the present.

Sharing history thus means sharing historical consciousness with a particular meaning. In the spirit of Emanuel Lévinas' ethics it is here a question of taking responsibility for the other's responsibility, of removing the preconceived per-spectives that we carry with us and thus finding new ways to deal with the past as sublime, practical and hybrid through *integration* in a coming historical future (Lévinas 1990: 116). On one level it is a question of thinking within the present, of understanding the present as something historical, but on another and more important level, shared history implies thinking the future as something new, or a new whole through *integration*, and exploring this possibility by sharing our histori-cal consciousness.

Thus, the theoretical strategies behind our discussions at Färgfabriken are to explore the possibilities of a new whole by taking integration seriously in a post-heritage future. Our discussion actively and explicitly turns against *heritage* and the idea of its a-historical usefulness. Instead we ask the question, among others, what might be achieved if *newly arrived* architects, artists and urban planners come together with *Swedish* architects, artists and urban planners, everyone with his or her own personal historical consciousness, with the purpose of integrating with each other and thereby addressing a future that we need to discuss so much in our present world. Here the idea of sharing historical consciousness – or history – in the sense mentioned above might open up a new understanding of art, architecture and urban planning, a new understanding based on the idea that sharing history through the process of integration will help create a new future whole.

The idea of the Färgfabriken discussion project is experimental. What is most important for us is not to finish with an exhibition for the public and decision mak-ers, even though this is one aim of our discussion, but the process leading up such an exhibition, and even more what happens after the project has ended.

Since Färgfabriken is an important opinion institution, our goal in the long run is that our discussion project will have some impact on Swedish migration and integration politics, but also on the issue of heritage politics, by redirecting the discussion from heritage to the question of history, shared history and historical consciousness, but as I have stated above, the project and discussion is an ongoing venture and must be understood as work in progress. What I have discussed here is therefore its theoretical framework, not its actual outcome. Yet this framework is open for anyone to explore its usefulness.

The Örebro project

As with the Färgfabriken project, here too I discuss a theoretical framework rather than an actual outcome of a long-running project. If Färgfabriken is a hyped international institution, Örebro County Museum can be viewed as almost the opposite. Örebro County Museum (Örebro läns museum in Swedish) is in a city approximately 160 kilometers west of Stockholm. County museums have played an important part in Swedish heritage management and nation-state-governed history writing. I mentioned earlier that in the late nineteenth century heritage management became more centralized and related to bureaucratic institutions and museums in Stockholm, a process criticized by private actors in the provinces. Many of these private collections later became the foundation of the county museums, and in the 1930s they were interconnected in a system of museums under the auspices of the Swedish History Museum in Stockholm. The county museums became important components in the *folkhemmet* ideology and in the creation of a new society, a society that understood itself as the truly perfect, homogenous and good society, with one history, one language, one religion and one race.

Today many county museums are struggling to become a part of a rapidly changing world and are unsure how to adjust to a change in population structures, partly due to migration and partly because of the *brain drain* of many young people moving to larger urban regions such as Stockholm. In Örebro County, smaller towns and villages are seeing a dramatic drop in population, and some places have almost turned into ghost towns.

Örebro city, and even more so the county, have problems with extreme right-wing groups and the Sweden Democrats have a stable position of 10 percent in Örebro Municipality, but have much higher levels in other municipalities in the county, in some over 30 percent. Örebro Municipality is also one of the municipalities in Sweden that has seen most people leaving for Syria and Iraq to fight for IS. The city also has problems with gentrification and segregation.

If the Färgfabriken project points to a future post-heritage world, the Örebro project returns to the past, to history. Every second year there is a big art exhibition in the city called "Open Art". Major contemporary artists are regularly invited to present their art in different outdoor spaces in the city.

This important work has created a dialogue among the citizens. The Örebro project is partly inspired by the Open Art project and involves, in the fall of 2016, staff from the museum, a curator from Färgfabriken and myself. In the process of the project the plan is to involve more and more people from the city, such as the municipal leadership, theaters, companies, minorities, *newly arrived* and of course everyone else through workshops and other activities with the purpose of opening the city to its history.

By history I, or we, do not mean a chronologically displayed historical narrative. Instead the aim is to point to different visible or invisible historical contexts in the city, through different techniques, for example placing large images in different spaces in the city, and thus making people aware that they share a history that is both a past not belonging to anyone and a present belonging to everyone. The museum will be turned into a meeting place where people will be able to deepen their understanding of the history of the city through interactive exhibitions, workshops and personal engagement. Regardless of where they come from, how long they have lived in Örebro, what their identity is, the history of Örebro belongs to everyone and at the same time to no one. Rather than being a property without ownership, history is time without ownership, past time, the yesterday of the city, a yesterday that we need to address to be able to understand the presence of the city. What we want to achieve is an integration of the city, its history and its inhabitants. History makes a difference, and through this I believe that we can attain a more comprehensive whole, a historical consciousness that hopefully will bridge over segregation and gentrification in a post-heritage future. I would stress that this will not be easily achieved, and the point of the project is not an ending but the creation of a new beginning.

The Örebro project, rather like the Färgfabriken project, is an experiment and very much based on discussions and workshops, and it is the process before and after any actual event that is the major focus; in other words, we see the work, for example in workshops, or meetings with museum staff and politicians, companies, minorities and *newly arrived*, as being an equally valuable part of the project, as important as any actual event, but we also want the project to have a future outside the museum, for example in the municipality's different organizations and to be useful in other cities too. We are moving from a present situation and into a future that we need to claim as a new whole beyond the rigid structure of heritage and identity politics.

Conclusion

As mentioned, these two separate projects are experiments. Whatever the outcome, we want to explore a post-heritage future. As I said, I am not claiming that this is an easy undertaking, but at least it will throw some critical light on the never-ending discussion of heritage, the narcissism of identity politics, the misuse of the concept of *integration*, the almost fundamentalist understanding of history as chronology, or past events locked in the past or a process of bringing the nation into being, to mention a few examples.

I introduced this chapter by pointing to the fact that Swedish politicians are addressing the issue of integration again after many years of oblivion. The question has become important due to the large flows of refugees arriving in Sweden in 2015. In the second part of the chapter, I discussed the history of Swedish heritage management. My intention was to describe the socio-political background of Swedish museum staff and heritage functionaries and how closely related heritage management has been to Swedish politics and the development of the welfare society. But I also showed the shift from heritage as homogeneity to multiculturalism and identity politics, which is very much the present state of the art. This political position is now discussed because of the real or imagined pressure from migration and the need for a more explicit relationship to integration. This new discussion of integration has opened up a discussion about what integration actually implies. In this discussion heritage has become central. However, as I have concluded above, it has never been a question of taking the word integration seriously, meaning the merging of two or more components into a new whole. As I stated earlier, in the discussion at Färgfabriken we actively and explicitly turn against *heritage* and the whole idea of its a-historical usefulness. Instead we ask the question what might be achieved if architects, artists and urban planners, as *newly arrived* or *Swedes*, each with their own personal historical consciousness, come together in order to integrate with each other and thereby produce a future whole that we need so much in our present world.

In Örebro, the second project that I have discussed, we are turning to history and again against heritage. Here we want to explore how history can be used as an instrument for integration. When heritage is stripped of its historical dimensions it becomes wide open for any interpretation and is effectively *misused* in political and economic discourse, while also creating a never-ending discussion among academics as to what *heritage* actually is and how it should be used. Instead of discussing Örebro as heritage we are addressing Örebro as history. If heritage can be used in whatever way suitable for the present opinion, history has a logic that makes it far more complicated to use. I understand shared history as a multi-layered and multitemporal complexion or perspective that cannot be violated the way heritage can.

In this chapter I have suggested that we leave the heritage issue behind and instead turn to history as historical consciousness and as shared. The question is complicated, and I am not claiming to have any clear and straightforward solutions. What I have presented here is a suggestion for further discussion in Sweden and beyond. The idea of shared history can be useful in other contexts too, and most of all in situations of heritage-related conflicts, because it opens up a deep and significant understanding of the concept of integration, something that may create a new whole and hopefully a more comprehensive, sustainable and peaceful future.

Acknowledgements

The section on "Swedish Heritage Management" is based on previous work published as Hegardt (2014). I would like to thank the editors for their almost Socratic patience.

Note

1 www.regeringen.se/regeringens-politik/kulturarvspolitik-for-ett-sverige-som-haller-ihop/ *I bred dialog med olika aktörer arbetar regeringen för att forma en kulturarvspolitik för ett Sverige där många berättelser ryms och olika röster hörs. Det gemensamma kulturarvet är i ständig utveckling och formas av människor tillsammans.* Accessed 14 May 2016.

242 Hegardt

References

Anderson, B. 1991. *Imagined communities: Reflections on the origin and spread of nationalism.* London & New York: Verso.

Ankersmit, F. 2005. *The sublime historical experience.* Stanford, California: Stanford University Press.

Appiah, K.A. 2007. *Cosmopolitanism: Ethics in a world of strangers.* London: Penguin Group.

Appiah, K.A. & A. Gutmann. 1996. *Color conscious: The political morality of race.* Princeton , NJ: Princeton University Press.

Bhabha, H.K. 2004. *The location of culture.* With a new preface by the author. London: Routledge.

Dagens Nyheter, 2016. "Slutet för tystnadens strategi", editorial, 25 February 2016.

de los Reyes, P. & M. Kamali. (2005) Bortom vi och dom: Teoretiska reflektioner om makt, integration och strukturell diskriminering, Rapport / av Utredningen om makt, integration och strukturell diskriminering. *Serie, Statens offentliga utredningar,* 0375-250X; *2005*:41.

Derrida, J. 2005. Lagens kraft: "Auktoritetens mystiska fundament". I översättning av Fredrika Spindler. *Med förord av Hans Ruin.* Stockholm, Stehag: Brutus Östlings Bokförlag Symposion.

Harrison, R. 2013. *Heritage: Critical approaches.* Abingdon, UK: Routledge.

Hegardt, J. 2005. Den existentiella möjligheten. *En studie över arkeologins samtidsrelevans.* Available at: www.raa.se/publicerat/den_existentiella_mojligheten.pdf

— 2011a. "Walking through history: Archaeology and ethnography in museum narration." Hans Ruin & Andrus Ers, (Eds.). *Rethinking time. Essays on historical consciousness, memory, and representation. Södertörns högskola 2011.* Södertörn Philosophical Studies 10. Huddinge. Available at: http://histcon.se/publications/rethinking-time-essays-on-history-memory-and-representation1319/

— 2011b. "Narrating a (new) nation? Temporary exhibitions at the Museum of National Antiquities in Stockholm, Sweden, between 1990 and 2009." Dominique Poulot, Felicity Bodenstein & José María Lanzarote Guiral, (Eds.). *Great narratives of the past. Traditions and revisions in national museums.* Conference proceedings from EuNaMus, European National Museums: Identity Politics, the Uses of the Past and the European Citizen, Paris 29 June – 1 July and 25–26 November 2011. EuNaMus Report No 4. Published by Linköping University Electronic Press. Available at: www.ep.liu.se/ecp_home/index.en.aspx?issue=078

— 2011c. "The marvel of cauldrons: A reflection on the United Stories of Archaeology." Anders Högberg & Anna Källén, (Eds.) 2011. *Current Swedish Archaeology. The Swedish Archaeological Society.* Vol. *19.* Available at: www.arkeologiskasamfundet.se/csa/vol19_2011.html

— 2014 "Sweden: Cultural heritage management". Claire Smith, (Ed.). *Encyclopedia of global archaeology.* New York Heidelberg Dordrecht London: Springer. pp. 7173–7181.

Hegardt, J. & A. Källén. 2011. "Being through the past. Reflections on Swedish archaeology and heritage management". Ludomir R. Lozny, (Ed.). *Comparative archaeologies. A sociological view of the science of the past.* New York: Springer.

Lévinas, E. 1990. Etik och oändlighet: Samtal med Philippe Nemo. Symposion.

Pred, A. 2000. *Even in Sweden: Racism, racialized space, and the popular geographical imagination.* Berkeley, CA: University of California Press.

Sandomirskaia, I. 2015. "Catastrophe, restoration, and kunstwollen: Igor Grabar, cultural heritage, and Soviet reuses of the past". *Ab Imperio, 2/2015,* pp. 339–362.

Smith, L. 2006. *Uses of heritage*. New York: Routledge.

Thomsen, C. J. 1836. Ledetraad til nordisk oldkyndighed, udgiven af det kongelige Nordiske oldskrift-selskab. Kjöbenhavn, Molles bogtr.

White, H. 2014. *The practical past*. Evanston, Illinois: Northwestern University Press.

Witoszek, N. 2002. Moral Community and the Crisis of the Enlightenment: Sweden and Germany in the 1920s and 1930s. Nina Witoszek & Lars Trägårdh. (Eds.). *Culture and crisis: The case of Germany and Sweden*. New York & Oxford: Berghahn Books.

INDEX

residence, ethics of 27–37; and cultural
identity 28, 29, 35, 37; familiar places
27, 30–3; and identity, national 29, 35,
37; and memory 29, 30, 36; obligations
of gratitude 34–5, 36, 37; and
predecessors 27–8, 29, 34–5, 36, 37
respect 172, 173, 174, 206; self-respect 14,
17–23, 24
reterritorialization, affiliative 110–25; *see
also* Inca people; Japanese migrants
(Peru); Peru
rhyolite 97, 107n40
Ricketson, Daniel 95
Riegl, Alois 235
Riksantikvaren (Norwegian Heritage
Directorate) 52, 58
rituals 221; and bread making 199, 200,
201, 203–4
roads *156*, 157, 160
Robbins, Caesar 99
Robbins, Roland Wells 102–3
Rodrigues, N. 185
Rohingya province, Myanmar 2
role of resident 32
rolling pins 207
Roman archaeology 182
Royall, Isaac 98
Rua Xic Project 188–91
Ruiz, Apen 188
rural areas 32, 211, 213
Russia 238

Saami people 55, 56, 57
sacred places 41, 49
sacrifice, human 3
Said, Edward 2
Saint-Denis, Paris 184–5
St. John, shipwreck 101–2, 104
Sanborn, Franklin B. 94–5
Sandomirskaia, Irina 235
Sant Boi, Catalonia 187, 188
Sasabe, Arizona 73
Scarre, Geoffrey 1–9
Schengen agreement 229
Schofield, John 150, 159, 160, 198
schools 57, 60, 61, 197, 199–207; *see also*
education
Schuback, Marcia Sá Cavalcante 235
Scottish independence campaign 50
Second World War 46
Seddon, Robert 39–50
Seglow, Jonathan 13–24
segregation 64, 239, 240
Selassie, Haile 177n15

self-esteem 19, 20, 25n2, 123
self-government, right to 16, 92, 175, 180
self-knowledge 132, 142n13
Seminario, Federico Elguera 115
sensoriums 216
sentimentality 75
Serbian empire 165
settlement 41–2, 45, 49–50
settlers 39; European migrants 70, 71,
90–2, 96, 97, 100–5, 106n30; and racism
96, 97, 106n30
Shattuck, Lemuel 91, 93
Sheller, Mimi and Urry, John 111
Shenley, United Kingdom 215
shipwrecks 101–2
shrines, religious 75, 82
Sierra Club 81
similarity 184, 200, 202
Simons, Martha 95
Sinclair, Murray 103
Siriusgatan, tomb of 184
slavery 3, 25n3, 170; United States 92,
98–100, 104, 108n71
Slavic people 166, 170, 171
Smith, Laurajane 15, 18, 234
Smyrna, Turkey 130; *see also* New Smyrna,
Athens
Smyrnian migrants 128, 130–1, 138–9, 140
social media 153, *156*, 157, 190
Sociedad Central Japonesa 115, 116, 118
societies, multicultural *see* multiculturalism
Socrates 34
Somalian migrants 57, 61
Sonoran Desert, Arizona 71, 72, 73, 80,
81, 82
Spanish migrants 115, 189, 195
stability, politics of 172–6, 229
stately homes 46
State of Exception exhibition 76–8, 82
Statistics Norway 57
stereotyping: and epistemic injustice 137,
141, 142n17; Norway 61, 66, 67;
undocumented migrants 78–9, 80–1;
United States 93, 104
Stonehenge 39–40
storytelling: and bread making 204, 205,
208n22; US/Mexico border 75, 76, 78
students 60, 232
suffering 75, 76
Suito, Enrique Ciriani 123
Sundberg, Juanita 79
Sweden 54, 57, 178, 228–41;
cosmopolitanism 230, 232–3, 237;
heritage management 229, 230–3, 234,